THE MOUNTAINS OF PHARAOH

THE MOUNTAINS OF PHARAOH

2,000 YEARS OF PYRAMID EXPLORATION

by

LEONARD COTTRELL

"I visited the Pyramids, called by the Arabs,
the Mountains of Pharaoh. . . ."
MELTON, *an English traveller*, 1661

BOOK CLUB ASSOCIATES
LONDON

This edition published 1975 by
Book Club Associates
by arrangement with Robert Hale & Company

Printed in Great Britain by
REDWOOD BURN LIMITED
Trowbridge & Esher

CONTENTS

To
URSULA

LIST OF ILLUSTRATIONS

DIAGRAMS AND MAPS

ACKNOWLEDGEMENTS

I would like first to express my special thanks to Mr. I. E. S. Edwards, Deputy Keeper of the British Museum, for the generous help he has given me during the preparation of this book, and for reading the manuscript. Mr. Edwards's book *The Pyramids of Egypt* is in my opinion the most readable, authoritative introduction to pyramid study written in recent years, and I would not have attempted the present work but for the fact that it deals specifically with pyramid exploration rather than the history and development of the Pyramids which is the subject of Mr. Edwards's book. Where I have dealt with these matters I have been happy to follow his interpretation.

I am also grateful to Mr. Zakaria Goneim, Chief Inspector of Antiquities at Saqqara, Egypt, who discovered the "new" pyramid of King Sekhem-khet. I was fortunate enough to enjoy Mr. Goneim's hospitality during one of the most interesting periods of his excavations in 1954. Some of the information which he has given me for this book will appear in a much fuller and more developed form in his own forthcoming publication of this great discovery, which places him beside the great pyramid explorers of the past.

My thanks are also due to Mr. Leslie Grinsell, F.S.A., for permission to reproduce some of the excellent plans from his book *The Egyptian Pyramids*, to Lady Flinders Petrie, for permission to reproduce some of her late husband's unpublished journals, and to the publishers of the books quoted in the text, and acknowledged in the footnotes.

Last, but not least, I owe a handsome debt to the British Broadcasting Corporation which first gave me the opportunity of visiting the Pyramids, thus fulfilling a childhood ambition which otherwise might never have been realized.

LEONARD COTTRELL

INTRODUCTION

Beginning a book on the Pyramids of Egypt is like being asked to describe the sun or the moon. During the past five thousand years, millions have seen them; thousands have written about them. Around me as I write are scores of books, some of them by learned men who have devoted a lifetime to the study of these monuments; Petrie, Borchardt, Reisner, Jequier, Vyse and Perring, Firth and Quibell. These are the relatively modern observers. Behind them are the curious travellers of the seventeenth and eighteenth centuries; Sandys, Pococke, Davison, Browne, Shaw; and beyond them the Arab historians of the Middle Ages; men like Abd-el-Latif, Yakut and Abou Mustapha Youssef Ben Kazil. Still more distant sound the faint but still audible voices of the Greek and Roman historians. Herodotus, in the sixth century before Christ, solemnly recording the information given him by an Egyptian dragoman of his time, who told him the precise amount paid for the garlic and radishes consumed by the 20,000 workmen who built the Great Pyramid; and the supercilious Pliny, who remarks:

"We will mention also cursorily the Pyramids . . . that idle and foolish exhibition of royal wealth . . ."

And, going still further back in time, more than a thousand years before Pliny, there are the comments of the Ancient Egyptians themselves, men who scrawled on the stones of the Pyramids *graffiti* which express the awe and wonder which men who may have been coeval with Abraham felt towards the mighty works of their remote ancestors:

"The scribe Aakheperkara-senb, son of Amenmesu the scribe and reader of the deceased king Tuthmosis . . .

*came here to see the beautiful temple of the Horus (king)
Snofru . . .*

*"He found it like Heaven within when the sun god is
rising in it; he exclaimed 'may Heaven rain with fresh
frankincense and drop incense upon the roof of the temple
of the Horus King Snofru . . .'"*[1]

"Remember," said the Emperor Napoleon when he addressed his troops before the Battle of the Nile, "fifty
centuries look down upon you." So must the modern
amateur of Egyptology feel when he dares to commence
yet another book on the Pyramids. What can he say that
has not been said, and perhaps better said, centuries before?

During my visits to Egypt I have, like other tourists,
climbed the sides, and scrambled through the subterranean
galleries, of a number of these monuments. In 1947 I had
the good fortune to be among the first Englishmen to enter
the "Bent Pyramid" at Dashur after Perring had entered
it in 1837, and in 1954 I was lucky enough to be staying
with Dr. Zakaria Goneim at Saqqara during the most
critical period of his excavations in the newly discovered
pyramid of Sekhem-khet. Also, while writing my various
books, I have enjoyed the friendship of a number of distinguished Egyptologists such as Professor Newberry,
Professor Fairman, Sir Alan Gardiner, Professor Emery
and Mr. I. E. S. Edwards, and through them have experienced, vicariously, the pleasures of Egyptological research.

However, none of these circumstances in itself justifies
an author in attempting yet another book on the Pyramids,
unless he feels that he can contribute something new or
little-known to the subject. Is this possible? I believe it is.

During the course of my work I have, throughout the
years, studied a very large number of books on this subject,
including many which, because of their formidable size and
apparent abstruseness, are little-known to the general
reader. These great works, by such men as Lepsius,
Maspero, Perring, Borchardt, Vyse and Petrie, are the

[1] Graffiti found by Petrie on the walls of the pyramid of Snofru at Medum.

familiar companions of the professional Egyptologist. They provide an almost everlasting mine of material which is regularly drawn upon by scholars and students.

But the scholar is usually seeking only for archæological data; dimensions, dates, diagrams, facts concerning when and in what position objects were found; and so on. He passes over, perhaps with an indulgent smile, the fascinating human anecdotes with which the old-time explorers used to enliven their heavy tomes. But the professional writer suffers from no such inhibitions, particularly if he finds archæologists almost as interesting as archæology, as I do. Thumbing through Vyse for information concerning the King's Chamber in the Great Pyramid, he comes across the following passage, in which the gallant Colonel momentarily turns aside from his measuring instruments to observe:

"The wedding of a Sheikh's son took place in an adjoining village, and in the morning an immense concourse of people came across the plain, no doubt in full expectation of *backshish*; they were accompanied by a band of music and dancing; and some of the performers were girls, who, in addition to their usual dress, were covered with a loose drapery composed of shawls and scarfs, which floated in the air, as they moved about with swords in their hands, which they brandished with violent gestures. The bride and her attendants were mounted on camels; and the horsemen fired and skirmished in various directions, and formed an escort, which was, probably, in other times, necessary as a defence. I gave them a few piastres, and a pound of English gunpowder. . . ."[1]

The Colonel was very handy with gunpowder, and it is salutary for the reader, accustomed to the lily-handed methods of the contemporary scientific archæologist, to note the determined way in which Colonel Vyse attacks the Great Pyramid.

"The mortar was nearly as hard as the stone itself, so

[1] The author saw an exactly similar ceremony in Syria in 1953.

that with Arab workmen, and common tools, it was a most tedious operation. To obviate some of these difficulties I ordered the people to get up to twenty or thirty feet, and to cut perpendicularly behind the stones; but very little advantage was gained in proportion to the increased number which required to be removed. Towards the end of this work gunpowder was used with great effect. . . ."

He was equally tough with his labour force.

"Not being aware of this circumstance, however, we lowered the granite portcullis, in order to break it, and, in doing so, endeavoured to shut in two of the Arabs, that they might work the harder to effect their escape; but no persuasion could induce them to remain, although Mr. Hill offered to stay with them. . . ."

The Colonel had a poor opinion of his Arab workmen:

"The Arabs can stand heat, but are feeble workmen, and have neither proper tools, nor skill for such undertakings. We had parties employed by night and day for many weeks, which required constant superintendence. I tried piece work, without success; and but little progress was made. . . ."

Clearly, gunpowder is the only answer.

". . . quarrymen arrived from the Mokkatam, who understood their business, and could use gunpowder; yet even then the joints were obliged to be cut to get room for the blasting; and the great fragments, immediately above the workmen, were afterwards drawn out with much difficulty, and in many instances with considerable danger."

The more one reads of the methods of the early Pyramid explorers, the more one marvels that so much of the Pyramids still remains. What with the Caliph Mahmoud with his battering-rams (which drove a great hole, still called "Mahmoud's hole", through the northern face of the Great Pyramid) and Vyse with his boring rods and blasting powder, one feels surprise and relief on arriving at Giza and finding the Pyramids still looking very much as they appeared to Herodotus two thousand five hundred years ago.

Then there is the question which has puzzled me for many years: "Why are Egyptologists so quarrelsome?" Those who have not had the opportunity of coming into close contact with archæologists may be forgiven for imagining, as I did, that the men and women who take up this profession are gentle, dedicated creatures, devoted to the pursuit of knowledge, remote from the animosities and jealousies which afflict ordinary mortals; men who deal with subjects which, in Sir Arthur Evans's words: "lie apart from the domain of human passions, in the silent avenues of the past".

Would that it were so! But it is not. Few archæologists go through life without arousing the enmity of some of their fellow-scholars. There is, for example, the traditional rivalry of the archæologist, who digs, and the philologist, who studies manuscripts in his library; I have known philologists who would like to shut down all excavation for half a century until all the existing inscriptions are copied and translated. And as for the Pyramids, probably more bitterness has arisen over the interpretation of these monuments than any buildings in the world. Often one finds echoes of these old quarrels in the works I have mentioned earlier, and in the pages of old antiquarian journals.

There is, to quote one case, a delicious row between Colonel Vyse, who excavated the Giza Pyramids in 1836, and one of his predecessors, Captain Caviglia, whom for a time Vyse employed but afterwards dismissed, on the grounds that the Italian was less interested in making a scientific survey of the Pyramids than in digging for mummies in the adjacent tombs. Years afterwards, a supporter of Caviglia wrote an anonymous letter to a Manchester journal in which he said:

"I there made the acquaintance of M. Caviglia . . . but I found that, both towards myself and others . . . he maintained a prudent reserve respecting the discoveries he expected to make, and the operations by which he hoped to effect them. I mention this to shew that, if he imparted his secrets to Colonel Vyse, it must have been in a spirit of confidence, springing from the intimate alliance they had entered into. How far that confidence has been abused, must be determined by other testimony than mine, as I have no means of judging of the circumstances of the case, excepting such as are given in M. Caviglia's own letters below . . ."

The translation of Caviglia's letters follows; they are too long to be quoted in this Introduction though they will be mentioned later. But the general gist of them is that, after obtaining Caviglia's confidence, the perfidious Colonel Vyse had obtained from the Italian certain secrets concerning the inner construction of the pyramid, after which the Colonel had dismissed the Captain and made use of the alleged "secrets" himself. In a portentous reply, Vyse denies that Caviglia had any secrets to impart, and implies that he was an unscientific bungler, besides being no gentleman:

"This 'amiable and enthusiastic devotee' who complains that I was 'allowed to trample under foot those courtesies of society which are reciprocally due from one individual to another' was so good as to tell me (in the presence of Mr. Perring) respecting the additional men whom I intended to employ, that he was master, and that no person dared to work there without his orders, with many other complimentary expressions; and, upon my desiring him to return a subscription of £40, which I had just advanced, he had the civility to throw it down most indignantly on the breakfast-table, tied up in an old stocking, which I carefully returned with my best compliments, as soon as I had taken out the money. . . ."

It is a beautiful picture. The Colonel at breakfast in his

tent; the Arabs squatting outside; the Pyramids golden in
the morning sun; and the irate Signor Caviglia storming
into the tent and tossing an old stocking on to the table.
. . . How undignified! How unbecoming to a scholar and
a "scientific investigator"! And how delightfully human!
But in the strict sense it has nothing to do with archæology,
and therefore I give due warning to any ultra-serious-
minded reader that if he dislikes digressions of this kind,
he had better read no further, because this book will contain
many of them.

Even at this early stage I cannot resist the temptation
to quote one more passage from the letter addressed to
Tait's Magazine by the anonymous champion of Captain
Caviglia, because it illustrates how politics can enter even
into archæology.

"One word as to the names with which the chamber[1]
discovered by M. Caviglia is to be christened; for it seems
that rival godfathers are disputing over the subject. It
appears that whilst the discoverer of the chamber in
question would give it the title of O'Connell, Colonel
Vyse, with an *esprit de corps* not a little natural, assigns
to it the name of Wellington. Neither name is, in my
opinion, well chosen; for the Liberator of Ireland, a fame
more imperishable than even the Pyramids themselves,
has already been secured at the hands of the historian;
whilst the hero of Waterloo, if he be not remembered in
the bridges, streets, and boots, which are named after
him, will for ever be preserved in our memory by those
annual instalments which, in the form of taxation, are
levied in payment for his glory. . . ."

These enchanting side-tracks, usually avoided by the
fact-seeking modern scholar, provide my main excuse for
adding yet another book to the great corpus of works on
the Pyramids. I have a feeling that there may be many
other camp-followers of Egyptology like myself who will
not mind being led astray occasionally, while the main body

[1] Above the "King's Chamber" in the Great Pyramid.—L.C.

of the army marches sternly on. I can promise them that they will never entirely lose sight of the main force; nor that our main objective, to find out why and how the Pyramids were built, will be obscured by a mass of irrelevant stories. For the pioneers of pyramid study, whom we follow in this book, were great men. Vyse and Perring, whom I have quoted, conducted the first really serious scientific survey of the Pyramids, and even to-day, more than one hundred and twenty years after they wrote, their *Pyramids of Gizeh*, with its meticulous plans and drawings, remains one of the standard works on the subject. Even John Greaves, whose book *Pyramidographia* was written in 1639, recognized that the Pyramids were tombs "intended for the security of the bodies entombed, whose preservation was supposed to have been connected with the existence of the soul", and his observations contain little that can be contradicted by modern archæologists who have had the advantage of working under conditions, and with instruments, which were denied to the seventeenth-century explorer.

Coming to more modern times we have the great Sir Flinders Petrie, the father of modern, scientific archæology, whose work *The Pyramids and Temples of Gizeh*, written when he was twenty-six, has never been surpassed for painstaking, accurate observation. Yet even Petrie could occasionally turn aside from his theodolite and measuring-rods to write:

"Beside the detective business over one's own men, there were sometimes sharp steeple-chases over Arab dealers. They know that their coming into the work is morally indefensible, and they have an indefinite dread of being caught. As however by law nothing whatever could be done to them the object is not to catch them, but only to act on their feelings so as to make them flee before you. The way is to walk straight at any suspicious character, openly and ostentatiously; he moves off; you quicken; he doubles; you cross to cut him off; then he fairly bolts; and off you go, with perhaps a furlong between; across fields, jumping canals, doubling, hiding behind bushes, and so forth; if once he gains a village it is useless to look for him in the houses, so the way is to keep him out in the open for as much time as you can spare for the game; two to four miles is a fair run. This exercise is valuable both morally and physically; the rascals are always laughed at by my diggers for running away, so their habit of flight is worth cultivating. . . ."

But enough; I must not give the impression that this book is merely a collection of frivolous anecdotes festooned like garlands around the solemn bulk of the Pyramids. They and their builders are the real heroes of my story. In my first book on Egyptology I wrote:

"The Giza Pyramids are beyond doubt the supreme expression of Pharaonic majesty and power, whether one sees them far across the valley, lifting their golden tips above the morning haze, or at glaring mid-day, when their huge limestone sides lean against the sky like a flight of heavenly stairs. . . ."

Since I wrote those words, six years ago, I have had the opportunity to read far more about the Pyramids, and to revisit them on several occasions. In spite of the importunate dragomans and the troops of tourists, in spite of the touts and the souvenir-sellers, in spite of the efforts—by scholars, by cranks, by religious fanatics—to explain away their mystery, each visit to the Pyramids only serves to deepen their spell. To the Ancients they were one of the Seven Wonders of the World. The other six have gone. Yet as long as the Pyramids endure, even the most ardent devotees of Space Fiction may be lured from a contemplation of Man's problematical future to a reverent study of his first attempt at civilization on this planet.

LEONARD COTTRELL

Highgate, London
January, 1955

CHAPTER ONE

TWILIGHT OF THE GODS

"The Gods that were aforetime rest in their Pyramids,
Likewise the noble and the glorified, buried in their
*   Pyramids.*
They that build houses, their habitations are no more.
What hath been done with them?

"I have heard the discourses of Imhotep and Hardedef
With whose words men speak everywhere.
What are their habitations now?
Their walls are destroyed, their habitations are no
*   more,*
As if they had never been.

"None cometh from thence that he may tell how they
*   fare,*
That he may tell us what they need, that he may set
*   our hearts at rest,*
Until we also go to the place whither they are gone."

WE, in the middle of the twentieth century, think of the
Pyramids as immemorially old; but perhaps we do not
always realize that they were very old even to the Ancient
Egyptians themselves. To the author of the above poem,
writing at about the time of Abraham, Imhotep, the architect of the first pyramid, was as remote as the Emperor
Nero is to us. As for Herodotus, the Greek historian who
saw the Pyramids in about 450 B.C., almost as great a span
of time separated him from Cheops, the builder of the Great
Pyramid, as separates us from Herodotus.

For the purpose of this book, we begin our story in the
twilight of Egyptian civilization, nearly 2,000 years after
Cheops, Chefren and Mycerinus raised their pyramids on
the Giza plateau. Yet there is still a Pharaoh on the throne,
wearing on his crown the same royal insignia—the serpent

of Lower Egypt and the falcon of Upper Egypt—which his predecessor Narmer wore when he unified the two kingdoms nearly twenty-five centuries before. The priests in their temples at Sais, the capital, still chant hymns to Osiris, god of the dead and the judge of souls, and when the dead are reburied they are mummified in the form of Osiris. The priests still watch the stars and calculate the annual rising of the Nile. The field labourers sow and reap the crops, using the same methods and the same implements which are depicted on the walls of their ancestors' tombs. On the surface nothing seems to have changed, except that to-day the Pharaohs' armies, instead of being recruited from Egyptians as were the armies of the Tuthmoses and the Ramesses, are mercenaries from Libya and hardy Greeks, descendants of the "fair-haired Achaeans" of whom Homer wrote.

Although the Pharaoh, Psamtik I, rules a prosperous and united kingdom; although the long, bitter period of foreign domination—by Libyans, Ethiopians and Assyrians—has at last ended; this Twenty-sixth Dynasty is really but the last flicker of the flame of Egyptian civilization before it sinks into ashes. Yet to the labourers in the muddy fields and the brown-skinned boatmen rowing upstream, Egypt is still what it was to their remote ancestors. Only the priests and learned scribes, poring over their temple records, know that Egypt has known better times.

Four hundred miles up the river lies Thebes, once capital of Egypt when her rulers stretched out their sceptres as far as the Euphrates in the north-east and the Sudan in the south. Those were the days of Egypt's imperial might, when Tuthmosis III led his armies into Asia and into Nubia, bringing back rich spoils to adorn the temple of Amun, King of the Gods. But Tuthmosis died more than eight hundred years ago and eight dynasties separate him from the present occupants of the throne. Eight hundred years during which Egypt has known long periods of civil anarchy and foreign invasion. But the priests also know that in the long scroll of history Tuthmosis was a relatively recent king. Behind him stretch eighteen earlier dynasties, for the records go back even as far as King Narmer, founder of the first dynasty 2,500 years before their own time. They look back with nostalgic pride to the Old Kingdom, to the days of the pyramid builders—Djoser, Cheops, Chephren, Mycerinus—deified kings whose monuments have outlived nearly 2,000 years. To the Ancient Egyptians, *these* were the "Ancient Egyptians".

It is difficult for the modern mind to grasp the immense age and conservatism of Egyptian civilization, but it will help if we try to imagine that we in Great Britain are still part of the Roman Empire, that we still speak Latin, and are still ruled by a remote successor of Cæsar Augustus. So it would seem if we were living in Egypt in the middle of the seventh century B.C.

The Pharaoh rules now from Sais, a town in the Delta, that broadening band of vegetation which lies like a green fan across the parched desert. Through it writhes the slow, turgid Nile, lapping reed banks, sliding past innumerable mud flats, dividing and redividing, until it merges at last in the Mediterranean.

Let us imagine that we are accompanying one of the Saitic nobles and his entourage on a visit to the pyramid plateau beside the ancient capital of Memphis. They frequently went there; sometimes to bury their distinguished dead in the ancient cemetery of Ptah-Soker (modern Saqqara) or near the Great Pyramid at Giza. At other times they sent expeditions to repair and restore the monuments of their forefathers, for the Saitic period was one of revived archaism, when the works of the Old Kingdom (2780–2100 B.C.) were not only revered but copied by the Saites, who studied and reproduced the ancient religious texts, revived the ritual and imitated the art of that far-off age. The Twenty-sixth Dynasty has been compared with the European Renaissance, but the comparison is misleading. The Saitic revival was not a starting-point from which new ideas could spring, but the last backward glance at glories which would never return.

Sais is on the western branch of the Nile, about fifty miles above the point at which the great river divides into its eastern and western arms. Rowing up-river our flotilla enters the main stream just beyond Letopolis, beyond which the green fan of the Delta narrows and the tawny desert begins to enclose it to right and left. The gong which gives time to the rowers sounds out its brazen clang, and myriads of water-fowl rise and hover above the reeds. A hunting party is out, tearing hither and thither on skiffs made of papyrus reeds, boomerangs hum through the air, stricken birds fall into the water across which the cries of the hunters sound clearly.

Gradually the brown river narrows until we can see either bank and the bare, fissured hills which rise above them on each side. We are approaching Memphis, capital of the old empire, although 1,500 years have passed since the last Pharaoh ruled there. But before we reach Memphis and the main group of pyramids, we see on our right a solitary structure, clearly intended as a pyramid but never finished. This is the tomb of Djedkare, successor of Cheops, builder of the Great Pyramid. The records state that this king, who reigned for only eight years, was implicated in the murder of Cheops' eldest son Kawa'ab, and there are some who say that for this reason the guilty monarch began to build his pyramid at a considerable distance to the north of that of his predecessor. It is the most northerly pyramid in Egypt, like an outpost guarding the great complex of royal tombs which begins at Giza and stretches southward for a distance of more than sixty miles.

Soon the Giza group looms up out of the heat haze, dominated by the greatest pyramid of all, that of Cheops, the most powerful monarch of the Old Kingdom. Behind it, smaller but still magnificent, are those of his successors, Chephren and Mycerinus; and on either side, like courtiers ranged around their king, are the hundreds of smaller tombs of the nobles, street after street of sloping sided *mastabas*,[1] each protecting the mummified remains of its noble owner, its four chambers adorned with sculptured and painted

---

[1] An Arabic word meaning "bench" from the bench-like seats which are found outside Arab houses. The *mastabas* were either of mud-brick or stone, of rectangular plan with sloping sides. They usually contained four chambers and a serdab, or chamber for the *ka* statue of the deceased, who was buried in a rock cut chamber deep beneath the structure.

frescoes setting out his dignities and titles, such as "fan bearer on the right-hand side of His Majesty". The wind-blown sand has piled itself in golden drifts against the smooth, limestone walls of these tombs—many of them plundered thousands of years ago and now restored and cared for, even though the religious texts which cover their walls are only dimly understood by the Saitic priests who reverently copy them.

Our party disembarks on the western bank of the Nile and makes its way slowly towards the Pyramids. As we draw nearer, the immense bulk of Cheops' monument over-shadows and awes us. Its gleaming, limestone sides, more than 450 feet high, fling back the glare of the sun as we toil up the huge causeway, also of finely masoned stone, which leads from the river to the high plateau. The Saites are fine masons and the temples of Sais are renowned, but they know that they could never have attempted such a monument as this which must indeed have been built by gods, not men.

The priests chant:

> *"The Gods that were aforetime rest in their Pyramids,*
> *Likewise the noble and the glorified, buried in their*
>   *Pyramids.*
> *They that build houses, their habitations are no more.*
> *What hath been done with them?"*

Compared with Cheops, Psamtik is a pygmy and none knows that better than Psamtik himself.

How was it done? What manner of men were they who raised these colossal structures in which stone blocks weigh-ing many tons were manœuvred into juxtaposition with such accuracy that a papyrus leaf would be too thick to pass between them? What giants planned the whole; with its cunningly contrived galleries which burrow deep beneath the rock; with its massive portcullis blocks of granite sealing off the royal tomb; its Main Gallery more than twenty-five feet high; with its high, corbelled roof; its sepulchral chamber in the heart of the pyramid, roofed with red granite from Assuan, five hundred miles away? How did the ancient workmen seal off the royal chamber with granite blocks each weighing scores of tons and then make their escape? To the Saites, such builders were giants, not men. They could only admire and feebly imitate.

As the Saites approach Cheops' pyramid, they see a far more smoothly-finished building than the one we know to-day. In our own time the angles of the building have a saw-like edge, and the sides resemble a giant's staircase, leading to a platform at the top. This is because quarriers have removed the outer casing of fine white limestone, leaving the inner blocks exposed. But as the Saites see it, each side of the building is dazzling white, smoothly polished and rising to a perfect point. The entrance, high up on the northern face, is sealed by a stone flap-door opening from the top. It had been open for centuries, and if the sepulchral chamber ever contained the body of the king and his funerary furniture, it must have been robbed many centuries ago. But the pious Saites have re-sealed it.

They have also restored and re-sealed the other pyramids, that of Chephren, which although somewhat smaller than that of Cheops, looks taller since it is built on higher ground, and the still smaller pyramid of Mycerinus, to which we now make our way. Mycerinus, the successor of Chephren, is greatly revered by the Saites, because the ancient records say that he was a just and merciful king, in contrast with his predecessors, who oppressed the people in order to build their monuments. Mycerinus, however, reopened the temples which had been closed by his father, and allowed the people, who were ground down to the lowest point of misery, to return to their occupations and resume the practice of sacrifice. His sense of justice, say the records, was so high that when anyone was dissatisfied with his sentence, the king made compensation to him out of his own purse.

None the less, Mycinerus was permitted only a short reign, for the gods had ordained that Egypt should suffer tyrannical rulers for one hundred and fifty years, and when he ascended the throne, forty-four years of this penance still remained to be served. The gods, therefore, decided that the reign of the "just and pious" Mycerinus should be cut short. "Six years only shalt thou live," said the oracle, "and in the seventh thou shalt end thy days."

Mycerinus was indignant and reproached the gods with their injustice.

"My father and uncle," he said, "though they shut up the temples, took no thought of the gods and destroyed multitudes of men, nevertheless enjoyed a long life; I, who am pious, am to die so soon!"

But the gods were adamant, saying that Egypt must endure affliction until the end of the stated time. Whereupon, the king, realizing that his doom was fixed, had lamps prepared and lighted every day at night-time, and feasted and enjoyed himself unceasingly by day and night, moving about in the marsh-country and the woods, visiting all the places that he found agreeable. In this way he hoped to prove the oracle false, turning nights into days and so living twelve years instead of six.[1]

So says the ancient legend, and certainly it would seem that Mycerinus enjoyed only a short reign, though probably longer than seven years. Either because of this, or because he did not command the resources of his predecessors, his pyramid is much smaller than the other two, though it is handsome enough, and the lower part is faced with blocks of polished granite. Like its companions it has a name— "Divine is Mycerinus", the others being called "Horizon of Cheops" and "Great is Chephren". Like them, too, it has its Mortuary Temple on the east side, and a long causeway leading down to the river's edge, where stands a second temple, the "Valley Temple". These causeways were originally built to facilitate the transport of building stone, and later were used for religious purposes. The "Valley Temples" were probably used for the ritual washing of the king's body before embalmment; the mortuary temples may have been used for offerings, and for performing the

[1] This legend is noted by Herodotus, who was told it by Egyptian priests in 450 B.C.

ceremony known as "Opening the Mouth" by which the mummy and the statues of the king were ritually given life.

These ancient ceremonies are known and imitated by the Saites, even though their meaning is only partially understood, but they bury their dead in rock-cut tombs, as their ancestors have done for centuries. The last pyramid to be built in Egypt was raised nearly fifteen hundred years before their time.

Now the nobles and their retinue pause at the entrance to the pyramid "Divine is Mycerinus". Workmen with ponderous levers raise the stone flap which seals the entrance, revealing a dark gallery lined with granite which slopes down through the masonry and then pierces the rock beneath the pyramid. The gleaming granite walls reflect the light of torches, and the voices echo eerily in the hollow depths. After descending for some hundred feet, the passage levels out, and the explorers can lift their heads and stand upright in a panelled vestibule.

Beyond this they enter a horizontal passage, originally barred by three huge granite portcullis blocks, but ancient plunderers have raised them and the visitors' passage is unimpeded. Next they enter a long rectangular chamber running from east to west, at right-angles to the corridor. At first sight it appears to be the burial chamber of the king; but no, at its western end another ramp dives down into the rock. On the right a flight of steps leads down to yet another chamber, also empty, but continuing westward we come to the sarcophagus chamber itself, with walls and an arched roof of smooth granite blocks.

The torches are lifted, and the visitors gather reverently around a magnificent basalt sarcophagus, the lid of which has been raised above it by lifting tackle. Inside is a wooden coffin of anthropoid design, bearing an inscription which reads:

"*Osiris King of Upper and Lower Egypt, Menkaure (Mycerinus) living for ever. Born of the sky, conceived of Nut[1] heir of Geb[1] of whom he is beloved. Thy mother Nut*

[1] For an explanation of these names, see "Egyptian Religion" in the Appendix.

*spreads herself over thee in her name of 'Secret of the Sky'.
She causes thee to be as a God in thy name of God, O King
of Upper and Lower Egypt, Menkaure (Mycerinus) living
for ever."*

The nobles in their long black wigs and rich robes of white
linen stand silently watching, as the shaven-headed priests
recite prayers. Then, at a signal, the workmen haul on the
ropes and the massive lid is lowered into position. More
prayers and chanting follow; then the procession, led by the
torch-bearers, makes its way slowly through the dark corridors and up the steep ramp into the sunlight. The outer
door of stone is lowered back into position and sealed. The
nobles mount their chariots and the party moves off down
the causeway and back to the river.

Why did the Saites perform this ceremony over the body
of a king who died nearly two thousand years before their
time? Because they revered the monarchs of the Old Kingdom, and when they entered the pyramid of Mycerinus,
neglected for centuries, they found his burial chamber in
confusion. Robbers, perhaps fifteen hundred years ago, had
stripped it of all valuables. They had taken the body out
of its original coffin, which was perhaps of gold, stripped it
of its rich ornaments, and left the bones scattered about the
floor of the chamber. The golden furniture with which it
was customary to bury a Pharaoh had been broken up and
taken away. But some bones remained, and whose could
they be except those of the mighty king, the "pious
Mycerinus", builder of the pyramid? So the Saites had a
new coffin made, which they then re-interred in the original
sarcophagus.[1]

Nor were the Saites the first restorers. The Sphinx, which
looks down on our party as it returns to the river-bank,
holds between its paws a slab of red granite put there over
a thousand years before by Tuthmosis IV. It bears an in-

[1] When Perring entered the pyramid in 1837 he found the lid of the Saitic coffin in the
long chamber at the end of the horizontal gallery, but there seems no reason to doubt that
it was originally re-interred in the sarcophagus which the explorer found in the lower
chamber, from which it may have been dragged by later robbers. The coffin lid and the
bones are now in the British Museum. The sarcophagus was lost in a shipwreck when it was
being brought to England.

scription stating how Tuthmosis, while still a prince, was hunting in the neighbourhood and decided to rest in the shadow of the monument. Falling asleep, he dreamed that the Sphinx, who was regarded as the embodiment of the sun-god Harmachis, spoke to him, promising that if Tuthmosis would clear away the sand which encumbered the statue, he would inherit the Double Crown of Egypt. The prince agreed to do so, and presumably on his accession, set up the inscription in gratitude to the god.

We cross the river to spend the night at Memphis, on the east bank. In the morning, re-embarking at the ancient quay we see, on the far bank of the river, an awe-inspiring sight. The sun, rising behind our backs, floods with glorious light a whole concourse of pyramids which stand on the high western plateau above the river. To the right rises the Giza group[1] which we visited yesterday. Then, sweeping southward we see ranged in splendid line the Abusir group,[1] built by four kings of the Fifth Dynasty—Nefer-efra, Nieuserra, Neferirkara and Sahura—and their adjoining sun-temples, for, when the Pyramids were built the principal Egyptian deity was Re (or Ra) the sun-god, whose name was incorporated in those of these four kings.

Still further to the left, surrounded by a high, white wall of gleaming limestone, we see the oldest pyramid of all, that of King Djoser. Unlike the others, which are straight-sided, Djoser's pyramid is built in a series of steps, also faced with smooth limestone. Djoser, first King of the Third Dynasty (2780–2720 B.C.), reigned more than sixty years before Cheops, and was especially revered by the later Egyptians. His chief architect, the great Imhotep who designed the first pyramid, renowned for his wisdom, is now deified, and the scribes are in the habit of pouring out a libation to him before commencing their work. It is this pyramid which we are going to visit, for the Saites have recently repaired it, and driven a new passage beneath the building, which connects the underground galleries made by the Third Dynasty workmen.

[1] These, of course, are the Arabic names by which the Pyramids are known to-day. But some of the names, e.g. Saqqara, are derived from the Ancient Egyptian language.

We disembark, cross the cultivated land and then begin
to climb the causeway which ascends to the plateau on
which the Step Pyramid stands. As we draw nearer, the
great white wall thirty feet high rises above us, its line
broken by shallow projecting buttresses and many "false
doors". It is said that this was built in imitation of the
wall which once surrounded Memphis, the old capital. We
pass through a high, colonnaded entrance and enter a
great courtyard, near the centre of which the pyramid rises
in six great steps of polished limestone to a height of over
two hundred feet. Three of its sides are in shadow, but the
eastern face is dazzling white in the sunlight.

East of this great court we enter a smaller enclosure. At
its southern end is a platform approached by two stairways,
and to the west a temple with three fluted columns and
roofed with limestone slabs shaped in imitation of palm
logs. In this respect the Step Pyramid of Djoser is quite
unlike the later pyramids of the Fourth, Fifth and Sixth
Dynasties, which had, as adjoining buildings, only their
mortuary temples, the causeways and the valley temples.
Djoser's monument is in the centre of a whole complex of
buildings, temples, shrines, niches for statues, passages,
courts, some half-ruined others restored. But there is one
strange feature which all these structures have in common.
They are not real buildings intended for living men. They
are dummies.

What appear to be rooms turn out on examination to be
almost solid blocks of masonry. The doors are of stone, but
though they are represented with hinges and jambs, they
stand perpetually ajar, solid and immovable. The whole
vast complex of buildings, surrounded by its high wall, is,
in fact, a representation in stone of the king's palace in
Memphis, but not intended for his living presence, but as
a dwelling for his *ka* or spirit in the after life.

The Saitic princes and their attendants stand in reverent
admiration of this work of the king and his great minister,
Imhotep, who died more than two thousand years before
they were born. Other pilgrims move in curious groups
about the half-ruined courts, for the later Egyptians made

pilgrimages to the Pyramids, just as pilgrims of the Middle Ages visited cathedrals. And like the medieval pilgrims, the Egyptians sometimes wrote their names on the walls to commemorate their visit. For instance, during the Eighteenth Dynasty, more than a thousand years after Djoser, the scribe Ahmose, son of Iptah, came to see Djoser's temple.

"I found it as though heaven were within it, Re rising in it"

he wrote on its walls, adding:

"Let loaves and oxen and fowl and all good and pure things fall to the ka *of the justified Djoser; may heaven rain fresh myrrh, may it drop incense!"*

Our party returns to the south side of the pyramid, and descends a ramp which leads to a low doorway at its base. Torches are lit; the door swings open, and we pass through into a long, curving corridor cut out of the rock, its roof supported by pillars. The Saites have made this corridor in order to penetrate to the burial chamber at the heart of the pyramid. The original entrance is on the north side, but for some reason, perhaps because it is blocked by fallen rock, they do not use it. Suddenly the party halts. Below them yawns a huge pit, more than eighty feet deep. One of the attendants lights a bundle of dried reeds and flings it down into the abyss. It burns brightly far below, lighting up the rugged sides of the shaft and revealing, at its base, a pavement of massive granite slabs, which form the roof of the burial chamber of Djoser. One of the slabs is pierced by a hole beside which lies the three-ton granite plug which once sealed it. Originally, after the builders had made the burial chamber, they filled the whole of the pit with stone rubble and above it built the two-hundred-foot bulk of the pyramid. All this filling the patient Saites have removed, using the newly-cut corridor to remove the rubble, and supporting the base of the pyramid with huge timber baulks which can be seen high above them in the torchlight. But when they entered the chamber, it was empty;[1] robbers had been before them, perhaps a thousand, fifteen hundred years ago, who knows?

Some of the more venturesome members of our party climb down a ladder to the base of the shaft, and explore the galleries which surround the burial chamber. They are lined with blue tiles, probably in imitation of the reed mats which used to hang on the walls of the Memphite kings' palaces. All is wondrous to the Saites, and they stand in admiration before a wall-relief in one of the galleries. It depicts the long-dead king, wearing the tall crown of Lower Egypt, in a running or dancing posture; every line of the almost naked body is alive with movement. One of the craftsmen has drawn a grid over the relief, in order to copy it. To the Saites, the art of the Old Kingdom represents perfection and they imitate it zealously.

They return to the surface, and pay a final visit to the statue of Djoser, which is enclosed in a walled-in chamber on the north side of the pyramid. The king is seated on his throne, wearing a long heavy wig and the Osirian false beard. The stone eyes gaze out through two holes in the wall of the chamber, out across the desert. The priests make offerings to the king's ka[2] and burn incense before the statue. Then they make their way back to the waiting boats.

As they leave the plateau, other pyramids look down upon them, all the burial places of long-dead kings, for pyramids were never built for anyone below the royal rank. Even the queens had to content themselves with very small pyramids crouched at the feet of their lords' monuments. The Saites know them all by their names; "Pure are the places of Userkhaf", the sepulchre of the first king of the Fifth Dynasty; "Enduring are the places of Teti"; "Beauti-

[1] It is generally assumed that the Saites found the tomb plundered, since it is extremely unlikely that it would have survived intact for two thousand years; but this, of course, cannot be proved.

[2] Authorities differ on the meaning which the Ancient Egyptians gave to the ka. Some believe that it was the spirit of the dead, others that it was his double, born simultaneously with his body but surviving in the after-life.

ful are the places of Unis". Then there is the pyramid of
Pepi; "Enduring is the beauty of Pepi" with its corridors
and sarcophagus chamber adorned with sacred texts, unlike
the earlier pyramids which contain no inscriptions.

The Saites have studied and copied these, though the meaning of many of them is lost. For though the main elements
of Egyptian religion have changed slowly through the centuries; though Re, the sun-god; Osiris, god of the dead;
Isis, his sister-wife and Horus, their son, continue to be
worshipped; yet there have been changes of emphasis.
Besides the principal deities, there are hundreds of minor
gods in the Egyptian pantheon, and sometimes one has
gained prominence, sometimes another, according to the
shift and sway of dynastic power, that, much as the Saites
revere and admire the Old Kingdom, imitating its religious
rituals and studying its texts, there are some elements of
its worship which they cannot understand.

For instance, in the pyramid of Teti I, there is the so-
called "Cannibal Hymn", in which the king is described as
"devouring the gods". In another, the spirit of the dead is
told to *"throw sand from thy face!"* and again, in a third,
the text says *"a brick is drawn for thee out of the great tomb!"*
The Saites may be forgiven if they do not understand these
texts which were archaic even before the Pyramids were
built. The first could refer to the practice of cannibalism
which the primitive, pre-Dynastic Egyptians may have
practised before they became civilized. The second is
probably an allusion to the pit-graves in which the remote
ancestors of the Egyptians were buried long before the days
of brick and stone tombs. The third is almost certainly a
reference to the very early brick-built tombs which came
after the pit-graves but before stone *mastabas* and their
successors, the Pyramids.

One element remains constant; the passionate desire for
survival after death, and the conviction that this can only
be achieved by the preservation of the body, and by providing it with food and other offerings. In this the Saites
of the Twenty-sixth Dynasty and the men who built the
great rock-cut sepulchres of the Eighteenth Dynasty and

the pyramid-builders of the Old Kingdom are one with their far-off ancestors who were buried crouching in a shallow pit in the sand, surrounded by a few pathetic little pots.

Further to the south are yet more pyramids. First, Dashur which has two great structures, smaller than that of Cheops himself, and probably built by his father, Snofru, the last king of the Third Dynasty. Then Lisht, with its pyramids of Amenehat and Senusret I, two Pharaohs of the Middle Kingdom (2100–1700 B.C.); and still further south our travellers see before them an enormous pyramid set well back from the edge of the desert plateau, bearing the name "Snofru appears". Probably begun by Huni but finished by Snofru, it stands in lonely magnificence, dwarfing the rows of small *mastaba*-tombs which huddle at its feet.

> "*I found it*," wrote an Eighteenth Dynasty visitor, "*like Heaven within when the sun god is rising in it . . . may Heaven rain with fresh frankincense and drop incense upon the roof of the temple of the Horus King Snofru . . .*"

Hawara . . . Illahun . . . on and on stretches the splendid line, always on the western bank, until at last we reach a point, nearly seventy miles south of the place where we caught our first glimpse of Dedefre's pyramid, where no more golden triangles pierce the empty sky, and there is only the silent desert and the bare stony hills.

There are over eighty pyramids, and all bear, or have borne, the names of kings.

* * *

Now it is evening, and the flotilla is moving downstream again, returning to Sais after its pilgrimage. One by one the Pyramids come back into view, but now they loom darkly against the sunset. Nowhere in the world is the death of the day more dramatic than in Egypt, and as the last dregs of colour fade from the sky, and the night-breeze stirs the reeds, the great monuments take on a strange, melancholy splendour. They seem to speak not of immortality, but its opposite. The Saitic nobles draw their cloaks more closely around their shoulders, thinking perhaps of the millions of dead, of so many generations, who lie silent in their tombs along the edge of the western desert.

> *"None cometh from thence that he may tell us how*
> *   they fare,*
> *That he may tell us what they need, that he may set*
> *   our hearts at rest,*
> *Until we also go to the place whither they are gone."*

The Egyptians believe that the west is the home of the dead, who are known as "the Westerners". In the west the sun-god's boat, having crossed the sky by day, enters upon its nightly journey through the Underworld.[1] So, too, man, at the end of his earthly life, is buried in the west.

The Saites do not know that the great civilization of which they are a part is also soon to go into its final decline; that within less than a century the Persians will invade and conquer their country, followed by the Ptolemies and the Romans. They do not know that a time is approaching when their ancient language will be forgotten, and their religion will die or survive only in folk-memories. A time will come when even the mighty names of Snofru, Djoser, Cheops and Mycerinus will be forgotten, and generation after generation of curious foreigners will peer and poke among their monuments, speculating, guessing at, but never fully understanding them. Two thousand five hundred years must pass before men from across the sea, from lands they never knew, will re-discover the ancient tongue, read the inscriptions, and dig from the sand and rock the forgotten history of their land.

---

[1] See "Egyptian Religion" in the Appendix.

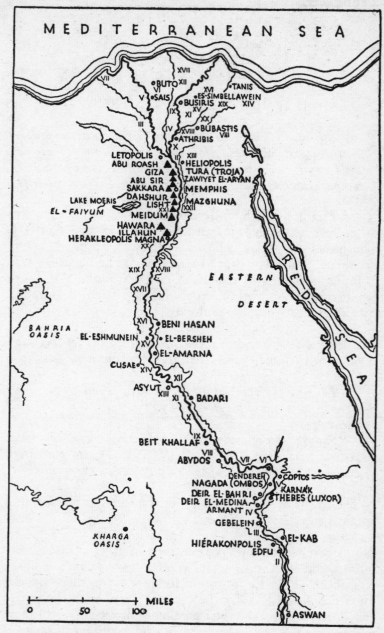

1. Egypt, showing the location of the principal Pyramids

CHAPTER TWO

HERODOTUS AND THE REST

"The word of the Lord that came to Jeremiah the prophet against the Philistines, before that Pharaoh smote Gaza . . . Baldness is come upon Gaza; Askelon is cut off with the remnant of their valley; how long wilt thou cut thyself?"

THE Pharaoh of whom Jeremiah spoke was Necho, another Twenty-sixth Dynasty king, successor to Psamtik I. The hated Assyrians, who had occupied Egypt and long oppressed Palestine, were in retreat. Their empire was crumbling under the attacks of the Medes and the Babylonians, and soon Nineveh would fall, as exultantly foretold by the Hebrew prophet Nahum:

"But Nineveh is of old like a pool of water; yet shall they flee away. Stand, stand, shall they cry; but none shall look back.

"Take ye the spoil of silver, take the spoil of gold; for there is none end of the store and glory out of all the pleasant furniture.

"She is empty, and void, and waste; and the heart melteth, and the knees smite together, and much pain is in all loins, and the faces of them all gather blackness. . . ."

The words of the Hebrew prophets, though they resound mightily in the Old Testament, were really only a loud voice in a puny body. For generations the petty Jewish state, perched on the Judæan hills, had been alternately subjugated by the powerful rival kingdoms to the north and south. First Egypt would conquer them, then Assyria, then Babylon. Usually they joined forces with the power which seemed to have the best chance of winning. But now Necho, profiting by the collapse of the Assyrians, was pushing into Palestine with a powerful army, hoping to win back the dominions of his forefathers. The wisest course for the Hebrews would have been to let him pass, but, urged on by the fanatical prophets, the young Josiah threw his puny forces into the path of the Pharaoh's army, which promptly annihilated it and killed Josiah. Necho pressed on to the Euphrates, where the Assyrians were too weak to oppose him, and at one stroke restored his forefather's Asiatic dominions. On his way back he took Jehoahaz, Josiah's son, whom the Jews had placed on the throne, put him in chains and carried him back to Egypt, where he died. The Hebrews had only exchanged one overlord for another.

But the Pharaoh's conquests were of short duration. After destroying Nineveh, the Babylonians met Necho's army at Carchemish on the Euphrates, and routed it. As the remnants of Pharaoh's forces straggled back to Egypt, the soured and vindictive Jeremiah gave vent to his usual spleen:

> "*Against Egypt, against the army of Pharaoh Necho king of Egypt, which was by the river Euphrates in Carchemish, which Nebuchadnezzor king of Babylon smote in the fourth year of Jehoakim the son of Josiah king of Judah. . . .*
>
> "*. . . Wherefore have I seen them dismayed and turned away back? and their mighty ones beaten down, and are fled apace, and look not back; for fear was round about, saith the Lord. . . .*
>
> "*. . . Come up, ye horses; and rage, ye chariots; and let the mighty men come forth; the Ethiopians and the Libyans that handle the shield, and the Lydians that handle and bend the bow.*
>
> "*For this is the day of the Lord God of Hosts, a day of vengeance, that he may avenge him of his adversaries; and the sword shall devour, and it shall be made satiate and drunk with blood. . . .*"

On and on he rants, like a little man who, having been knocked down by a big one, crows with joy when his adversary is beaten by an even bigger opponent. But his outburst is interesting because it shows that at this period the Pharaoh's armies were not Egyptian levies, as in earlier days, but mercenaries: Libyans, Ethiopians, and "the Lydians that handle and bend the bow".

Lydia, in Asia Minor, was a Greek colony—it was in Lydia that Hercules became the slave of Queen Omphale —and no doubt there were many Greeks in the Pharaoh's army, as there were in that of his father, Psamtik I; in fact they had helped to put Psamtik on the throne. At this period, the seventh century B.C., the Greeks had established trading colonies in the Delta, just as, in modern times, Europeans settled on the Chinese coast. And, like the Europeans in China, the Greeks, while enjoying the protection of the Egyptian rulers, were not assimilated by the mass of the people, who remained apart from them.

"Before the impact of the foreign life, which thus flowed in upon Egypt, the Egyptian showed himself entirely unmoved, and held himself aloof, fortified behind his ceremonial purity and his inviolable reserve. If he could have had his way he would have banished the foreigners one and all from his shores. . . . Thus, while the Saitic Pharaohs . . . were profoundly influenced by the character of the Greeks, the mass of the Egyptians were unscathed by it. On the other hand, the Greeks must have profited much by the intercourse with the Nile valley civilization, although it will have been chiefly material profit which they gained. They found there, perfected and ready at hand, the technical processes which their unique genius was so singularly able to apply to the realization of higher ends than those governing the older civilization."[1]

If the Greeks learned from the Egyptians the arts and technical processes, they taught the Egyptians much about the art of war, which had been forgotten after long centuries of peace and foreign oppression. When Necho returned in

[1] Prof. Charles Breasted, *History of Egypt*, London, 1924.

triumph from his first Asiatic campaign he dedicated to the Milesian Branchidae the corselet he had worn on the campaign—in appreciation of the Greek mercenaries to whom his success was due. His ancestors would have dedicated it to Amun.

Yet, even with the aid of foreign troops, the Pharaohs were not able to hold their own against the empire of Babylonia. Psamtik II, who succeeded Necho about 593 B.C., made no attempt to win back the territories lost by his father, though he made an expedition into Nubia, to the south. He was followed by Apries (Hophra to the Hebrews), who made an alliance with Tyre and Sidon, Moab and Ammon when they attempted to throw off the sovereignty of Babylon. This time the Hebrews came out on the side of Egypt which they had previously opposed. Nebuchadrezzar,[1] the Babylonian king, had already put down a revolt by Jehoiachin in Necho's time, and had carried off nine or ten thousand of the better class of Jews into exile, leaving only "the poorest sort of people in the land". Zedekiah, Nebuchadrezzar's puppet, was placed on the throne in place of Jehoiachin, but when, nine years later, he threw in his lot with Apries and his allies, and the Babylonians besieged Jerusalem, the Pharaoh's armies could do nothing to help them and the city again fell. Zedekiah's fate was worse than that of Jehoiachin. He was taken to Nebuchadrezzar's camp at Ribleh, where his sons were slain before his eyes, after which he was blinded. Once again the Hebrews had backed the wrong horse.

The usual lamentations followed.

Within her own border, Egypt continued to enjoy prosperity, though Apries had great difficulty in controlling his foreign troops. On one occasion a large contingent of Greeks, Libyans and Syrians attempted to desert to Nubia, but were prevented and punished. Later, in attempting to suppress the Greek colony of Cyrene, which he thought was becoming too powerful, his Egyptian troops were badly mauled by the Greeks, and when the survivors returned to Egypt they accused Apries of sending them to Cyrene in

[1] Nebuchadnezzor to the Hebrews.

order to get rid of them. A revolt followed in which Apries was killed.

Under his successor, Amasis, Greek influence in Egypt continued to grow. At Naucratis, in the Delta, Amasis founded a new city as a home and market for the Greeks which became the most important commercial centre in Egypt, if not in the whole Mediterranean. The Greeks, of course, had their own temples to their national gods at Naucratis, to which such Ionian cities as Chios, Teos, Phocaea and Clazomenae contributed, together with Cnidus, Phaselis and Halicarnassus.

In Halicarnassus, a Greek colony in Asia Minor, was born the first European visitor to Egypt who has left us an account of the Pyramids; the "father of history"— Herodotus. In fact, most of what we know of the history of Egypt at this period—including the material of this chapter—comes from him. When he was born, round about 484 B.C., Amasis had been dead some forty years, and Egypt had entered upon her final decline. Psamtik III, the last king of the Twenty-sixth Dynasty, had been pushed off the throne within a few months by the Persians, who invaded and occupied Egypt.

". . . the old Egyptian world . . . has already ceased to be. Its vitality, which flickered again into a flame, in the art of the Saitic age, is now quenched for ever. . . . With the fall of Psamtik III, Egypt belonged to a new world, toward the development of which she had contributed much, but in which she could no longer play an active part. Her great work was done, and unable, like Nineveh and Babylon, to disappear from the scene, she lived an artificial life for a time under the Persians and the Ptolemies, ever sinking, until she became merely the granary of Rome, to be visited as a land of ancient marvels by wealthy Greeks and Romans, who have left their names scratched here and there upon her hoary monuments. . . ."[1]

[1] Prof. Charles Breasted, *History of Egypt*, London, 1924.

It is fortunate that the first of these visitors to leave a comprehensive record was the "father of history" because, unlike many historians, he did not write only from other men's books, but spent a large part of his youth in visiting the countries whose history he was to write. He visited Babylon, Persia, the remoter parts of Egypt, Scythia (south-western Russia), Macedonia, Greece, and Italy. He covered within his travels a space of thirty-one degrees of longitude (above 1,700 miles) from east to west, and twenty-four of latitude (1,660 miles) from north to south. Within these limits his knowledge is close and accurate.

One of the reasons why Herodotus is a delight to read is that, again unlike many historians, he loved a good story; legends, folk-tales, court gossip fascinated him, and he was not above relishing a juicy bit of scandal. Humourless sobersides have sometimes condemned him for credulity, not realizing that Herodotus did not necessarily believe in the historical accuracy of all the tales he was told, but re-told them because he enjoyed them, and wanted his readers to share his enjoyment.

Take, for instance, the delightful story of King Rhampsinitus (the Greek name for one of the great Ramesses).

"Rhampsinitus was possessed, they said, of great riches in silver—indeed to such an amount, that none of the princes, his successors, surpassed or even equalled his wealth. For the better custody of this money, he proposed to build a chamber of hewn stone, one side of which was to form a part of the outer wall of his palace. The builder, therefore, having designs upon the treasures, contrived, as he was making the building, to insert in this wall a stone, which could easily be removed from its place by two men or even by one. So the chamber was finished, and the builder fell sick, when finding his end approaching, he called for his two sons, and related to them the contrivance he had made in the king's treasure chamber, telling them it was for their sakes he had done it, so that they might always live in affluence."

So, from time to time, the two sons would visit the chamber and help themselves to the money. After a time, the king noticed that his treasure was disappearing, so he laid traps.

". . . when the thieves came, as usual, to the treasure-house, and one of them entering through the aperture, made straight for the jars, suddenly he found himself caught in one of the traps. Perceiving that he was lost, he instantly called his brother, and telling him what had happened, entreated him to enter as quickly as possible and cut off his head, that when his body should be discovered it might not be recognized, which would have the effect of bringing ruin upon both."

When the king came to the chamber he was astonished to find a headless body, while the building remained whole and there seemed no way in which the thief could have got in. So he commanded that the body should be hung on the palace walls and if anyone was seen lamenting near it he or she should be brought in. The mother of the dead thief, hearing of this, upbraided her surviving son and threatened to expose him if he did not recover the body. The son did all he could to dissuade her, but in vain. Somehow he had to retrieve the body without revealing himself. How was he to do it? Herodotus explains the stratagem he adopted.

"Filling some skins with wine, he loaded them on to donkeys, which he drove before him till he came to the place where the guards were watching the dead body, when, pulling two or three skins towards him, he untied some of the necks which dangled by the asses' sides. The wine poured freely out, whereupon he began to beat his head, and shout with all his might, seeming not to know which of the donkeys he should turn to first. When the guards saw the wine running, delighted to profit by the occasion, they rushed one and all into the road, each with some vessel or other, and caught the liquor as it was spilling. The driver pretended anger, and loaded them with abuse; whereupon they did their best to pacify him, until at last he appeared to soften, and recover his good humour, drove the asses aside out of the road, and set to work to re-arrange their burdens; meanwhile he talked and chatted with the guards, one of them began to rally him, and make him laugh, whereupon he gave them one of the skins as a gift. They now made up their minds to sit down and have a drinking bout where they were, so they begged him to remain and drink with them."

Of course the thief let himself be persuaded, and "they drank so copiously that they were all overcome with the liquor, and growing drowsy lay down, and fell asleep on the spot". Then, at dead of night, the thief took down the body of his brother and took it away on one of the asses, after first shaving off the right side of all the soldiers' beards in mockery.

Still not to be outdone, Rhampsinitus devised another trick "which," says Herodotus, "I can scarcely credit."

"He sent his own daughter to the common stews, with orders to admit all comers, but to require every man to tell her what was the cleverest and wickedest thing he had done in the whole course of his life. If any one in reply told her the story of the thief, she was to lay hold of him and not to allow him to get away."

The cunning robber, well aware of the king's plan, enjoyed the embraces of the princess, and even had the audacity to tell her the true story of his exploit.

"As he spoke, the princess caught at him, but the thief took advantage of the darkness to hold out to her the hand of the corpse. Imagining it to be his own hand, she seized and held it fast; while the thief, leaving it in her grasp, made his escape by the door."

The end of the story shows Rhampsinitus sending messengers to all the towns in Egypt to proclaim a free pardon for the thief, and promising him a rich reward as the boldest and most sagacious man in his dominions. The man came boldly into the king's presence, was pardoned, loaded with riches and given the king's daughter in marriage. "The Egyptians," said Rhampsinitus, "excel all the rest of the world in wisdom, and this man excels all other Egyptians."

The story is almost certainly a legend, though it may have a slight basis of truth. The fact that the original builder of the chamber left a secret entry chimes very well with what we know of the Ancient Egyptian tomb-robbers; they must have had some prior knowledge of concealed burial chambers, to which they usually found their way with unerring accuracy, to the discomfiture of modern archæologists.

When Herodotus is re-telling an ancient legend given him by the priests of Memphis he tells it for what it is worth, sometimes warning his readers against undue credulity. But when he is describing what he has seen with his own eyes, his accurate observation commands respect. Here he is describing how the Egyptians catch the crocodile.

"The modes of catching the crocodile are many and various. I shall only describe the one which seems to me most worthy of mention. They bait a hook with a chine of pork and let the meat be carried out into the middle of the stream, while the hunter upon the bank holds a living pig, which he belabours. The crocodile hears its cries, and, making for the sound, encounters the pork, which he instantly swallows down. The men on the shore haul, and when they have got him to land, the first thing the hunter does is to plaster his eyes with mud. This once accomplished, the animal is despatched with ease, otherwise he gives trouble."

Nothing is too small or insignificant to escape his notice. He has the true reporter's eye for detail. Therefore, when, like all Greek travellers, he approaches the Pyramids, we can be certain that, so far as his observation is concerned, we can rely on him. Unfortunately, when he comes to describe by whom and why the Pyramids were built he can only repeat what the priests tell him, drawing partly on their records, but largely, one imagines, on tradition.

This is how he describes the Giza pyramids in about 450 B.C.:

"Till the death of Rhampsinitus, the priests said, Egypt was excellently governed, and flourished greatly; but after him Cheops[1] succeeded to the throne, and plunged into all manner of wickedness. He closed the temples, and forbade the Egyptians to offer sacrifice, compelling them instead to labour, one and all, in his service. Some were required to drag blocks of stone down to the Nile from the quarries in the Arabian range of hills; others received the blocks after they had been conveyed in boats across the river, and drew them to the range of hills called the Libyan. A hundred thousand men laboured constantly, and were relieved every three months by a fresh lot. It took ten years oppression of the people to make the causeway for the conveyance of the stones, a work not much inferior, in my judgement, to the pyramid itself. This causeway is five furlongs in length, ten fathoms wide, and in height, at the highest part, eight fathoms. It is built of polished stone, and is covered with carvings of animals. To make it took ten years, as I said—or rather to make the causeway, the works on the mound where the pyramid stands, and the underground chambers, which Cheops intended as vaults for his own use; these last were on a sort of island, surrounded by water introduced from the Nile by a canal. The pyramid itself was twenty years in building. It is a square, eight hundred feet each way, and the height the same.[2] It is built of polished stone, fitted together with the utmost care. The stones of which it is composed are none of them less than thirty feet in length."

[1] There is some confusion of dates here, since Ramesses (Rhampsinitus) reigned long after, and not before, Cheops.

[2] The latest survey gives the following as the original dimensions of the Great Pyramid. Width of the four sides at the base: north, 755.43 ft., south 756.08 ft., east, 755.88 ft. west, 755.77 ft. Height: 481.04 ft.

From the reference to walls of "polished stone" it is clear that when Herodotus saw it, the Great Pyramid still had its original casing of polished limestone, of which to-day only a few fragments remain at the base. The causeway, which has now practically disappeared, also seems to have been intact, or practically so. He was also right in ascribing it to Cheops, as we know now from stone blocks which bear his name. We also know that the stones for the facing blocks were wrought from the opposite banks of the Nile, as he states, though the stones for the interior were quarried locally. His account of the time taken to build the pyramid, and the number of men employed, may also be considered reasonably correct.

He obviously knew of the existence of inner and underground chambers, though it seems doubtful if he saw them. Such an eager inquirer would surely not have missed the opportunity had it been available. But probably the pyramid was closed in his time. Nothing has ever been found of the "island, surrounded by water" on which Cheops was alleged to have been buried, though at Abydos, in Upper Egypt, archæologists have discovered a temple of Osiris which does seem to have incorporated an inner sanctuary surrounded by water.

His account of the method of building is particularly interesting. Clearly it is traditional, but modern research has shown that part of it, at any rate, may be true.

"The pyramid was built in steps, battlement-wise, as it is called, or, according to others, altar-wise. After laying the stones for the base, they raised the remaining stones to their places by means of machines formed of short wooden planks. The first machine raised them from the ground to the top of the first step. On this there was another machine, which received the stone upon its arrival, and conveyed it to the second step, whence a third machine advanced it still higher.[1] Either they had as many machines as there were steps in the pyramid, or

[1] Some archæologists suggest that these "machines" may have been wooden "rockers", models of which have been found in Middle Kingdom tombs. See Chapter 11, "How They Were Built."

possibly they had but one machine, which, being easily moved, was transferred from tier to tier as the stone rose—both accounts are given, and therefore I mention both. The upper portion of the pyramid was finished first, then the middle, and finally the part which was lowest and nearest the ground. There is an inscription in Egyptian characters on the pyramid which records the quantity of radishes, onions, and garlic consumed by the labourers who constructed it; and I perfectly well remember that the interpreter who read the writing to me said that the money expended in this way was 1,600 talents of silver. If this then is a true record, what a vast sum must have been spent on the iron tools used in the work, and on the feeding and clothing of the labourers, considering the length of time the work lasted, which has already been stated, and the additional time—no small space, I imagine—which must have been occupied in quarrying of the stones, their conveyance, and the formation of the underground apartments."

The "interpretation" of the inscriptions can be taken with a large pinch of salt. As Herodotus could not read the Ancient Egyptian writing he was at the mercy of any guide who chose to tell him a tall story. Possibly he was taken round by one of the ancestors of those glib-tongued, resourceful gentlemen, the Egyptian dragomans who pester the modern tourist. No doubt there were writings on the smooth limestone facing, but they would probably be *graffiti*—inscriptions left by some of the millions of pilgrims and visitors who had visited the pyramid during the two thousand years of its existence.

Herodotus mentions the Second Pyramid and rightly ascribes it to Chephren, but says that it "has no subterraneous apartments, nor any canal from the Nile to supply it with water, as the other pyramid has". Here he is wrong; there *are* subterraneous apartments, but the entrance must have been closed in Herodotus' day, probably by the Saites.

But if we—smug in our archæological knowledge—can afford to smile at some of Herodotus' statements and deplore his ignorance, how one envies him his opportunity of chatting with the Egyptian priests at a time when the ancient civilization, though moribund, was still alive, a time when the true history of the Old Kingdom had been metamorphosed into legend and fantasy; fairy stories which may still contain fragments of fact. Reading the Greek historian's pages one feels he would not have envied our superior knowledge of pyramid architecture, our measuring rules and our theodolites—when we cannot, as he could, listen to the Memphite priests telling the tale of Mycerinus and his daughter.

"Mycerinus had established his character for mildness, and was acting as I have described, when the stroke of calamity fell on him. First of all his daughter died, the only child that he possessed. Experiencing a bitter grief at this visitation, in his sorrow he conceived the wish to entomb his child in some unusual way. He therefore caused a cow to be made of wood, and after the interior had been hollowed out, he had the whole surface coated with gold; and in this novel tomb laid the dead body of his daughter.

"The cow was not placed underground, but continued visible to my times; it was at Sais, in the royal palace, where it occupied a chamber richly adorned. Every day there are burnt before it aromatics of every kind; and all night long a lamp is kept burning in the apartment. In an adjoining chamber are statues which the priests of Sais declared to represent the various concubines of Mycerinus. They are colossal figures in wood, of the number of about twenty, and are represented naked. Whose images they really are, I cannot say—I can only repeat the account which was given to me."

It is difficult to believe that a golden statue of the time of Mycerinus should have survived two thousand years into Saitic times, through all the periods of anarchy and civil chaos into which Egypt was regularly plunged, but Herodotus clearly saw such a statue, and we do know that

Hat-hor, the Egyptian goddess of love, was sometimes represented in the form of a cow. Perhaps this was such a shrine, and the naked goddesses were her attendants, or representations of Hat-hor in human form. No doubt the priests knew this well, but they guarded the secrets of their religion and told the tale of Mycerinus' daughter to entertain an ignorant foreigner.

But this is not the only story of Mycerinus with which they regaled Herodotus. "Concerning these colossal figures and the sacred cow, there is also another tale narrated, which runs thus:

"Mycerinus was enamoured of his daughter, and offered her violence—the damsel in grief hanged herself, and Mycerinus entombed her in the cow. Then the mother cut off the hands of all her tiring-maids, because they had sided with the father, and betrayed the child; and so the statues of the maids have no hands."

But Herodotus is not taken in this time. "I could plainly see," he goes on, "that the figures had only lost their hands through the effect of time. They had dropped off, and were still lying on the ground about the feet of the statues.

"As for the cow," he continues, "the great portion of it is hidden by a scarlet coverture; the head and neck, however, which are visible, are coated very thickly with gold, and between the horns there is a representation in gold of the orb of the sun. The figure is not erect but lying down, with the limbs under the body; the dimensions being fully those of a large animal of the kind. Every year it is taken out of the apartment where it is kept, and exposed to the light of day[1]—this is done at the season when the Egyptians beat themselves in honour of one of their Gods, whose name I am unwilling to mention in connection with such a matter.[2] They say that the

[1] It is interesting to note how pagan religious customs have survived under a Christian veneer. Compare the draped and gilded statues of Christian saints which are annually paraded through the streets.
[2] This was Osiris, god of the dead.

daughter of Mycerinus requested her father in her dying moments to allow her once a year to see the sun."

Herodotus also relates the tale of Cheops' daughter. At the foot of the Great Pyramid are a number of small pyramids which we now know to have been made for his queens. One of these, says the historian, was built by Cheops' daughter under somewhat unusual circumstances.

"The wickedness of Cheops reached such a pitch that, when he had spent all his treasures and wanted more, he sent his daughter to the stews, with orders to procure him a certain sum, how much I cannot say, for I was not told; she procured it, however, and, at the same time, bent on leaving a monument which should perpetuate her own memory, she required each man to make her a present towards the works which she contemplated. With these stones she built the pyramid which stands midmost of the three that are in front of the great pyramid, measuring along each side a hundred and fifty feet."

Yet even this scandalous tale contains a fragment of historical truth. For years writers on the Pyramids were misled by the middle of the three chambers it contains into believing that this was intended for Cheops' queen. In fact, it is still wrongly called the "Queen's Chamber". Scientific archæologists have established beyond doubt that queens were never buried in their husbands' pyramids but in smaller structures of the same form, built near the king's monument. The priests were right in saying that the pyramid was built for a female member of Cheops' family; and we know that the Pharaohs did sometimes marry their own daughters.

But, reluctantly, we must turn from these enchanting stories quoted by Herodotus to the more arid accounts of the later Greek and Roman explorers, which, though more rational, are much duller, so I shall mention them only briefly.

Between Herodotus and the next European writer to

leave a record of his visit to the Pyramids is a gap of over four hundred years. Obviously many other visitors to Egypt must have written about the Pyramids—in fact we know the names of several quoted by Pliny—but their works have perished. When the curtain rises again the scene is much changed. The Persian Empire has fallen. Alexander the Great has conquered the east and founded an empire, which was afterwards divided up among his generals. Among these, Ptolemy took Egypt and founded a dynasty which lasted for three hundred years, until, in 30 B.C., Egypt became a Roman province. It was during the Roman occupation that a Greek historian from Sicily, Diodorus Siculus, visited the Pyramids.

Diodorus says little that had not already been said by Herodotus, four centuries before him, and whom he had obviously read, even repeating the story of the radishes and garlic consumed by the workmen who built the Pyramids.

"The largest," he writes, "is quadrangular; each side at its base is seven hundred feet long, and more than six hundred high; it gradually contracts to the top, where each side is six cubits; it is built entirely of solid stone, of a difficult workmanship, but eternal duration; for in the thousand years said to have elapsed since their construction, which some make more than three thousand four hundred, the stones have not moved from their original position, but the whole remains uninjured. The stone is said to have been brought from a great distance in Arabia, and raised on mounds; for machines, in those days, had not been discovered."

By "mounds" he means, presumably, construction ramps up which the blocks were hauled. This is now generally accepted to be the way in which the Pyramids were built.

"But the most wonderful thing in the construction of a work of such magnitude is this—the whole tract around is sand, yet no trace either of the mound or of the working of the stone is left, so that the whole fabric appears to have been placed on the surrounding sand, not gradually, by the workmanship of man, but by the instantaneous agency of a Deity. Some Egyptians affect to tell wondrous tales about this, and pretend that the mounds were made of salt and nitre; the river was then let out upon them, melted them, and caused them to disappear without manual labour. This is not the truth; but the same number of hands which raised the mounds, restored the whole work to its original state. For three hundred and sixty thousand men are said to have been occupied on the work, which was scarcely terminated in twenty years."

He gives the names of the builders of the three pyramids as Chembes (Cheops), Chephren and Mykerinos, and tells the story of Cheops' tyranny and the clemency of Mycerinus which he has obviously taken from Herodotus. But it is apparent that in the time of Diodorus less was known by the Egyptians concerning the Pyramids than was known when Herodotus visited Egypt.

". . . there is absolutely no agreement amongst the natives, or amongst writers on the subject of the Pyramids. They are ascribed both to the above mentioned kings, and to others; for instance, Armæus is said to have built the greatest; Amasis, the Second, Inaron, the Third. Some say this latter is the sepulchre of the courtesan Rhodopis; she was beloved by certain of the Prefects of the Districts, whose affection induced them to construct this at their common expense."

The long night has fallen, and from now on for many centuries all will be speculation and the re-hashing of Herodotus. But two other classical writers have left records of their visits to the Pyramids, and while they add nothing to our knowledge of their history, their personal observations are interesting. The Greek geographer, Strabo, who lived between *circa* 63 B.C. and A.D. 25, travelled in Greece, Italy, Egypt, Sardinia and Ethiopia. In Book XVII of his

Geographia there is a brief mention of the Pyramids. When Strabo saw the Great Pyramid it could be entered, for he writes:

". . . the one slightly larger than the other . . . has, about half-way up its sides, a removeable stone. On taking this away there is a winding gallery to the vault."

The galleries are not described, and one wonders if Strabo even entered them, since if he had one cannot see why he should have described straight-sided passages as "winding".

Then, some half a century later, came Pliny, a more interesting, though irritating, writer, and one who, like Herodotus, had travelled widely in order to obtain his material. Pliny, besides being a scientific writer, had served in Africa, commanded a cavalry troop in Germany, and held high office under the Emperor Vespasian. His scientific curiosity in the end brought about his death, for he was suffocated by the fumes of Vesuvius when exploring the volcano during the eruption of A.D. 79.

In the sixth volume of his *Natural History* he begins loftily:

"We must make mention, too, however cursorily, of the Pyramids of Egypt, so many idle and frivolous pieces of ostentation of their resources, on the part of the monarchs of that country. Indeed, it is asserted by most persons, that the only motive for constructing them was either a determination not to leave their treasures to their successors or to rivals that might be plotting to supplant them, or to prevent the lower classes from remaining unoccupied. There was great vanity displayed by these men in constructions of this description, and there are still the remains of many of them in an unfinished state. . . ."

There are two interesting points to note; for the first time the "treasure" motive makes its appearance—the idea that such enormous structures could be merely tombs becomes increasingly difficult for later generations to swallow, and this led to the Pyramids being repeatedly hacked about by vain seekers after plunder. Pliny also mentions that there were other pyramids beside the Giza group, a fact which his predecessors ignored.

He mentions the names of a number of writers on the Pyramids whose works have since been lost; Euhemerus, Duris of Samos, Aristogoras, Antisthenes, Demetrius, Demoteles and Apion (all, it should be noted, Greek names).

> "These authors," he continues in his pompous way, "are disagreed as to the persons by whom they (the Pyramids) were constructed; accident having, with very considerable justice, consigned to oblivion the names of those who erected these stupendous memorials to their vanity."

Like Herodotus and Diodorus, he gets his dimensions wrong. He gives the width of each side of the Great Pyramid as eight hundred and thirty-three feet and the height from ground to summit seven hundred and twenty-five feet (see footnote 2, page 49). He must have entered the Great Pyramid, because in his description of it we find the first mention of the so-called "well" which was to intrigue travellers for two thousand years, and which will crop up several times in this story.

> "In the interior of the largest pyramid there is a well, eighty-six cubits deep, which communicates with the river, it is thought."

Pliny also mentions the Sphinx, "a still more wondrous work of art, but upon which silence has been observed, as it is looked upon as a divinity by the people of the neighbourhood. It is their belief that King Harmais was buried in it, and they will have it that it was brought there from a distance. The truth is, however, that it was hewn out of the solid rock; and, from a feeling of veneration, the face of the monster is coloured red."

He concludes his observations by repeating the legend that the smallest pyramid was built by Rhodopis, the courtesan.

"Such are the marvels of the Pyramids; but the crowning marvel of all is, that the smallest, but most admired of them—that we may feel no surprise at the opulence of the kings—was built by Rhodopis, a courtesan! This woman was once the fellow-slave of Aesop the philosopher and fabulist, and the sharer of his bed; but what is much more surprising is, that a courtesan should have been enabled, by her vocation, to amass such wealth."

During the early part of the Roman occupation the Egyptians retained their ancient customs and religion. Some of the Egyptian deities, such as Isis and Osiris, were adopted by the conquerors and temples were dedicated to them in many parts of the Roman Empire, including Britain. Most of the Roman Emperors from Tiberius onwards adopted Egyptian titles in Egypt. But when Christianity appeared, which was probably very early, it attracted many adherents whose fanatical faith was only increased by repeated savage persecutions. With its message of redemption and resurrection the new faith satisfied the Egyptian longing for an after-life.

When at last Christianity was recognized the long-persecuted turned on their persecutors, and the remaining followers of the old paganism were vigorously attacked. During the persecution of the Christians, the faithful fled to the hills and the desert, setting up monasteries and establishing hermitages, often in the tombs of their long-dead ancestors. Now they came out into the open, destroying the sanctuaries of the ancient gods, or adapting them to Christian usage. It was Christianity more than Græco-Roman paganism which was most bitterly opposed to the ancient faith. And yet it helped to save the language.

The reason for this was that the Coptic Christians (Copt is the old name for Egyptian) retained the old language in their religious ritual, and when, in the seventh century A.D.,

Egypt fell to the Moslems, the pagan Egyptians adopted the Islamic faith and language. The Copts, a minority, remained Christians, and though they learned to speak Arabic for their daily intercourse, they retained, in their religious ceremonies, a debased form of their ancient tongue. It was this fortunate accident which helped Young and Champollion to decipher the Ancient Egyptian writing, twelve centuries later.

Meanwhile, the Moslems invaded the ancient land, intermarrying with the inhabitants, and bringing in an uncompromising, monotheistic religion which forbade the representation of any living thing. Families living in the ancient tombs thought it a religious duty to destroy, when they could, the painted and sculptured faces of their long-dead ancestors. Statues were broken, temple records lost or destroyed, and a generation arose to whom the ancient inscriptions were meaningless, for they no longer understood the system of writing which had been current in Egypt for four thousand years.

But on the plateau opposite Memphis the Pyramids still stood, ageless, eternal, though the sepulchral chambers lay empty, their temples overthrown, their causeways stripped of stone for the building of Arab houses. The sand drifts piled against their neglected sides, clogged their underground passages, buried their streets of attendant *mastabas*.

Far away in Palestine, wailing beside the ruined wall of Solomon's temple, the Hebrews had their long-awaited revenge. The prophecy of Ezekiel had been fulfilled, that—

"There shall be no more a prince out of the land of Egypt."

CHAPTER THREE

ARABS WITH BATTERING-RAMS

SINCE the Arab Conquest a large number of Arab writers have left records of the Pyramids, though one looks in vain among them for a single example of a serious, scientific survey. Their appeal, which is considerable, is of a different kind. In the Arab accounts one enters the world of the "Thousand and One Nights"; the Pyramids become treasure-houses in which fabulous wealth in gold and jewels is guarded by mechanical sentries which slay all who attempt to approach it. The Second Pyramid is guarded by a spirit in the form of a naked woman "with large teeth" who enchants trespassers and drives them insane; within the Great Pyramid a would-be thief falls down the "well" for three hours without reaching the bottom then reappears to his companions outside the pyramid, mad and gibbering in an unknown tongue. The tales with which Scheherezade beguiled the Caliph Haroun-al-Rashid[1] are not more wonderful than those which gather around the Pyramids during the Arab occupation.

The first Arab account which I have been able to trace is by Abou Ma'sher Ja'fer Ben Mohamed Balkhi, in the Bodleian Library. This, and other accounts which I shall quote, are given in the Appendix to Vyse and Perring's great work, *The Pyramids of Gizeh*. The author, an astrologer, died in the year 272 A.H. (*anno hegiræ*) towards the end of the eighth century after Christ.[2]

"The wise men, previous to the flood, foreseeing an impending judgement from heaven either by submersion or by fire, which would destroy every created thing, built

---

[1] Haroun-al-Rashid himself attempted to enter the Pyramids.

[2] Since A.D. 640, when the Moslem calendar was introduced, Moslems have dated the years from the Hejira—September 13, A.D. 622—the date of Mohammed's flight from Mecca.

upon the tops of the mountains and in Upper Egypt[1] many pyramids of stone, in order to have some refuge against the approaching calamity. Two of these buildings exceeded the rest in height, being four hundred cubits high, and as many broad, and as many long. The length and breadth of each stone was from eight to ten cubits square; and they were so well put together that the joints were scarcely perceptible. Upon the exterior of the building, every charm and wonder of physic was inscribed in the Mosannad character, and likewise this declaration—'I have built them, and whoever considers himself powerful, may try to destroy them; let him however reflect, that to destroy is easier than to build'."

Another Arab writer of this period was Masoudi, who died in 345 A.H., about one hundred years before the Norman Conquest of Britain. He professes to relate the Coptic tradition which says:

"That Surid, Ben Shaluk, Ben Sermuni, Ben Termidun, Ben Tedresan, Ben Sal, one of the kings of Egypt before the flood, built two great pyramids; and, notwithstanding they were subsequently named after a person called Sheddad Ben Ad, that they were not built by the Adites, who could not conquer Egypt, on account of their powers, which the Egyptians possessed by means of enchantment; that the reason for building the pyramids was the following dream, which happened to Surid three hundred years previous to the flood. It appeared to him that the earth was overthrown, and that the inhabitants were laid prostrate upon it, that the stars wandered confusedly from their courses, and clashed together with tremendous noise. The king though greatly affected by this vision, did not disclose it to any person, but was conscious that some great event was about to take place. . . ."

But later Surid gathered together the chief priests from all the nomes (districts) of Egypt, and related the vision to

[1] Actually Lower (i.e. northern) Egypt.

them. The wise men then informed the king that a great catastrophe would overtake the earth, but that after it would again become fruitful. They also told him that during the period of calamity "a stranger would invade the country, kill the inhabitants and seize upon their property". The king then ordered the Pyramids to be built:

". . . and the predictions of the priests to be inscribed upon columns, and upon the large stones belonging to them; and he placed within them his treasures, and his valuable property, together with the bodies of his ancestors. He also ordered the priests to deposit within them, written accounts of their wisdom and acquirements in the different arts and sciences. Subterraneous channels were also constructed to convey to them the waters of the Nile. He filled the passages with talismans, with wonderful things, and idols; and with the writings of the priests, containing all manner of wisdom, the names and properties of medical plants, and the science of arithmetic and geometry; that they might remain as records, for the benefit of those, who could afterwards comprehend them."

Masoudi then goes on to describe each of the Giza pyramids in turn, and the methods used in their construction. Here he is hopelessly wrong. He writes of "porticoes composed of stones fastened together with lead" which observation would have shown him to be untrue, and says that the western—i.e. Mycerinus's—pyramid contained "thirty repositories for sacred symbols, and talismans formed of sapphires, for instruments of war composed of iron, which could not become rusty, and for glass, which could be bent but not broken. . . ." Iron was unknown to the Egyptians of the Old Kingdom, and so were sapphires.

The only fragments of truth in the narrative are that the Pyramids had once contained treasure—we know that the Pharaohs were buried with rich funerary equipment—that there were "subterraneous channels", though unconnected with the Nile, and that some pyramids—though not those at Giza—contained inscriptions. These, however, were not "predictions of the priests" but religious texts intended to assist the king's spirit in its passage through the Underworld. But the legend is interesting in that it shows how, in the Christian and Moslem period, the Pyramids became associated with the Hebrew (or Babylonian) story of the Flood.

He continues, "within the coloured (Third) pyramid were laid the bodies of the deceased priests, in sarcophagi of black granite; and with each was a book, in which the mysteries of his profession, and the acts of his life were related." This, though untrue of the Pyramids, may be a dim memory of the days when the Ancient Egyptians of a later period were sometimes buried with a papyrus roll containing religious texts, the so-called "Book of the Dead", though again it may be a pure coincidence. But after several paragraphs devoted to astrology, Masoudi embarks on a piece of pure and delightful fantasy, which is by far the most interesting part of the document.

"The king assigned to each Pyramid a guardian; the guardian of the eastern Pyramid was an idol of speckled granite, standing upright, with a weapon like a spear in his hand; a serpent was wreathed around his head, which seized upon and strangled whoever approached, by twisting round his neck, when it again returned to its former position on the idol.[1]

"The guardian of the western Pyramid was an image made of black and white onyx, with fierce and sparkling eyes, seated on a throne, and armed with a spear; upon the approach of a stranger, a sudden noise was heard, and the image destroyed him. To the coloured (that is, the Third Pyramid) he assigned a statue, placed upon a pedestal, which was endowed with the power of entrancing every beholder till he perished. When everything was finished, he caused the Pyramids to be haunted with living spirits; and offered up sacrifices to prevent intrusion by strangers, and of all persons, except those who, by their conduct, were worthy of admission."

[1] One of the royal insignia worn on the crowns of the Ancient Egyptians was the uræus or sacred snake.

1. Chephren, builder of the Second Pyramid

2. The Giza Pyramids from the air. Furthest from camera is the Great Pyramid of Cheops, next Chephren's Second Pyramid, then (nearest) the Third Pyramid of Mycerinus with those of his Queens. Near the Great Pyramid are streets of mastaba-tombs

3. The Second Pyramid of Chephren at Giza

(Photo: Exclusive Photo Agency)

4. In foreground a typical stone-built "mastaba" tomb. Behind it, Chephren's
Second Pyramid with remains of limestone casing at top

5. The Third Pyramid, built by Menkaure (Mycerinus). Note the forced passage on the northern side

(Photo: *Exclusive Photo Agency*)

6. The Step Pyramid of Djoser with its temples to the south-east

7. Mr. Sandys and his companions approaching the Giza Pyramids in 1610 (from Sandys' "Travells")

(By courtesy of the Ashmolean Museum)

Pyramidographia:

OR A
DESCRIPTION
OF THE
PYRAMIDS
IN ÆGYPT.

By IOHN GREAVES, Profeſſor
of Aſtronomy in the Univerſity
of OXFORD.

*Romanorum Fabricæ & antiqua opera (cum veniâ
id dictum ſit) nihil accedunt ad Pyramidum ſplendo-
rem, & ſuperbiam.* Bellon. lib. 2. Obſerv. cap. 42.

LONDON,
Printed for *George Badger*, and are to be ſold at
his ſhop in St *Dunſtans* Churchyard
in Fleet-ſtreet 1646. 7÷

8. Title page of Professor Greaves' "Pyramidographia" (1646)
(*By courtesy of the Ashmolean Museum*)

And the author adds that Surid then had inscribed on the Pyramids, in Arabic, the words:

"I, Surid, the king, have built these Pyramids, and have finished them in sixty-one years. Let him, who comes after me, attempt to destroy them in six hundred. To destroy is easier than to build. I have clothed them with silk; let him try to cover them with mats."

Masoudi also relates that "the spirit of the northern pyramid has been observed to pass around it in the shape of a beardless boy, with large teeth, and a sallow countenance; that the spirit of the western pyramid was a naked woman, with large teeth, who seduced people into her power, and then made them insane; she was to be seen at midday and sunset; and that the guardian of the coloured pyramid, in the form of an old man, used to scatter incense round the building with a thuribulum, like that used in the Christian churches." (Notice again the Christian influence.)

In another manuscript the same author tells the story of twenty men of the Fayum (a district to the north-west of Giza) who came to examine the Great Pyramid.

"One of them was accordingly lowered down the well by means of a rope, which broke at a depth of one hundred fathoms, and the man fell to the bottom; he was three hours falling. His companions heard horrible cries; and, in the evening, they went out of the Pyramid, and sat down before it to talk the matter over. The man, who was lost in the well, coming out of the earth, suddenly appeared before them, and uttered the exclamations 'Sak, Sak, Saka, Saka', which they did not understand; he then fell down dead, and was carried away by his friends. The above-mentioned words were translated by a man from Said as follows: 'He who meddles with, and covets what does not belong to him, is unjust.' "

Another Arab author, Muterdi, tells a similar story about the "well". A party of explorers went down the first and second descents, and passed along the base of the pyramid—

"until they came to a narrow passage, whence a cold wind proceeded, and multitudes of bats, as big as black eagles; one of the party was sent forward to explore it, with a cord fastened to his waist by which, in case of necessity, he could be withdrawn. After he had gone a short distance, the passage closed, and crushed him to death, and a dreadful sound scared the rest of the party out of the Pyramid, of whom several died; as the rest were consulting about what had happened, their lost companion appeared, and spoke to them in an unknown tongue."

Masoudi's description of a great chamber found by some other explorers reads more like the story of Aladdin's cave.

"The walls of the chamber were composed of small square stones of beautiful colours; and a person, having put one of these stones in his mouth, was suddenly seized with a pain in his ears, which continued until he had replaced it. They also discovered, in a large hall, a quantity of golden coins put up in columns, every piece of which was the weight of one thousand dinars. They tried to take the money, but were not able to move it. In another place they found the image of a sheikh, made of green stone, sitting upon a sofa, and wrapped up in a garment. Before him were statues of little boys, whom he was occupied in instructing; they tried to take up one of these figures, but they were not able to move it. Having proceeded further to a quadrangular space, similar to that which they had previously entered, they met with the image of a cock, made of precious stones, and placed upon a green column. Its eyes enlightened all the place; and upon their arrival, it crowed and flapped its wings. Continuing their researches, they came to a female idol of white stone, with a covering on her head, and stone lions on each side, attempting to devour her, upon which they took flight. . . ."

Of course, one can dismiss all these stories as Oriental fairy-tales. Perhaps they are. Certainly I do not believe that they bear any relation to what was actually found in the Pyramids, which must have been robbed many centuries before the Arab conquest.

Yet, again and again, myths and fairy-stories have been found to have a kernel of truth. One has only to recall the poems of Homer, which generations of scholars regarded as pure invention. Yet Heinrich Schliemann and Sir Arthur Evans discovered that there had existed, in Greece and the Aegean islands, a great civilization which flourished more than a thousand years before the days of classical Greece, and that folk memories of this civilization survived in the epics of Homer, like flies embedded in amber. Architecture, furniture, dress and weapons long forgotten by the Greeks of Homer's day are described in these poems, and when the archæologists dug out of the earth examples of these objects, Sir Arthur Evans was able to say with pride and truth: "We know now that the old legends were true."[1]

If one approaches these Egyptian stories in a spirit neither of scepticism nor credulity, I think it is possible to discern within them a core of reality. We know from the ancient records and from the evidence of the plundered sepulchres, that the Ancient Egyptians were determined and skilful tomb-robbers. Rich treasures *were* buried with the Pharaohs and the great ones of Egypt, though they did not stay there long. Some of the robbers were caught—as we know from the Ramesside papyri describing the trials of certain of these thieves—but how many thousands must have gone undetected! The work was secret, known only to the companions and the families of the men who carried out the dangerous task; yet, perhaps on their death-beds, old men like the builder of the treasure house of Rhampsinitus may have whispered to their sons the stories of their exploits.

So these stories would be handed on among the people from generation to generation, becoming more and more garbled and distorted as time passed, until the statue of an Egyptian noble became "the image of a sheikh in green stone", the golden image of Horus, in the form of a hawk,

[1] See *The Bull of Minos* by the present author.

became "the image of a cock, made of precious stones, which crowed and flapped its wings", the serpent on the crown of a Pharaoh became a magical reptile which destroyed the intruders, and the mysterious, undecipherable writing on the walls of the tombs became the records of priestly wisdom. One does not know; one is groping in the darkness like the tomb-robbers themselves. Yet I believe that this is the way in which these Arabic legends should be interpreted. Scholars may disagree with me, but scholars have sometimes been proved wrong.

Some of the Arab accounts are much more factual, and indicate that the authors have entered the pyramids, though even in these narratives the element of fable creeps in. Vyse quotes another Arab writer with the formidable name of Abou Abd Allah Mohammed Ben Abdurakim Alkaisi, who died about 565 A.H., that is towards the end of the twelfth century A.D. He repeats a statement made by many of his compatriots, that the Great Pyramid was entered by the Caliph El Ma'mun, or Mahmoud, who forced a passage through the northern side, which can still be seen, and is called "Mahmoud's hole" to this day.

The Caliph, it is said, attacked the pyramid with battering rams "at a point somewhat to the east of the original entrance, which had been re-sealed by the Saites and was not detected by the Arabs. They also used hot vinegar to crack the huge stone blocks. But the attackers had chosen the wrong spot and would probably never have found the entrance gallery had not their battering dislodged the granite plug-block which sealed the entrance to the ascending passage. It must have been a dramatic moment when Ma'mun's men heard the great stone fall in the depths of the pyramid. Guided by the sound they started tunnelling west and finally broke through into the original entrance passage."[1]

When the Arab author quoted by Vyse entered the pyramid he found—

". . . a square chamber with a coved roof, and in it a

[1] Cottrell, *The Lost Pharaohs*, Evans Bros., London, 1950.

well, ten cubits deep, large enough for a person to enter; from whence, at each angle, doors opened into large apartments, in which bodies had been deposited, enveloped with many wrappers, that had become black through length of time; they were entire and retained their hair, and as none of it was grey, they appeared to have belonged to young persons; they were stiffened so that their joints could not be moved, and they had become as light as air; he likewise says, that there were four circles filled with human bodies in the well, and that the whole place was infested with bats. He also observes that various animals were buried there. And he says, that he found a bundle above a cubit long, in the form of a turban composed of very white cotton interwoven with red silk; and that, upon opening it, he found a dead lapwing completely covered with feathers as if it had just died."

"From the vaulted chamber above-mentioned the higher point of the pyramid was accessible by a passage above five paces wide, but without stairs or steps."

Up to this point all is credible, but afterwards one begins to have doubts.

"He was informed that those who went up there in the time Al Mamoon, came to a small passage, containing the image of a man in green stone, which was taken for examination before the caliph; and that when it was opened a human body was discovered in golden armour, decorated with precious stones, in his hand was a sword of inestimable value, and above his head a ruby of the size of an egg, which shone like fire, and of which Al Mamoun took possession. The author states that he himself saw the case, from which the body was taken, and that it stood at the door of the king's palace at Cairo, in the year 511."

All the earlier part of this story has the ring of truth. The "square chamber with a coved roof" is clearly the so-called "Queen's Chamber" (see diagram of the Great

Pyramid opposite page 74). The "bodies . . . enveloped in
many wrappers" were probably interments made by the
Saites when they restored and re-sealed the pyramid. They
often buried their dead in the tombs of their remote forefathers, and the presence of mummified animals and birds
again suggests Saitic burials, for at this time the cult of
animal-worship, which had existed for centuries, reached
its peak in Egypt.

The "passage, about five paces wide, but without stairs
or steps" is obviously the Grand Gallery (see diagram) leading to the "King's Chamber" in the heart of the pyramid.
To-day, this chamber contains an empty, lidless sarcophagus of granite. Was it intact when the Caliph Ma'mun
entered it? Did he find the body of Cheops? It is extremely
doubtful. In view of the fact that other, cunningly concealed tombs of later periods were almost invariably robbed
by the Ancient Egyptians, it seems incredible that so
obvious a monument as that of Cheops could have remained unplundered for nearly three thousand years. Yet
the "human body in golden armour, decorated with
precious stones" could have been a golden or gold-plated
coffin, and the mention of the mummy case which stood
outside the door of the king's palace, has an authentic ring.
Perhaps the Caliph found a later Saitic burial. Could it
have been a re-burial of Cheops' remains? It is a fascinating
question.

Such is the Arab fondness for romantic embroidery, that
even the historical fact of Ma'mun's forcing the Great
Pyramid acquired, in time, a magical element. In the
thirteenth century A.D., when Henry III was building Westminster Abbey, a certain Arab explorer named Sibt el Janzi
visited the pyramids of Giza, and in his account re-tells the
tale of Ma'mun's exploit with a difference.

". . . the Caliph Mamoun Ben Haroun al Raschid came
to Egypt and wished to take down one of the Pyramids
to see what it contained. He was told that it was impossible; he answered, that at least it must be opened. He
made a chasm, which the author says was to be seen in

the Great Pyramid. Having penetrated twenty cubits, a vessel was found full of coined gold, each piece of which was a dinar in weight, one thousand dinars in all, and two hundred dinars beside. There was also a tablet, according to some accounts, of gold, to others, of coloured marble, with an inscription in ancient characters, as follows. 'King ——, son of King —— in the year ——, will open this Pyramid and will expend in doing so a certain sum. We here repay him what he has laid out; if he continues his researches, he will be at great expense, and will obtain nothing more.' The Caliph was greatly astonished; he admired the beauty and excellence of the money, and ordered an account to be drawn up of the expenses of the excavation, which, to his surprise, exactly amounted to the money he had discovered; he therefore observed that the ancient people were very wise, and had a knowledge of future events, to which no other persons could ever attain."

This story is repeated by several other Arab authorities. Some also assert that when he entered the King's Chamber and forced open the sarcophagus he found nothing "excepting some bones completely decayed by time; upon which the Caliph declined any further examination, as the expenses had been very great, particularly in provisions for the workmen."

Another, Edresi, who died in the thirteenth century A.D., says of the Great Pyramid:

"They worked at it with axes for six months, and they were in great numbers. They found in this vessel, after they had broken the covering of it, the decayed, rotten remains of a man, but no treasures at his side, except some golden tablets inscribed with characters of a language nobody could understand."

One could devote many pages to these Arab writings but at the risk of becoming monotonous, because in the main they repeat the same legendary stories again and again. Here and there, however, one finds odd facts which are worth noting. One is the tradition, obviously of Hebrew origin, that the Pyramids were granaries built by Joseph during his sojourn in Egypt, but this the Arabs do not accept, for the obvious reason that the Pyramids are practically solid. Another is that the Sabæans, the pagan ancestors of the Arabs, performed regular pilgrimages to the Great Pyramid, and also visited the others.[1]

The frequency with which the Pyramids are associated with the story of the Flood is interesting. In a flat country such as Egypt, it is easy to see how the Christians, reading the story of the Deluge, might come to think that these great buildings were erected to preserve records of man's achievements in the arts and sciences against the time when the waters should subside.

But the most frequent note is one of awe and admiration for skill, craftsmanship and engineering genius which they could never hope to imitate.

"The extreme exactness with which they (the stones) have been worked and laid," wrote Abd-el-Latif, "is worthy of the utmost admiration. The joints are so perfect that it would be impossible to pass a needle or even a hair between them. They are cemented together by a layer of mortar not thicker than a sheet of paper; with the composition of which I am totally unacquainted. The stones were inscribed with ancient characters, now unintelligible. The inscriptions are so numerous, that copies of those alone, which may be seen on the surface of the two pyramids, would occupy above ten thousand pages.[2] I have read in some of the books of the ancient Sabeans, that one of these two pyramids is the tomb of Agathodæmon, and the other of Hermes, who are said to have been two great prophets, of whom Agathodæmon was the most famous and the most ancient." (Note the Hellenic influence.) "It is also said, that people used to come from all parts of the world on a pilgrimage to these tombs."

[1] Shehab Eddin Ahmed Ben Yahya, died *circa* 745 A.H.
[2] Showing that at this period the Pyramids still retained their outer covering of polished limestone.

Abd-el-Latif concludes with an account of the futile attempt of one of the Caliphs, Malek-Al Aziz Othman Ben Youssef, to demolish the Third Pyramid.

". . . he was prevailed upon by some persons of his court —people totally devoid of sense and judgement—to attempt the demolition of the Pyramids. He accordingly sent miners, and quarrymen, under the superintendence of some of the principal officers and emirs of his court, with orders to destroy the *red* pyramid,[1] which is the least of the three. They encamped near it, collected labourers from all parts of the country at a vast expense, and endeavoured with great assiduity for eight months to execute the commission, with which they were intrusted, removing each day, with great difficulty, one or two stones, which were forced out of their places by levers and wedges, and afterwards drawn down with cords. When at last one of these enormous blocks fell, the tremendous noise was heard at an immense distance, and the concussion shook the ground, and made the mountains tremble. . . . At length, having exhausted their resources, their resolution grown proportionately weaker as their labour and difficulties increased, and they were at last obliged to give up the undertaking as hopeless."

The chasm made in the side of the Third Pyramid can be seen to-day, but only from close quarters, for, as the writer says,

". . . so immense is the pile, that the stones are scarcely missed; and it is only on one of its sides that any trace of the impression, which was attempted to be made, can be discovered."

The Arab treasure-seekers and would-be despoilers had had their day. Now it was to be the Europeans' turn.

---

[1] So called because the lower part was faced with red granite.

CHAPTER FOUR

EUROPEAN EXPLORERS

From the fifteenth century onwards we have numerous accounts by European travellers of their visits to the Pyramids. Most of these deal only with the Giza group, no doubt because they were the most easily accessible from Cairo. It is not surprising that Europeans rarely ventured into the interior of the country to view the other pyramids, since infidels were hated, and unless travellers were strongly guarded they were liable to be attacked by bands of robbers. A few bold spirits who did make these dangerous journeys in the eighteenth century have left spirited accounts of the hazards they ran; and even as late as the 'eighties of the last century archæologists such as Sir Flinders Petrie used to carry a gun, which was sometimes needed.

Since the bulk of these early accounts describe the Giza pyramids and particularly the Great Pyramid, I have included in this book diagrams of these monuments. If the reader will occasionally refer to these, he will find it easier to understand the descriptions of the various galleries and chambers, which otherwise tend to become confusing.

After Breydenbach, a German scholar (1486), and Bartholomeus de Salignace (1550) who gave only a few lines to the Pyramids, the first account mentioned by Vyse of a visit by a European traveller is that of Bellonius, who visited Egypt in 1553.

After quoting Herodotus and giving the rough dimensions of the Great Pyramid, the explorer . . .

"entered it by a square aperture in the northern side, which was more dilapidated than the others . . . and . . . having descended by the inclined passage for a considerable distance, he arrived at the well, said by Pliny to have contained, at a depth of eighty-six cubits, the

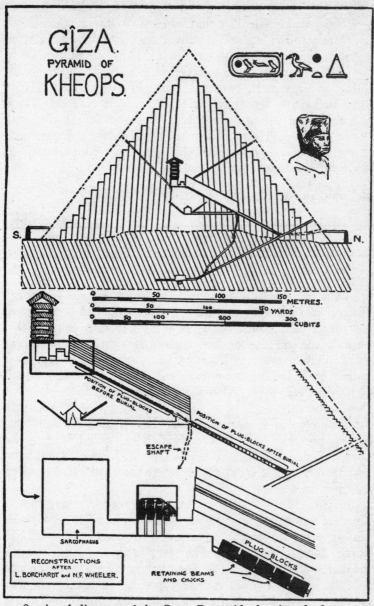

GÎZA.
PYRAMID OF
KHEOPS.

S.   N.

50   100   150 METRES.
50   100   150 YARDS
50   100   200   300 CUBITS

POSITION OF PLUG-BLOCKS BEFORE BURIAL

POSITION OF PLUG-BLOCKS AFTER BURIAL

ESCAPE SHAFT

SARCOPHAGUS

PLUG - BLOCKS

RECONSTRUCTIONS
AFTER
L. BORCHARDT and N.F. WHEELER.

RETAINING BEAMS
AND CHOCKS

2. Sectional diagram of the Great Pyramid, showing the layout of
its galleries and chambers

waters of the Nile, but that when he saw it, it was almost entirely filled up with stones and rubbish. He then ascended, by a passage on the left hand, to a chamber in the centre of the Pyramid, six paces long, and four broad. It was lined with polished stone, and contained a large tomb twelve feet long and six wide, formed of black marble,[1] in which he was told that an ancient king had been buried. He mentions that the passages were much encumbered with rubbish, and infested with great quantities of bats which had long tails."

Bellonius also mentions the Second Pyramid.

". . . the summit ended in a point, but was inaccessible; it was solid, had no opening, and was said to have been covered with marble, and to have been intended for a tomb."

He says little about the Third Pyramid, except to repeat the old story that it was built by Rhodope, the courtesan.

From this account it seems pretty certain that at this period, the middle of the sixteenth century, the Great Pyramid had been at least partially stripped of its outer casing, since Bellonius writes of the "dilapidated condition" of its northern side. Also the main galleries were open, as they probably had been since the entry of the Caliph Ma'mun several centuries earlier. The Second Pyramid was closed, possibly by drift-sand which had piled against the northern side and hidden the entrance; for we know, from inscriptions inside its chamber, that the Arabs had entered this pyramid also.

At this point I suggest that the reader consults the diagram opposite page 74 in order to familiarize himself with the layout of the galleries. The entrance is on the north face, about fifty-five feet above ground level, measured vertically. It is not exactly mid-way along the face, but about twenty-four feet east of the centre. It was this fact that misled Ma'mun's men, who, imagining that it would be exactly in the centre, forced their passage through

[1] Actually granite.

the masonry at that point. If their battering had not dislodged the stone plug which sealed the entrance to the Ascending Corridor, they might never have discovered the original entrance.

From the entrance a long corridor plunges down at an angle of 26° 31' 23", first through the masonry and then through the rock beneath. It is 3 feet 5 inches wide and 3 feet 11 inches high. At a distance of 345 feet from the entrance the corridor becomes level. It continues horizontally for another 29 feet and then enters a roughly-cut, unfinished chamber, which, according to Vyse,[1] who entered it in 1838, measures 11 feet 6 inches in height, 27 feet in width (north-south) and 46 feet long (east-west). Thus it will be seen that its longest axis is at right angles to the horizontal corridor.

In the south wall of the chamber, opposite the entrance, is a blind passage extending for a score or so feet further, and then ending. This too is unfinished. In the floor of the chamber is a square pit, also unfinished, and, just before the entrance, on the west side of the corridor, is a roughly-cut recess.

So much for the descending corridor and the subterranean chamber beneath the pyramid. Now look at the Plan again. At a distance of about 60 feet from the entrance there is a hole in the roof of the Descending Gallery leading to an *Ascending* Gallery, which is *hewn out of the masonry*. It is 129 feet long, and in width and height corresponds to the Descending Gallery. Also the gradient is almost exactly the same—26° 2' 30"—only 7" different from the Descending Gallery. At its lower end, just above the gap left by the missing limestone slab which originally sealed the entrance in its ceiling, are three large granite plug-blocks placed one behind the other. When the tomb-robbers encountered these granite blocks they by-passed them by cutting through the softer limestone on the west, till they got beyond the uppermost plug.

An interesting point, observed by Borchardt, is that

[1] The chamber is inaccessible now, Vyse and Perring having filled most of it with stone blocks which they removed during the course of their subsequent excavations.

whereas the stones in the walls of the lower part of the gallery are laid approximately horizontally, those in the upper part are laid parallel with the angle of the corridor.

"The only stones which are not laid parallel with the gradient," writes Edwards in his *Pyramids of Egypt*, "are the so-called 'girdle-stones', a name used to describe either single stones or two stones, one above the other, through which the corridor has been hewn. These 'girdle-stones' placed at regular intervals of 17 feet 2 inches may offer a clue to the structural composition of the Great Pyramid. . . ."

But that will form the subject of a much later chapter. For the moment, let us see the pyramid galleries as they were known to European travellers from Bellonius onwards, and observe how they interpreted them.

At the top of the Ascending Gallery (see Plan) just before it enters the Grand Gallery—which continues upwards at the same angle—there is a horizontal corridor leading to what is called by the Arabs "The Queen's Chamber". This, as we now know, is a misnomer, as the queens were never buried in their husbands' pyramids. At first the corridor is only 3 feet 9 inches high, but as it approaches the Chamber the floor level drops approximately two feet. The Chamber is exactly between the north and south sides of the pyramid. It measures 18 feet 10 inches from west to east and 17 feet 2 inches from south to north. The roof—20 feet 5 inches at its highest point—is pointed. In the east wall there is a niche, 15 feet 4 inches high and 5 feet 2 inches wide at the base. The original depth was 3 feet 5 inches but treasure-seekers have cut away the back.

The floor of the "Queen's Chamber" is very rough and unfinished. In the thickness of the northern and southern walls are narrow shafts sloping upwards at an angle of about 30°, but not leading to the outer surface of the pyramid. They are blind alleys. The existence of these shafts was not known until 1872, when they were discovered by an engineer named Waynman Dixon.

Returning to the Ascending Gallery we see in front of and above us the entrance to the so-called Grand Gallery. This is one of the most awe-inspiring achievements of the Old Kingdom architects, and though the walls have been worn to a fine polish by the passage of millions of tourists—Ptolemaic, Roman, Arab, European and American—this lofty granite corridor strikes reverence into the heart of the most insensitive visitor.

Above the first 7 feet 6 inches of the limestone walls, the ceiling rises in a series of projecting steps or "corbels", each projecting inwards about three inches beyond the course below, thus forming a vault of gigantic dimensions. The lower edge of each stone hitches like a pawl into a ratchet cut in the tops of the walls. "Hence," wrote Sir Flinders Petrie, "no stone can press on the one below it, so as to cause a cumulative pressure all down the roof; and each stone is separately upheld by the side-walls across which it lies."

Cut out of the very heart of the pyramid, the Grand Gallery rises to a height of nearly 30 feet, planing upwards through the masonry as if eager to reach the chamber of the great king. Like the last thrilling bars of a Beethoven symphony, it soars onwards and upwards until it reaches the Finale—the King's Chamber.

There are no steps in the steeply-sloping floor. On each side is a flat-topped ramp, 2 feet high and 1 foot 8 inches wide, and between the two ramps is a passage of exactly the same width as the roof, 3 feet 5 inches. At the very top there is a high step leading to a low-ceilinged gallery which admits first to an antechamber of which the west, east and south walls are of granite. On each side four wide slots have been cut in the granite to take portcullis blocks, though these were removed many centuries—perhaps thousands of years—ago. So at last we enter the King's Chamber.

It is built entirely of granite, black and highly polished; the mammoth blocks are placed so close together that there is less than a hair's breadth between them. 34 feet 4 inches from west to east, 17 feet 2 inches from north to south, and just over 19 feet in height, the King's Chamber is hollowed out of the heart of the pyramid—not at its exact centre but some distance to the south. Its ceiling is flat, composed of nine slabs of granite weighing in aggregate about 400 tons. Above it, one above the other, are five "relieving chambers" each with a roof of granite slabs, the uppermost being pointed. In this way the Old Kingdom architects solved the problem of supporting the immense superincumbent weight above the chamber (See Vyse's Plan opposite p. 131).

In each of the north and south walls are small rectangular apertures leading to shafts which pierce the thickness of the pyramid at an angle of about 30° till they reach the outer surface (see Plan opposite p. 74). These are the so-called "Ventilating Shafts" though whether they were really intended for this purpose, or had some ritual function, is unknown.

Near the west wall is a simple sarcophagus of granite, uninscribed, and without a lid, made of polished granite, still bearing the marks of the tubular drills used by the ancient workmen. It is rough and unfinished, even the saw-marks being visible. Its width is one inch greater than the width of the Ascending Corridor, so it must have been placed in the chamber before the rest of the pyramid was built.

Now we retrace our steps, down the Grand Gallery and the narrower Ascending Gallery below it, slipping and sliding and groping, until we reach the point where the Ascending Gallery debouches into the Descending Gallery (see Plan). At the foot of the Gallery, the lowest stone in the western ramp has been removed, and below is a black hole. Below it a shaft descends, almost perpendicularly, through the masonry. (See the diagram opposite p. 105.) Our guide flings down a stone, and we hear it ricocheting off the walls of the shaft, down, down, and it seems seconds pass before the noise ceases. This is the "well" which Pliny saw, and which the old chroniclers said led to the Nile. The Arabs are afraid of it. One man tried to explore it, they say, and fell for three hours before reaching the bottom, while the pyramid echoed to his dreadful cries. They nervously lower a candle into it to show its fearful depths, haunted by "afrits" (evil spirits).

It is important to remember, also, that when the pyramid was finished by the Old Kingdom builders, both the Ascending and Descending Galleries were sealed with huge blocks of stone which fitted them accurately.

These, then, are the main features of the Great Pyramid which Bellonius saw, four hundred years ago. And, in the main, this is what we see to-day.

Twenty-eight years after Bellonius, the Pyramids were honoured by a visit by Monsieur Jean Palmerme, Secretary to the Duke of Anjou and of Alençon—the brother of Henri III of France. Vyse, in his paraphrase of M. Palmerme's account, remarks:

"The entrance, he says, was about the seventh and eighth range of stone, and was small and square. He slid down the inclined passage, and found that the bottom was built up with a wall. He then crept through a small hole, and climbed up, but not to so great an height as that from which he had descended; and then he came to a large space, where he found, on the right, a long gallery, which he entered with the help of torches, which were with difficulty kept alight, on account of the multitude of bats; the examination was, therefore, attended with some danger, for if the torches had gone out, he might have missed the way, or have fallen into hollows, or down the different descents. He mentions an echo in this place, and also the well; and describes the Queen's Chamber to have been empty, to have a pointed roof (*voûtée en dos d'âne*) and to have been five or six paces long. . . ."

There is little else which the Frenchman observed that had not already been noted by previous explorers. He climbed to the King's Chamber "which he states to have been a handsome apartment" and notes that the sarcophagus, when struck, "sounded like a bell." He goes on to say that the pyramid "is superior to the antiquities of Ancient Rome". The Second Pyramid he describes as "a solid mass, no entrance or chambers have been discovered in it; and as the surface is smooth, and without steps, it is impossible to arrive at the top, which ended in a point."

This indicates that, whatever the condition of the First or Great Pyramid, the Second Pyramid still retained its smooth limestone casing, and that the entrance was concealed.

In the year 1610, when James I was on the throne of England, and Shakespeare had retired to spend his last years at Stratford-upon-Avon, a sturdy Englishman named Sandys arrived on the Giza plateau. He had already had a look at Egypt and did not think much of it.

"The Egyptian Moors," he writes, "(descended of the Arabians) are men of a mean stature, tawny of complexion, and spare of body, shrill-tongued, and nimble-footed; naturally industrious, affecting more their profit than their ease, yet know they how to live of a little, as in nothing riotous. Rather crafty are they than wise; more observant than faithful; and by much more devout than the Turks in the Mahometan Religion.

". . . the poorer people wear long garments of hair, streaked with black and white; and in winter, side coats of cotton. The beggars by singing, both get relief, and comfort in their poverty; playing withall upon drums which are fashioned like sieves. A number here are afflicted with sore-eyes, either by the reflecting heat, the salt dust of the soyle, or excessive venery; for the pocks is uncredibly frequent amongst them. . . ."

There is a great deal in this vein. For example:

"The countrey people do follow husbandry. They are not long in dressing themselves, being only wrapt in a russet mantle; nor have the women any better coverture; hiding their faces with beastly clouts, having holes for their eyes; which little is too much to see, and abstain from loathing. Over their heads the men wear rounds of stiffened russet; to defend their brains from the piercing fervour. A people breaths not more savage and nasty; crusted with dirt, and stinking of smoke, by reason of the fuel and their houses which have no chimneys. Some of them dwell under beggarly tents, and those esteemed of the olde inhabitants. . . ."

When he approaches the Pyramids (see Illustration 7) he is still determined to be unimpressed.

"Full West of the City, close upon those desarts, a-loft on a rocky level adjoyning to the valley, stand those three Pyramides (the barbarous monuments of prodigality and vain-glory) so universally celebrated."

Although most of what Sandys wrote about the pyramid galleries has been described by earlier and later writers, I make no apology for quoting it at length, if only for the sake of the lusty Jacobean prose in which it is written.

"Descending again, on the east-side below, from each corner equally distant, we approached the entrance, seeming as heretofore to have been closed up, or so intended, both by the place itself, as appeareth, by the following picture, and conveyances within. Into this our Janizaries discharged their harquebuses, lest some should have skult within to have done us a mischief; and guarded the mouth whilst we entered, for fear of the wild Arabs. To take the better footing, we put off our shoes, and most of our apparel; fore-told of the heat within not inferiour to a stove. Our guide (a Moor) went foremost; everyone of us with our lights in our hands. A most dreadful passage, and no less cumbersome; not above a yard in breadth, and four feet in height, each stone containing that measure. So alwaies stooping, and sometimes creeping, by reason of the rubbidge, we descended (not by stairs but as down the steep of a hill) a hundred feet; where the place for a little circuit enlarged; and the fearful descent continued, which they say none ever durst attempt any farther."

This is obviously the "well" near the bottom of the Descending Gallery. Sandys repeats a story told him by the Arabs, that

"... a Bassa (Pasha) of Cairo, curious to search into the secrets thereof, caused divers condemned persons to undertake the performance, well stored with lights, and other provision, and that some of them ascended again well nigh thirty miles off in the Desarts."

But this tale does not impress Mr. Sandys. "A fable," he scoffs, "devised only to beget wonder. ..."

He then approaches the so-called "Queen's Chamber".

"A turning on the right hand leadeth into a little room; which by reason of the noysome savour and uneasie passage, we refused to enter. Clambering over the mouth of the aforesaid dungeon, we ascended as upon the bow of an arch, the way no longer than the former, about an hundred and twenty feet. Here we passed thorow a long entry, which led directly forward, so low, that it took even from us that uneasie benefit of stooping. Which brought us into a little room with a compact roof; more long than broad, of polished marble; whose grave-like smell half full of rubbidge, forced our quick return."

Holding his nose, he retreats from the "little room" and ascends the Grand Gallery to the King's Chamber.

"Climbing also over this entrance, we ascended as before, about an hundred and twenty feet higher. This entry was of an exceeding height, yet no broader from side to side as a man may fathome; benched on each side, and closed above with admirable architecture; the marble so great and so cunningly joyned, as it had been hewn thorow the living rock. At the top we entered into a goodly chamber, twenty foot wide, and forty in length, thereof of a marvellous height; and the stones so great, that eight floors it; eight flag the ends and sixteen the sides; all of well-wrought Theban marble. Athwart the room at the upper end there standeth a tomb (sarcophagus) uncovered, empty and all of one stone; breast high seven feet in length, not four in breadth, and sounding like a bell. In this (no doubt) lay the body of the

builder. They erecting such monuments, not onely out
of vain ostentation; but being of opinion, that after the
dissolution of the flesh the soul should survive; and when
the thirty-six thousand years were expired, again be
joyned unto the self-same body restored unto his former
condition."

The interesting point about Sandys' commonsense account is that practically everything he says concerning the
Great Pyramid is true. Other facts have been discovered
since by excavators who had more time and opportunity
than he had for studying and measuring the monument.
Yet, within the limitations imposed by circumstance, this
seventeenth-century traveller gives us a clear, accurate
description of the interior of the pyramid, and makes a
shrewd estimate of its purpose. Not for him the "granaries
of Joseph" theory; there is no suggestion that the pyramid
was an astronomical observatory or the repository of sacred
mysteries. It was a tomb, he says. The sarcophagus was
intended for the body of the builder, "they erecting such
costly monuments . . . being of the opinion, that after the
dissolution of the flesh the soule should survive. . . ."
Nothing that has been discovered since by the most scientific archæologists contradicts his opinion.

Six years after Sandys' visit, an Italian traveller, Pietro
della Valle, came to Giza. He remarked that the Great
Pyramid was not much inferior in height to St. Peter's,
Rome, and "did not measure it himself, as he believed that
the dimensions taken by Bellonius were correct". Pietro
della Valle's account adds little new to the descriptions of
the earlier travellers. He says that the "tomb at the end
of this chamber", i.e. the King's Chamber, "was made of so
hard a stone that he tried in vain to break it with a hatchet.
It must have been placed in the chamber when the Pyramid
was built."

Thirty years passed before another Englishman left an
account of the Giza pyramids. His name was John Greaves,
Professor of Astronomy at the University of Oxford—the
first Englishman to make a serious survey of the Giza

pyramids and to write a book about them. It is called:

PYRAMIDOGRAPHIA
OR A
DESCRIPTION
OF THE
PYRAMIDS
IN EGYPT

and was published in the year 1646, a year after Cromwell won the battle of Naseby. But Professor Greaves owed his trip to Egypt to the patronage of Laud, Archbishop of Canterbury under Charles I.

"His grand design," writes his biographer, "was to visit the Eastern countries, which by means of the Archbishop he was enabled to do. Mr. Wood observes that His Grace sent him to travel into the Eastern parts of the world, to obtain books of the languages for him. Dr. Smith informs us that Mr. Greaves furnished himself with quadrants and other instruments necessary for taking the altitudes and distances of the stars, and the latitude of cities, for measuring the Pyramids, and making observation of the eclipses, at his own expense, having in vain applied for the patronage and assistance of the magistrates of the City of London. . . ."

In his book Greaves begins by referring to the high estimation in which the Pyramids were held by the Ancients:

". . . as appeares by several testimonies of Herodotus, Diodorus, Strabo and Pliny . . . for Herodotus acknowledges that although there was a Temple at Ephesus very renowned, as also at Samos; yet the Pyramids are worthier of relation; each of which single might be compared with many of the most sumptuous structures of the Græcians. Diodorus Siculus confirmes as much; also as he preferres the wonders of the Aegyptians for magnificence, before those of other nations, so he preferred the Pyramids before the rest of the Aegyptians. . . ."

After regretting the loss of many sacred writings referred to by the Ancients, and the loss of the "sacred commentaries of the Ancient Egyptians, so often cited by Diodorus", he writes:

". . . it will be no superfluous labour to imitate the examples of the Ancients, and to supply the losse of them, by giving a distinct narration of the severall respective dimensions, and proportions of these Pyramids, in which I shall tread in as even a path as I can, between truth, and the traditions of such of the Ancients as are still extant. First, putting downe those relations, which of them have been transmitted to us; and next, shewing in what manner upon examination, I found the Pyramids in the yeares one thousand six hundred thirty eight, and one thousand six hundred thirty nine or in the thousand forty and eighth year of the *Hegira*. . . ."

Greaves is anxious to assure us that he was not a mere casual visitor but a scientific observer . . . "for I twice went to Grand Cairo from Alexandria for the greater certainty, to view them; carrying with me a radius of ten feet most accurately divided, besides some other instruments, for the fuller discovery of the truth. . . ."

As an illustration of the care with which this seventeenth-century *savant* carried out his work, I suggest that the reader studies the engraving (9) reproduced opposite page 80 from page 48 of *Pyramidographia*. Here he will see all the main elements of the Great Pyramid faithfully reproduced and described in Greaves' original caption as: "*The inside of the first and fairest pyramid.*" It clearly shows the ascent into the First Gallery, the "Well", the passage to the Queen's Chamber, the Second Gallery, the first antechamber, and the King's Chamber.

"The structure of it (the Descending Gallery) hath been the labour of an exquisite hand, as appeares by the smoothnesse and evenesse of the work, and by the close knitting of the joints. . . . Having passed with tapers in

our hands this narrow streight, though with some difficulty (for at the farther end of it we must serpent-like
creep upon our bellies) we laid in a place somewhat larger
and of a pretty height, but lying incomposed; having
been dug away, either by the curiosity or avarice of some,
in hope to discover an hidden treasure; or rather by the
command of Alamoun (el Ma'mun) the deservedly renowned Calife of Babylon. By whomsoever it were, it is
not worth the inquiry, nor doth the place merit describing, but that I was unwilling to pretermit any thing;
being only an habitation of bats, and those so ugly, and
of so large a size (exceeding a foot in length), that I have
not elsewhere seen the like."

Continuing along the Ascending Gallery, Greaves describes his ascent into the Grand Gallery.

". . . a very stately piece of work, and not inferiour,
either in respect of curiosity of Art, or richnesses of
materials, to the most sumptuous and magnificent of
buildings. . . . At the end of it, on the right hand, is the
well mentioned by Pliny: the which is circular, and not
square, as the Arabian writers describe. . . . By my
measure sounding it with a line it containes twenty feet
in depth. The reason of the difference between Pliny's
observation and mine, I suppose to be this, that since his
time it hath been almost dammed up, and choaked with
rubbage, which I plainly discovered by throwing down
some combustible material set on fire."

"Leaving the well and going on straight upon a levell,
the distance of fifteen feet, we entered another square
passage, opening against the former, and of the same
bignesse. The stones are very massy and exquisitely
joined, I know not wither of that glittering and speckled
marble, I mentioned in the columns, of the cisterns of
Alexandria. This leadeth (running in length upon a levell
an hundred and ten feet) into an arched vault or little
chamber; which by reason of its grave-like smell and
half-full of rubbage, occasioned my lesser stay. . . ."

He is greatly impressed by the fineness of the granite masonry in the Grand Gallery.

". . . the coagmentation, or knitting of the joints, is so close that they are scarcely discernable by a curious eye, and that which adds grace to the whole structure, though it makes the passage the more slippery and difficult, is the acclivity and rising of the ascent."

After giving the dimensions of the Grand Gallery, he mentions that it is "bounded on both sides by two banks (like benches) of sleek and polished stone; each of these hath one foot seven hundred seventeen of a thousand parts of a foot in breadth, and as much in depth". (Note the precision of his measurements when he has opportunities to measure.) Then he mentions a curious feature which no other writer had described before, but which was to have great significance in later years when archæologists were trying to discover how the Ancient Egyptians sealed the Ascending Gallery with the giant plug-blocks.

"Upon the top of these benches near the angle, where they close, and join with the wall, are little spaces cut in right-angled parallel figures, set on each side opposite to one another; intended, no question, for some other end than ornament. . . ." (In this he was right.)

He carefully measures and describes the antechamber, with its grooves for portcullis blocks—which he illustrates with engravings, and then he enters the King's Chamber.

"This rich and spacious chamber, in which art may seem to have contended with nature, the curious work being not inferiour to the rich materials, stands as it were in the heart and centre of the Pyramid, equidistant from all the sides, and almost in the middle between the *basis* and the top. The floor, the sides, the roof of it, are all made of vast and exquisite tables of *Thebaick* marble, which, if they were not veiled and obscured by the steam of tapers, would appear glittering and shining. From the

top of it descending to the bottom, there are but six
ranges of stone, all of which, being respectively sized to an
equal height, very graceful in one and the same altitude,
run round the room. The stones, which cover this place,
are of a strange and stupendous length, like so many huge
beams lying flat, and traversing the room, and withal
supporting that infinite mass, and weight of the Pyramid
above.

"... Within this glorious room (for so I may justly call
it) as within some consecrated oratory, stands the monument of Cheops, or Chemmis, of one piece of marble,
hollow within, and uncovered at the top, and sounding like a bell. ... The depth is two feet, and eight hundred and sixty of the thousand parts of an English
foot."

It may be a fancy, but it seems to me that this passage
from Greaves' *Pyramidographia* epitomizes the English approach to Ancient Egypt, as distinct from, say, that of the
Latins and the Germans. The Latins are usually either
coolly scientific or supercilious and flippant. The Germans
—among whom may be numbered the greatest Egyptologists—are painstaking, thorough, but sometimes ponder-
ously dull. But among most of the Englishmen who have
gained distinction as archæologists, one finds again and
again a rather endearing mixture of common sense and
romanticism. Petrie had it. So had Carter. So had Sir
Arthur Evans. They are careful, usually scientific, with a
strong practical bent. Yet, every now and then the plod-
ding prose of their narratives is suddenly enriched by
passages of quite unseltconscious poetry. You can see it in
the passage I have just quoted, when, after telling us that
the depth of the sarcophagus is "two feet, and eight hundred
and sixty of the thousand parts of the English foot", this
Oxford astronomer suddenly breaks into the cadences of
Sir Thomas Browne:

"A narrow space, yet large enough to contain a most
potent and dreadful monarch, being dead, to whom,

living, all Egypt was too streight and narrow a circuit. . . ."

But common sense is uppermost. Reading through Greaves' carefully-documented, tightly-reasoned book, written more than three hundred years ago, one marvels at the way in which, with only the ancient authorities to guide him, and a very brief and necessarily incomplete survey of the Pyramids, he came so near to the truth. Hampered as he is by having to allay the religious prejudice of his day, with its insistence on the literal truth of the Old Testament, he yet manages to avoid the major pitfalls.

"It is the opinion of some modern writers, that the Egyptian pyramids were erected by the Israelites, during their heavy pressure under the tyranny of the Pharaohs. . . . But the sacred scriptures clearly expressing the slavery of the Jews, to have consisted in making and burning of brick . . . whereas these Pyramids consist of stone, I cannot be induced to subscribe to their assertion. . . ."

Nor is he content with this slender argument, but goes on to demolish the theory that the *Hyksos*, or Shepherd Kings, who were driven out of Egypt by Tuthmosis I were, in fact, the Israelites.

"The whole force of his (Josephus's) opinion, is this, that Manetho mentions the expulsion of the nations of shepherds by Tethmosis; but the Hebrews were a nation of shepherds, therefore the Hebrews were expelled out of Egypt, or, in the scripture-phrase, departed out of Egypt. . . . By way of answer to Josephus (a Jewish historian) we say, that though the Israelites might properly be called shepherds, yet it cannot hence be inferred out of Manetho, that these shepherds were Israelites. Nay, if we compare this relation of Manetho, with that in Exodus, which Josephus, being a Jew cannot but approve of, we shall find the contrary. For there they live under a heavy slavery and persecution, whereas here they are the persecutors and afflictors; there they groan under their task-masters, here they make Egypt to groan under them. . . ."

Nearly all the fanciful theories revived by religious cranks two hundred years later are known to Greaves, who gives them a short shrift. The "granaries of Joseph" theory:

". . . besides that this figure is most improper for such a purpose (a Pyramid being the least capacious of any regular mathematical body) the streightness and fewness of the rooms within (the rest of the building being one solid and entire fabrick of stone) do utterly overthrow this conjecture."

The "astronomical observatory" theory:

"That the priests might, near these pyramids, make their observations, I in no way question; this rising of the hill being, in my judgment, as fit a place as any in Egypt for such a design; and so fitter by the vicinity of Memphis. But that these Pyramids were designed for Observatories (whereas by the testimonies of the ancients I have proved before, that they were intended for sepulchres) is in no way to be credited. . . . Neither can I apprehend to what purpose the priests with so much difficulty should ascend so high, when below with more ease, and as much certainty, they might from their own lodgings hewn in the rocks, upon which the Pyramids were erected, make the same observations. . . ."

His more positive conclusions have been abundantly borne out by more modern observers, writing with a knowledge of Ancient Egyptian history of which he—not understanding the inscriptions—was ignorant.

". . . I conceive the reason why they made these Sepulchres in the figure of a Pyramid, was either as apprehending this to be the most permanent form of structure, as in truth it is (for, by reason of the contracting and lessening of it at the top, it is neither over-pressed with its own weight, nor is it so subject to the sinking in of rain as in other buildings); or hereby they intended to represent some of their gods."

As to the reason why the Egyptians should have built such mighty monuments to contain their royal dead, he has no doubts that:

". . . this sprang from the theology of the Egyptians, who, as Servius shews in his comment upon these words of Virgil, describing the funeral of Polydorus, '——— Animamque sepucro Condimus ———' believed, that *as long as the body endured, so long the soul continued with it* . . . not as quickening and animating it, but as an attendant or guardian, and, as it were, unwilling to leave her former habitation."

The extraordinary point of this passage is that it accurately describes what some modern Egyptologists, after studying the ancient religious texts, think the Ancient Egyptians believed regarding the *ka*, or "double" of the deceased.

But here, alas, we shall have to leave Professor Greaves, struggling perspiringly out of the pyramid gallery into the sunlight, clutching his "radius of ten feet most accurately divided", his quadrant, and his notes for Archbishop Laud.

"We are now come abroad into the light and sun, where I found my jannizarry, and an English captain, a little impatient to have waited above three hours without, in expectation of my return; who imagined what they understood not, to be an impertinent and vain curiosity."

CHAPTER FIVE

PYRAMID PUZZLES

THROUGHOUT the seventeenth and eighteenth centuries the number of European visitors to the Pyramids increased. Most of them repeat each other, and are not worth quoting. But from time to time some explorer more enterprising, curious or observant than the rest notices something that his predecessors have missed, and so a little knowledge is gained. One can liken the search to a detective story. The puzzles to be solved are: (a) who built the Pyramids? (b) why were they built? and (c) how were they built? To most of us to-day—with the exception of a few eccentrics—the answer to the first two questions is beyond doubt. They were built by the Pharaohs as tombs, as Greaves and others before him recognized. The most interesting question is the third—how were they built?—and this involves a number of equally interesting subsidiary questions.

The most puzzling pyramid of all is the Great Pyramid. Please glance again at the Plan (2) opposite page 74. What was the reason for the building's complicated inner structure? Why did it have a Descending Gallery leading to an empty, unfinished chamber cut in the rock, as well as an Ascending Gallery hewn out of the masonry leading (a) to the Horizontal Gallery ending in the so-called Queen's Chamber and (b) the Grand Gallery, much higher than the first part of the Ascending Gallery which leads to it, and admitting first to a short passage with grooves in the side walls, and thence to the King's Chamber which alone contains a sarcophagus? What was the purpose of the holes in the northern and southern walls of the King's Chamber leading to oblique shafts which penetrate the pyramid structure until they reach the outer air? What was the reason for the three main chambers when other pyramids rarely have more than one, at the most two? What was the function of the mysterious "well" which descends through the masonry at the foot of the Grand Gallery?

Again, having built the pyramid and interred the king, how did the ancient builders seal the Ascending Gallery with close-fitting granite blocks? It would have been impossible to have pushed them up from below. And having sealed this Gallery, how did the workmen escape? Or did they escape?

Most, though not all, of these questions can now be satisfactorily answered, but—unless he wishes to cheat by reading the end of the book first—the reader must at present content himself with the clues discovered by the various explorers I have quoted and shall quote in succeeding chapters. They will all be given!

Other questions which have to be answered were how the Ancient Egyptians raised the enormous blocks into position without the aid of machinery, how they achieved such precise orientation of these buildings—the maximum error in the orientation of the Great Pyramid is 5' 30", or a little over *one-twelfth of a degree*. The magnetic compass was unknown to the Ancient Egyptians. By what means did they achieve such fineness of workmanship that, in the words of Sir Flinders Petrie:

". . . the mean thickness of the eastern joint of the northern casing stones is .020" (1/50th of an inch)."

Therefore the mean variation of the cutting of the stone from a straight line is but .01" (1/100th part of an inch)—

". . . of 75 inches up the face . . . these joints, with an area of 35 square feet each, were not only worked as finely as this, but cemented throughout. Though the stones were brought as close as 1/500th of an inch, or, in fact, into contact, the mean opening of the joint was 1/50th of an inch, yet the builders managed to fill the joint with cement, despite the great area of it, and the weight of the stone, some 16 tons. . . ."

When Greaves drew up his plan of the Galleries (No. 9,

opposite page 80) he saw almost as much of the interior of the pyramid as we can see to-day. The only parts he was unable to explore were the "relieving chambers" above the King's Chamber, the bottom of the "well" and, most important, the lower part of the Descending Gallery and the chamber to which it leads.

Subsequent travellers in the seventeenth century saw little more than he did, and most failed to observe as much. There was, for instance, a M. de Monconys, who paid a visit in 1647, who adds nothing to our knowledge. The next visitor to leave an account was another Frenchman, M. Thevenot (1655) who, although he did not venture down himself, tells us that a certain anonymous Scotsman tried to explore the "well".

". . . A Scotch gentleman was let down with some other persons, which was the second time it had been entered. . . . The well was not entirely perpendicular; it went down about sixty-seven feet to a grotto, from whence it again descended to the depth of one hundred and twenty-three feet, when it was filled up with sand. It contained an immense quantity of bats, so that the Scotchman was afraid of being eaten up by them, and was obliged to guard the candle with his hands. This well, he conceives, was made for the conveyance of mummies into the cavern under the Pyramid."

After him came a Mr. Melton, an English traveller, who wrote an account in Dutch in which he mentions that the Pyramids are called by the Arabs "the mountains of Pharaoh" but he adds nothing to what previous explorers had written. Like other seventeenth- and eighteenth-century travellers, he treated the great monument with scant respect. He tried to break the sarcophagus with a hammer "which he brought with him for the purpose", but failed, though, as usual, the granite chest "sounded like a bell". He and his companions also "discharged firearms into the entrance to drive away serpents", which seems to have been the usual practice.

However, he does mention the *mastaba* tombs of the nobles near the pyramid, which other travellers usually ignored.

". . . these monuments were regularly placed; each of the three larger were at the head of ten smaller, many of which had been destroyed."

After Greaves, the first explorer to make a positive contribution to our knowledge of the pyramids was a Mr. Maillet, who was Consul-General in Egypt from 1692 to 1708. No doubt he had more frequent opportunities to examine them than had most of his predecessors.

Maillet is the first writer I have found who seriously tackles the problem of how the men who first entered the Great Pyramid, whether they were Ancient Egyptians or Arabs, removed the great blocking stones which sealed the Ascending and Descending Galleries.

Vyse, in his paraphrase of Maillet's report, writes:

"He conceives that these blocks had been loosened by means of hot water, and says that they had, at all events, been taken out without injury to the walls of the passage, where notches had been cut in the floor to assist the descent. It was evident that, at the end of this passage, attempts had been also made to remove the stones where another, ascending at nearly the same angle and in a direct line with the former, had been closed up[1] and he describes the difficulty attending the supposed search for this communication. . . . He conceives that when the granite blocks, which filled up the ascending passage, were discovered, an excavation had been made to the right to get round them, and to re-enter it at a higher point, and that, as the granite blocks, at present seen at the bottom of this passage, do not exactly fit, that those originally placed there had been broken up and removed,

---

[1] As Vyse remarks, it does not appear why any ascending passage should have been expected. "It has, therefore, been supposed that the calcareous stone which concealed the granite blocks in it, must have accidentally fallen out of the ceiling of the descending passage, and have led to the discovery."

and that the rest had slid down from the upper part; and he concludes that, with the exception of these three, all the blocks with which this passage had been filled, were successively broken up and carried away."

It may be imagined what a Herculean task this must have been, in a passage in which it is barely possible for a man to stand upright.

"He adds that it was evident, from the ruined appearance of this passage, that great violence had been employed on the occasion."

He then describes the Horizontal Gallery leading to the Queen's Chamber:

". . . and is of the opinion that the slight projection, on the right side of the entrance into this chamber, was intended to prevent the stones, with which the horizontal passage had been filled, from being forced beyond the entrance of this room, and that the stone originally placed there fitted it exactly."

After describing the Ante-chamber, suggesting that the portcullis was constructed in the passage leading to the King's Chamber, and that the grooves over the entrance were "to facilitate the insertion of the stone which closed it", the so-called "Ventilating Shafts" in the King's Chamber lead him to a strange conclusion.

"He conceives that the king was buried in it (the sarcophagus) and that many of his attendants were also enclosed alive in the chamber, who were successively buried by each other in separate coffins, excepting the last one, who, M. Maillet remarks, could not have received any assistance, and must therefore have buried himself. He was led to this conclusion by observing the air-holes, which he states to have been exactly in the middle of the opposite walls, and at a height of $3\frac{1}{2}$ feet from the pavement."

Maillet could not have seen the mouths of these air-shafts on the outer surface of the pyramid because he states that the one of the northern side penetrated "in a horizontal direction" to the outside of the building, and that the other descended towards the bottom of the pyramid. Actually each shaft inclines upwards at an angle of about 30 degrees.

These contradictory accounts given by various travellers, few of whom ever seem to agree on dimensions, show the necessity for a really accurate scientific survey and measurement of the monument, which was not accomplished until the young Flinders Petrie spent two years at Giza between 1880 and 1881.[1]

Maillet also has the distinction of being the first writer partially to recognize the true function of the so-called "well".

". . . when the funeral had taken place, the workmen closed up the passages with the stones contained in the Great Gallery, and descended by the shaft, the upper part of which was afterwards, by some contrivance, closed with machinery. He remarks that this communication had never been properly explored, and that the Pyramid has always been entered by the regular passage" (i.e. by the Descending Gallery and from them into the Ascending Gallery).

By this presumably he implies that the "well" led to some concealed, separate exit from the pyramid as described in the Arab romances quoted earlier. But here Maillet was wrong. The "well" was used to enable the workmen to escape but not by the route he imagined.

Meanwhile, eighteenth-century travellers continued to confuse their readers with differing opinions as to who built the Pyramids. Egmont (1709) cites various traditions that they were built by Joseph, by Nimrod, by Queen Dalukah (whoever she was) or by the Israelites. Perizonius (1711) ascribes them to the Hebrews. And, of course, they all quote Herodotus, Pliny and Diodorus Siculus.

[1] Though Vyse and Perring did sound work in 1833-38.

Other writers question the belief that the Pyramids were tombs. Shaw, who visited Giza in 1721, "considers that the internal construction of the Great Pyramid ill-adapted for a sepulchre, and thinks that it was a temple". The sarcophagus, he says, "was intended for the celebration of the mystical worship of Osiris," and supposes that it contained "images, sacred vestments, and utensils, or water for lustration". On what authority he does not tell us.

Shaw's account, though not very interesting in itself, is contained in his *Travels in Barbary*, which is well worth reading for its descriptions of Bedouin customs, and of the perils and hardships endured by European travellers who ventured into the remoter parts of the Middle East in the early eighteenth century.

"In travelling along the sea coast of Syria, and from Suez to Mount Sinai, we were in little or no danger of being either robbed or insulted, provided we kept company with the caravan and did not stray from it; but a neglect of this kind, through too great a curiosity in looking after plants and other curiosities, may expose the traveller, as it once did myself, to the great danger of being assassinated. For whilst I was thus amusing myself, and had lost sight of the caravan, I was suddenly overtaken and stripped by three strolling Arabs; and had not the divine Providence interposed in raising compassion in one, whilst the other two were fighting over my clothes (mean and ragged though they were) I must inevitably have fallen sacrifice to their rapine and cruelty."

His travelling conditions are vividly described in the Preface:

"In our journies between Kairo and Mount Sinai, the heavens were every night our covering; the sand, with a carpet spread over it, was our bed; and a change of raiment, made up into a bundle, was our pillow. And in this situation we were every night wet to the skin, by the copious dew that dropt upon us, though without the least danger (such is the excellence of the climate) of our catching cold. The continued heat of the day afterwards, made us wish that these refrigerations could have been hourly repeated. . . . Yet the cold and the dews that we were every night exposed to, in the deserts of Arabia, did not incommode us half so much as the vermin and insects of all kinds, which never failed to molest us. . . . Beside fleas and lice, which might be said, without a miracle, to be here in all their quarters, the apprehensions we were under . . . of being bitten or stung by the scorpion, or the viper, or the venomous spider, rarely failed to interrupt our repose. . . ."

Shaw was more interested in people than their monuments.

"The dancing girls form a distinct class. They are always attended by an old man and woman, who play on musical instruments, and look to the conduct of the girls, that they may not bestow their favours for an inadequate reward; for though not chaste, they are by no means common. Their dances exhibit all that the most luxurious imagination can picture—all the peculiar motions and arts for which Martial has remarked the Egyptians are celebrated,

Nequitias Tellus scit dare nulla magis."

Merely to read the chapter summaries alone of some of these early travel books compels admiration and respect for these pioneers of Middle Eastern travel. Here are the subheadings of one chapter of Browne's *Travels in Africa, Egypt and Syria* (1792–98):

"*Departure from Assiut—Journey to El-Wab—Mountains—Deserts . . . Difficulties—Enter the Kingdom of Fur . . . Detention—Representation to the Malek—Residence—New Difficulties—Villainy of Agent—Illness—Robbery—Atrocious Conduct of my Kahirene Servant*" etc., etc.

Among the most indefatigable of these travellers was Richard Pococke, LL.D., F.R.S., who saw the Pyramids during the middle of the eighteenth century. Unlike most of his predecessors, he was not content only to see the Giza group but visited scores of others. (See Illustration 10.) In his great folio volume, Plate 18 shows eighteen pyramids, at Saqqara and Dashur, all of which he visited and examined as far as he was able. Not only did he visit them but he made measurements and drew plans. This book contains the first account I have been able to discover of the "Step Pyramid" of Djoser.

"Near these is the pyramid (F) called by the Arabs the 'pyramid with steps'. I omitted to measure it any otherwise than by paces, by which I computed the measure to be three hundred feet to the north, and two hundred and seventy-five to the east. This is . . . a hundred and fifty feet high consisting of six steps or degrees, eleven feet broad and twenty-five feet deep in the perpendicular, being, I suppose thirty-five in the inclined plane on some of the sides, as I measured it in some parts . . . the outer casing is of hewn stone, twenty tiers to each degree, each tier being one foot three inches deep. . . ."

At Giza he not only examines the pyramids but also the attendant *mastabas*, and correctly recognizes their purpose.

"They might be the sepulchres of the near dependants, or possibly of some of the relations of the Kings who were buried in the great pyramids."

Also he mentions the causeways described by Herodotus, parts of which were visible in Pococke's time.

"For at this time there is a causeway . . . extending about a thousand yards in length, and twenty feet wide, built of hewn stone; the length of it agreeing well with the account of Herodotus is a strong confirmation that this causeway has been kept up ever since."

The industrious explorer gives sixty-one sets of dimensions of the Great Pyramid, in feet and inches, though he admits to taking some of these from Greaves, Maillet and Sicard.

And then, in the middle of measurements and computations he describes a little incident which illustrates only too clearly the conditions under which he and other pioneers worked.

"Returning from visiting the catacombs (at Sakkara) sooner than was expected, when I unlocked the door of the room the Sheikh had put me into at his house, a little girl about eight years old ran out of the room against me; laying hold of her, she cried out, but I had presence of mind enough to let her go, it being a great affront in these countries for anyone to lay hands on the fair sex; and discovering any roguery (which I immediately apprehended), would have caused an embroil in the family, had the Sheikh taken my part or not. As soon as I came into the room, I saw a hole had been broke through the ceiling, though the room was ten feet high, and as I supposed, the mother had let the child down by a rope to rifle my baggage. . . ."

A few years after Pococke another traveller, Davison (1763) won the distinction of being the first explorer in modern times to penetrate nearly to the bottom of the mysterious "well", or at least the first explorer to leave an account of his adventure.[1] It was an intrepid performance, well described in a letter to a Mr. Varsey—which I have been unable to trace—but which is paraphrased in an article from the *Quarterly Review* of 1817.

"In a short but comprehensive letter addressed to Mr. Varsey, the author observes that, as he conceived the supposed well to be of vast depth, he provided himself with a large quantity of rope, which turned out to be no useless precaution, for though he found a sort of steps or holes in the rock, yet the lower part of them was so worn away, as to risk a fall and consequent destruction by trusting to them alone. To avoid so calamitous an event, Mr. Davison tied a rope round his middle; and previously to his descent let down a lanthorn attached to the end of

[1] The "Scotchman" mentioned by Thevenot may have performed this feat.

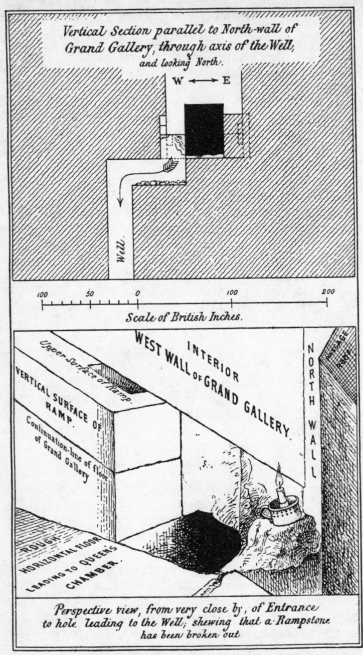

Vertical Section parallel to North-wall of
Grand Gallery, through axis of the Well,
and looking North.

W ←——→ E

Well.

100   50   0   100   200

Scale of British Inches.

INTERIOR
WEST WALL OF GRAND GALLERY.
NORTH WALL
PASSAGE ROOF
Upper Surface of Ramp.
VERTICAL SURFACE OF RAMP.
Continuation-line of floor of Grand Gallery.
ROUGH HORIZONTAL FLOOR LEADING TO QUEEN'S CHAMBER.

*Perspective view, from very close by, of Entrance
to hole leading to the Well; shewing that a Rampstone
has been broken out*

3. The entrance to the "Well" in the Great Pyramid
(explored by Davison)

a small cord, which, on finding it soon to stop, he prepared to follow. With much persuasion he prevailed on two of his servants and three Arabs to hold the rope; the Arabs assured him that there were ghosts below, and that he never could hope to return.

"Mr. Davison laughed at their timidity; and taking with him a few sheets of paper, a compass, a measure, and another lighted candle, commenced the descent, and soon reached the bottom of the first well or shaft. Here he found, on the south side, at a distance of about eight feet from the first shaft, a second opening which descended perpendicularly, to the depth of five feet only; and at four feet ten inches from the bottom of this a third shaft, the mouth of which was nearly choked up with a large stone, leaving only a small opening, barely sufficient to allow a man to pass."

Here Davison thought it prudent to pause and let down his lantern:

". . . not only to discover to what depth he was about to proceed, but also to ascertain if the air was pernicious. The shaft, however, was so tortuous that the candle soon became invisible; but Mr. Davison was not to be discouraged—nothing less than a journey to the bottom would satisfy his eager curiosity; the difficulty was how to prevail on the Arabs to come down and hold the rope. To all his entreaties they only answered that, a few years before, a Frank having got to the place where he then was, let down a rope to discover the depth, when the devil caught hold of it, and plucked it out of his hands. 'I was well aware,' says Mr. Davison, 'to whom they were indebted for this story—the Dutch consul swore that the thing happened to himself.' After many prayers, and threats and promises of money, and all the treasure that might be discovered at the bottom of the well, the avarice of one man got the better, in some degree, of his terrors, and he ventured to descend. 'On reaching the bottom,' writes Mr. Davison, 'he stared about him pale and trembling, appearing more like a spectre than a human being.'

"Our enterprising adventurer now hastened on his journey, with the rope round his body; and the sight of the lantern, which he had just let down, convinced him that this well was somewhat deeper than the first. . . ."

So, swinging on his rope, and occasionally snatching a foot-hold on the rough, rocky sides of the shaft, Davison descended, deeper and deeper, until he came to "a grotto, about fifteen feet long". But this was not the bottom. Below it yawned an even deeper shaft, in which the candle glimmered far below.

"Throwing down a stone he ascertained it to be of much greater depth than the others; pushing the lantern a little before him he set out afresh on his journey; and calling to the Arab to loosen the rope gently, with the help of the little holes made in the rock, he gradually proceeded, without the least appearance of reaching his journey's end. At length the shaft beginning to incline a little more to the perpendicular, brought him speedily to the bottom, where he ascertained it to be completely closed by sand and rubbish."

Actually Davison had not quite reached the bottom, though he was very near it, but sand at the foot of the shaft blocked further progress. Resting from his exertions in that four-thousand-year-old, man-made chasm, he thought of two unpleasant possibilities.

"The first was, that the multitude of bats might put out this candle" (which he could not re-light), "and the second that the immense stone at the mouth of the shaft might slip down and close the passage for ever."

When at last he climbed back to the foot of the first shaft, where he had left the Arab, the candle *did* go out.

"Then says he 'the poor Arab thought himself lost. He laid hold of the rope as I was about to ascend, declaiming that he would rather have his brains blown out than be left alone with the devil. I therefore permitted him to go before, and though it was much more difficult to ascend than descend, I know not how it was, but he scrambled up a hundred times more quickly than he had come down.' "

The depth of the first shaft was twenty-two feet; of the second twenty-nine; and of the third ninety-nine; making a total with the five feet between the first and second shafts, of 155 feet.

After reading Davison's account we can appreciate more readily the boldness of Captain Caviglia, who, in 1817, finally cleared the "well" and solved the mystery of its purpose. Caviglia, who will appear later in this book, was the owner of a trading vessel. Like his fellow-countryman, Signor Belzoni, he appears to have been one of those enter-prising amateurs of uncertain status, who established a reputation as pyramid excavators. The only account I can find is given in the *Quarterly Review* (1818) and is based on a report by a Mr. Salt who was British Consul-General in Egypt at the time. It is so dramatic that I make no apology for quoting it almost in full.

Incidentally, it may arouse in us a certain sympathy for the unfortunate Egyptian workmen who, like their remote ancestors who built the Pyramids, found themselves driven on by stern (and contemptuous) taskmasters. After being lowered to the bottom of the well, as Davison had been fifty years before, Caviglia was not content, but "from the circumstance of the ground giving a hollow sound under his feet, he was satisfied that there must be some concealed outlet". Now read on.

"With the view of making further discovery, he pitched his tent in front of the entrance of the Great Pyramid, determined to set about excavating the bottom of the Well. He hired some Arabs to draw up the rubbish with baskets and cords; but from the extreme reluctance of these people to work, notwithstanding the enormous wages given to them, he was compelled to suspend his operations and give up the enterprise, till an order from the—*Kiaya*—bey, had the effect of subduing their indolence, and, to a certain degree, of removing their prejudices. 'It is still,' says Mr. Salt, 'almost inconceivable how he could so far surmount the prejudices of these people as to induce them to work in so confined a space, where a light, after the first half-hour, would not burn (owing to the impure air) and where, consequently, everything was to be done by feeling and not by sight; the heat at the same time being so intense and the air so suffocating that, in spite of all precautions, it was not possible to stay below for more than an hour at a time without suffering from its pernicious effects. At length, indeed, it became so intolerable that one Arab was brought up nearly dead, and several others, on their ascending, fainted away.

" 'So that at last, in spite of the command laid upon them, they almost entirely abandoned their labour, declaring that they were willing to work but not die for him.' "

"Thus discouraged, Mr. Caviglia next turned his attention to the clearing of the principal entrance or passage of the pyramid which, from time immemorial, had been so blocked up as to oblige those who entered to creep on their hands and knees; hoping by this to give a freer passage to the air. He not only succeeded in carrying out his purpose, but, in the course of his labours, made the unexpected discovery that *the main passage, leading from the entrance, did not terminate in the manner asserted by Maillet, but* (having removed several large masses of calcareous stone and granite, apparently placed there to obstruct the passage) *that it still continued in the same angle downwards, was of the same dimension, and had its sides worked with the same care, as in the channel above,*[1] though filled up nearly to the top with earth and fragments of stone

"Having proceeded to the length of 150 feet in clearing

[1] Our italics.

out this passage, the air began to be so impure and the heat so suffocating that he had the same difficulties again to encounter with regard to the working Arabs. Even his own health was at this time visibly impaired, and he was attacked with a spitting of blood; nothing, however, could induce him to desist from his researches.

"By the 14th March, 1817, he had excavated as low down as 200 feet in the new passage without any thing particular occurring, when shortly afterwards a doorway on the right side was discovered, from which, in the course of a few hours, a strong smell of sulphur was perceived to issue. Mr. Caviglia having now recollected that when at the bottom of the well, in his first enterprise, he had burned some sulphur for the purpose of purifying the air, conceived it probably that this doorway might communicate with it, an idea which, in a little time, he had the gratification of seeing realized, by discovering that the channel through the doorway opened at once upon the bottom of the well, where he found the baskets, cords and other implements which had been left there on his recent attempt at a further excavation. This discovery was so far valuable as it afforded a complete circulation of air along the new passage, and up the shaft of the well into the chamber, so as to obviate all danger for the future from the impurity of the atmosphere."

Another pyramid puzzle—one which had perplexed generations of travellers—was solved at last. The "well" was, as Maillet suspected, an escape shaft. But it did not communicate with a separate entrance, but linked up with the Descending Gallery, which, unknown to Maillet and those who came before him, extended *beyond* the entrance to the Ascending Gallery for several hundred feet. Thus, after sealing the Ascending Gallery the ancient workmen could make their escape down the shaft, returning to the light along the Descending Gallery, which they afterwards sealed with more plug-blocks inserted through the entrance. There was only one entrance to the pyramid. (See Plan 2 opposite page 74.)

CHAPTER SIX

BELZONI OPENS THE SECOND PYRAMID

W H E N Caviglia discovered that the Descending Gallery extended beyond the entrance to the Ascending Gallery, and proved that the "well" was an escape shaft connecting the two, it seemed that the Great Pyramid had no further secrets to reveal. All the galleries were open, and subsequent excavations have failed to disclose the existence of any others.

Yet still the explorers were not satisfied. It seemed inconceivable to rational minds that such an enormous mass of masonry should be *solid*. Surely there must be other chambers elsewhere? Colonel Howard Vyse expresses this point of view very clearly in his *Pyramids of Gizeh*, an account of the survey which he carried out with Mr. Perring, a civil engineer, in 1837–38.

"I had not at that time any idea that the stupendous masses of the pyramids were composed of solid masonry, and that (with the exception of the King's and Queen's Chambers, and the adjoining passages and chambers of construction afterwards discovered in this pyramid) the apartments were invariably excavations in the solid rock. Indeed, after having ascertained the fact almost beyond the possibility of doubt, it was difficult to believe it, or to comprehend an adequate motive for the construction of these magnificent buildings merely as sepulchral monuments over a tomb, unless it was the all-powerful influence of superstitious feelings."

This reluctance to accept the buildings as they stood resulted in a further onslaught on the unfortunate Pyramids. But whereas the Arabs had used battering rams the European explorers of the early nineteenth century employed gunpowder; though before this stage was reached one or two minor attacks were made with conventional weapons.

Mr. Davison, who in 1793 explored the "well", was also responsible for finding the "relieving chambers" above the King's Chamber (see Plan opposite p. 131). There are five of these, one above the other, empty chambers roofed and floored with granite blocks, the uppermost having a pointed roof, and their purpose was clearly to prevent the superincumbent weight of the pyramid crushing in the roof of the King's Chamber. Davison discovered the lowest of them (which, in the old books, is called "Davison's Chamber") by entering through a hole at the top of the Grand Gallery, and his account of this exploit is worth quoting.

The first problem was to get up to the hole.

"For this purpose I made seven short ladders in such a manner as to fasten one to another by means of four wooden pins, the whole together, being joined, being about twenty six feet long. As soon as the rubbish was cleared from the straight passage at the bottom I caused the ladder to be brought in by two carpenters, who accompanied me. When they had conveyed them to the platform at the top of the gallery, tying two long canes together I placed a candle at one end, and gave it to a servant to hold near the hole in question. The platform being very small there was no thinking of fixing the ladders to the ground, as it would have been very difficult, not to say impossible, to raise them. We took the only method which seemed practicable; namely, that of placing the first ladder against the wall; two men raising it up, a third placed another below it, and having fastened them together were raised from the ground, and the rest in the same manner fixed one after another. The ladder entered enough into the hole, when all the parts were joined together, to prevent it sliding on the side of the gallery.

"I then instantly mounted, and found a passage two feet four inches square which turned immediately to the right. I entered a little way, with my face on the ground but was obliged to retire, on account of the passage being in a great measure choked with dust and bats' dung, which, in some places was near a foot deep. I thought of clearing it by throwing the dirt down into the gallery, but foreseeing that this would be a work of some time, besides the inconvenience of filling the gallery with rubbish, and perhaps rendering the descent more difficult, I determined to enter, which was accompanied by more success than the first. I was enabled to creep in, though with much difficulty, not only on account of the lowness of the passage, but likewise the quantity of dust which I raised.

"When I had advanced a little way, I discovered what I supposed to be the end of the passage. My surprise was great, when I reached it, to find to the right a straight entrance into a long, broad, but low place, which I knew as well by the length as the direction of the passage I had entered at, to be immediately above the large room" (i.e. the King's Chamber). "The stones of granite, which are at the top of the latter, form the bottom of this, but are uneven, being of unequal thickness. This room is four feet longer than the one below; in the latter you see only seven stones, and a half of one, on each side of them; but in that above, the nine are entire, the two halves resting on the wall at each end. The breadth is equal with that of the room below. The covering of this, as of the other, is of beautiful granite; but it is composed of eight stones, instead of nine, the number in the room below. One of the carpenters entered with me, and Mr. Maynard came into the passage, near the door, but being a good deal troubled with the dust and want of air, he retired. Having measured and examined the different parts of it we came out and descended the ladder."

The Great Pyramid had revealed its last secret. No more "rooms" remained to be discovered, apart from the upper relieving chambers which Vyse was to find, seventy years later, by the adroit use of blasting-powder. They contained no treasures, and generation after generation of frustrated explorers were to hack and blast at the ancient stones before giving up the struggle and accepting Vyse's reluctant conclusion, that "the stupendous masses of the pyramids were composed of solid masonry".

* * *

But, before the scientific archæologists arrived with their theodolites and measuring tapes, the Pyramids were to see one more adventurer of the old school—ebullient, unscientific, imbued with a sense of wonder and adventure, and not very respectable.   His name was Giovanni Belzoni, an Italian engineer who had lived in Britain for a time, and then arrived in Egypt in 1815 hoping to sell to the Sultan Mahomet Ali a new hydraulic machine of which he was the inventor.   The Sultan wasn't interested, so Giovanni found himself stranded in Egypt with no cash, and only his fertile brain to support him.   He was a man of enormous physique and uncertain temper.   Among other things he had been for a time a weight-lifter in a circus.

By this time (1816) interest in Ancient Egypt had become much more widespread.   In 1798 the Pyramids had seen Napoleon's armies defeat the forces of Murad Bey and Ibrahim Bey, and during the three years of French occupation which followed the Emperor sent an expedition of *savants* to study and survey the monuments of the ancient land, and it is from this period that modern Egyptological research truly begins.   In 1799 was found the famous Rosetta stone, with its bilingual inscription, and philologists had begun to struggle with the decipherment of the hieroglyphs.   Beginning in the studies of the scholars, a wave of interest in Ancient Egypt spread outwards until it engulfed cultivated European society.   Ancient Egyptian motifs decorated Empire furniture.   European museums began to demand Ancient Egyptian objects; mummies, sarcophagi, statuary, obelisks.

This gave Belzoni his chance.   He decided to make a journey through Egypt in search of antiquities, partly sponsored by the British Consul-General in Egypt, Henry

Salt, with whom he afterwards quarrelled. He spent about five years in Egypt and the Sudan and has left a charming account of his travels in his book *Narrative of the Operations and Recent Discoveries within the Pyramids, Temples, Tombs and Excavations in Egypt and Nubia.* From this I quote the story of how he penetrated to the inner chambers of the Second Pyramid, which, for hundreds of years, had been regarded as a solid block of masonry.

"My undertaking was of no small importance, it consisted of an attempt to penetrate into one of the great pyramids of Egypt, one of the wonders of the world. I was confident that a failure in such an attempt would have drawn on me the laughter of all the world for my presumption in such a task. . . ."

Notice the heroic strain which runs through all the accounts of pyramid exploration at this period, Davison, Belzoni, Caviglia approach their task with the gusto of Don Quixote tilting at the windmills.

"I examined every part, and almost every stone. I continued to do so on the west—at last I came round to the north. Here the appearance of things became to my eye somewhat different from that of any of the other sides. . . ."

The *savants* smiled, to Belzoni's irritation. Essentially a practical man, an engineer (as were the builders of the Pyramids), he often found himself in conflict with the academicians who theorized from their study desks.

"I certainly just beg leave to say, that I often observed travellers who, confident of their knowledge, let slip opportunities of ascertaining whether they were correct in their notions, and if an observation was made to them by any one, who had not the good fortune of having received a classical education, they scorned to listen to it,

or replied with a smile, if not a laugh of disapproba-
tion. . . ."

With Salt's assistance, Belzoni managed to enrol a gang
of Arab workmen whom he set to work clearing the sand
which had accumulated on the north side of Chephren's
Pyramid. At last, after weeks of labour, he came upon the
entrance to a "forced passage" probably made by the same
men who forced an entrance into the First Pyramid. At
first he was unsuccessful and the work became dangerous.

"A large block of stone, no less than six feet long and
four feet wide, fell from the top, while the man was digging under it . . . the man was so incarcerated that we
had some difficulty in getting him out . . . the falling of
the stone had moved many others in this passage; indeed
we were so situated that I thought it prudent to retreat
out of the pyramid . . . the danger was not only from
what might fall upon us, but also what might fall in our
way, close up the passage and bury us alive. . . ."

Then Belzoni remembered that the entrance to the Great
Pyramid was not exactly in the centre of the northern face
but some distance to the east. Perhaps the same applied to
the Second Pyramid? He examined the building again,
and was . . .

"not a little astonished when I perceived the same marks,
which I had seen on the other spot in the centre, about
thirty feet distant from where I stood. This gave me no
little delight, and hope returned to my pyramidical
brains. . . ."

"*Magnoon*" (madman) murmured the Arabs sullenly,
but Giovanni was undeterred. On the first of March
he discovered three large blocks of granite, and next
day . . .

"we came at last to the right entrance to the pyramid.
. . . Having cleared the front of the three stones, the
entrance proved to be a passage four feet high, which
descended towards the centre for a hundred and four
feet five inches at an angle of twenty-six degrees."

Diodorus Siculus was wrong. So was Pliny, and Sandys,
and Greaves, and Thevenot, and all the other explorers who,
during the last two thousand years, had said that there
was no entrance to the Second Pyramid. Ahead of the
Italian and his workmen rose the forbidding mass of a
granite portcullis, one foot three inches in thickness.

"The raising of it was work of no small consideration.
The passage is only four feet high and three feet six inches
wide. When two men are abreast of each other they
cannot move, and it required several men to raise a piece
of granite but less than six feet high . . . the levers could
not be very long, otherwise there was not space to work
with them and if they were too short I could not employ
men enough to raise the portcullis."

The only method was to raise the portcullis a little at a
time, and at last Belzoni made an entrance large enough to
squeeze through. He hurried down the corridor with a
torch held above his head, hoping that this time he, alone
among pyramid explorers, would find an intact tomb of a
Pharaoh. It had taken him thirty days to get beyond the
portcullis and he was full of hope. After descending a long,
sloping corridor he found himself in a horizontal passage
which led him to "a large chamber".

"My torch formed of a few wax candles, gave but a
faint light, I could however clearly distinguish the principal objects. I naturally turned my eye to the west end
of the chamber, looking for the sarcophagus, which I
strongly expected to see in the same situation as the First
Pyramid, but I was disappointed when I saw nothing
there. . . . On my advancing towards the west end, how-

ever, I was agreeably surprised to find that there was a sarcophagus buried on a level with the floor."

But on looking inside he found only a mound of rubbish and a few bones. And above, on the walls of the dark chamber, dimly lit by the light of the torches, he read an Arabic inscription left there nearly a thousand years before his time.

The Master Mohammed Ahmed, lapicide, has opened them; and the Master Othman attended this (opening) *and the King Ali Mohammed at first from the beginning to the closing up.*

*　　*　　*

Sadly Belzoni returned to the surface, paid his workmen and sat in the shade of Cheops' pyramid, reflecting on his adventure. Before him to the east, stretched the broad deep green floor of the valley, mud-brick villages, canals, more villages, then the Nile, and far beyond the arid slopes of the Arabian desert. He was facing the same disappointment which generations of future Egyptologists were to experience; of finding an apparently intact tomb, only to discover that someone had been there before. Who had been the first to enter the Second Pyramid? Almost certainly not the Arabs who had by-passed the ancient entrance by another route. Ages ago someone, perhaps from one of the villages at which he was looking now, had discovered the secret of the pyramid, had entered it and removed the treasure. Later, perhaps the Saites may have re-sealed it.

Another robust character, contemporary with Belzoni, was Captain Caviglia, whom we have already met in the "well". He was a Genoese mariner, the owner and master of a trading ship operating in the Mediterranean. As his home port was Malta he liked to regard himself as a British subject. He also worked for Salt, who employed him in the excavation of the Great Sphinx, where he discovered the pavement between its paws, and the steps leading to it.

He was an Old Testament literalist, besides being something of a mystic. He won the friendship of many distinguished men, and when he retired to Paris in 1837, enjoyed the patronage of Lord Elgin.

The occasion of Caviglia's retirement was probably his quarrel with the next notable pyramid explorer to appear on the scene, Colonel Richard Howard-Vyse, an Army officer. But Howard-Vyse and his collaborator, John Perring, deserve a chapter to themselves.

CHAPTER SEVEN

THE FALL OF SIGNOR CAVIGLIA

COLONEL RICHARD HOWARD-VYSE, son of General Richard Vyse (1798–1853), came of a military family, with a country seat at Stoke, in Buckinghamshire. From his writings he appears to have been a man of cultivation, though somewhat deficient in humour and—one suspects— rather a martinet. When he arrived in Egypt in 1835 he was thirty-seven, with nearly twenty years of military service behind him. It is not clear whether his visit was made in the course of his military duties, or as the result of a prior interest in the country—probably a mixture of both.[1]

Perhaps his interest in Egypt had been aroused by two contemporary travellers, Edward Lane, an Arabic scholar, who wrote *The Manners and Customs of the Modern Egyptians*, and Sir J. Gardner Wilkinson, the Egyptologist, who spent from 1821 to 1833 travelling throughout the country, making excavations and gathering material for his great work *Manners and Customs of the Ancient Egyptians* (1837).

Vyse was well acquainted with the works of both these authors, and also those of Jean Francis Champollion, the great French philologist who has been justly called "The Father of Egyptology". It was Champollion who, in his famous *Lettre à M. Dacier relative à l'alphabet des Hieroglyphes phonetiques* (1822) laid the foundation stone of modern Egyptian philology and archæology.

By the time Vyse arrived on the pyramid plateau, the Ancient Egyptian writing, dead for more than fifteen hundred years, had begun to yield its secrets. Seven years earlier Champollion, with the Italian archæologist Rosellini, had conducted a scientific expedition to Egypt, studying, copying and translating some of the inscriptions. He had succumbed to a stroke in 1832, while preparing the

[1] General Sir Richard Howard-Vyse, descendant of the Colonel, tells me that the great pyramid-explorer was better at archaeology than soldiering, and was "rather a trial to his family".

results of this expedition for publication but his works were published posthumously by his brother, and other scholars were following with success the new roads which he had opened. A new impetus had been given to the study of Ancient Egypt, and as the years passed a more scientific approach to archæology began to replace the old, amateur bungling.

Vyse stands mid-way between these two worlds. On the one hand he has no compunction about using blasting powder on the Pyramids in his vain search for concealed apartments, and possibly treasure. On the other he employs a qualified surveyor to measure and draw the Pyramids and leaves a careful record of his investigations, which were extended over two years.

In Vyse one sees again the blending of practicality and romanticism which, as I remarked in an earlier chapter, characterizes many British Egyptologists. He has no use for theories concerning the "granaries of Joseph" or "astronomical observatories".

"It appears," he writes, "that the Pyramids were tombs; that the inclined passages were for the purpose of assisting the conveyance of the sarcophagi, and for the better arrangement of the solid blocks with which part at least, if not the whole, of the long entrances were closed up; and also to increase the difficulty of disinterment and violation. Having been closed with solid masonry, they could not have been used for astronomical observation, nor yet for initiation or mysterious purposes, as some have fancifully supposed.

"It would indeed seem, from the great care and precautions taken to ensure the preservation of the body at an expense so vast, and by means so indestructible, that in these early ages there was a settled conviction, not only of an after-existence of lengthened duration, but also of the resurrection of the body—a belief which, however obscured by imperfect tradition and by superstitious ceremonies, could only have had its origin in direct revelation."

The last line provides another clue to the Colonel's character. He was a deeply religious man, with a profound faith in the literal truth of the Old Testament. It was this which led him so far astray as to write:

"An additional interest arose from the great probability that they [the Pyramids] were the mighty works of the Shepherd Kings, whose descendants, according to Manetho, after their expulsion from Egypt, under the denomination of Philistines built in Syria, Jerusalem, and also many defensive towns. . . . This extraordinary people appear to have been of the same race with the Cyclopes and heroic adventurers, whose enormous structures and architectural skill, and whose wanderings and misfortunes, have been celebrated by the ancient poets."

In another passage he tries to reconcile his admiration for the Ancient Egyptian civilization with his faith in Holy Writ.

". . . Egypt possessed a considerable degree of civilization and knowledge at a very remote period; and from various expressions in the Holy Scriptures, it may be collected that it was a country peculiarly favoured of the Almighty."

He then quotes Isaiah (xix, 25):

"*Whom the Lord of Hosts shall bless, saying Blessed be Egypt my people, and Assyria the work of my hands, and Israel mine inheritance.*"

This, incidentally, is a most curious passage, in which the prophet seems to be foretelling a time of international amity, when even the old enemies, Egypt ann Assyria, are reconciled.

"*In that day shall there be a highway out of Egypt to Assyria, and the Assyrians shall come into Egypt, and the*

*Egyptian into Assyria, and the Egyptians shall serve with
the Assyrians.*

*"In that day shall Israel be the third with Egypt and with
Assyria, even a blessing in the midst of the land."*

But as for Egypt being "peculiarly favoured by the
Almighty" Vyse could have set against that one conciliatory
text fifty in which the Hebrew prophets called down curses
on the Egyptians. However, the Colonel continues:

"From the time of Our Saviour the connexion is kept
up, chiefly, however, as a prohibited land, in contrast
with that of Judea; neither is the extreme state of corruption and idolatry, in which it afterwards fell, at all
inconsistent with the supposition that, when most other
nations were living in darkness, Egypt, and perhaps some
portions of the East, preserved distinct and accurate
traditions of the antidiluvian world,[1] originally derived
from revelation. . . ."

It is ironical that Vyse's interest in the Pyramids, which
almost certainly sprang from a desire to confirm his religious beliefs, led him to make the first serious near-scientific
study of the monuments. What led him to undertake this
work? He certainly did not come to Egypt with any such
intention.

"After a tour in Syria, Asia Minor, etc. . . . I arrived at
Alexandria . . . with the intention of going to Thebes
and Wady Halfa, and, if an opportunity offered, of visiting also Mount Sinai, and then returning to England by
Italy and the Rhine; for, at that time, I had not the
remotest idea of engaging in any operations at the
Pyramids."

My own view is that the man who aroused the Colonel's
interest was the Genoese mariner, Signor Caviglia, whom

[1] It is worth reminding ourselves that to Vyse's generation the word "antediluvian" did
not merely mean "antiquated" as it does to most of us to-day, but literally "before the
Deluge".

Vyse had met in Alexandria in 1836. Caviglia was also a religious man, well versed in the Old Testament.

". . . on the 23rd," writes Vyse, "I had the pleasure of being introduced to Mr. Caviglia, with whom I had a long conversation. He informed me that he had made the excavation in the Subterraneous Chamber; that to the south of Davison's Chamber, and one also along the Northern Air Channel; and that he had attempted to force the mouth of the Southern Air Channel in the King's Chamber. He stated his belief that these channels led to other apartments, which, by excavating in their direction, might easily be discovered. He also mentioned the vertical direction he supposed the Southern Air Channel to take. He was so good as to allow me to read some papers he had written on the mystical purposes for which he believed these buildings to have been applied; together with a printed account of his discoveries some years since at the Sphinx. I proposed that he should go to the Pyramids, and carry on operations at the Air Channels at my expense, but he declined doing so. . . ."

Vyse then went off to Syria, but on his return in October, Mr. Sloane, the vice-consul, who was a friend of Caviglia's, told him that it was proposed to procure a *firman* (permit) from the Government to enable Colonel Campbell, Vyse and Sloane to excavate in the Pyramids, each paying equal shares. And Caviglia, who, as we have seen, had had considerable previous experience, had agreed to superintend the work.

"The following day I paid my first subscription (200 dollars) to Mr. Caviglia; Colonel Campbell paid the same sum, and I conclude, Mr. Sloane did likewise. . . . The following day I left Alexandria for Cairo, Mr. Caviglia remaining behind to buy various articles, such as ropes, etc., which could there be best obtained."

Then Vyse set off on a tour of Upper Egypt, of which he

left a fascinating account in his book *Operations Carried on at Gizeh* from which, as it has nothing to do with the Pyramids, I should not quote. However, the temptation is too great. Here is the Colonel's description of an encounter with the Dancing Dervishes.

"I observed three or four men entirely naked, excepting a cloth around their waists, dancing upon some mats, and amongst them a man, with a white cotton cap, and a short apron, exerting himself in the most furious manner, foaming at the mouth, and brandishing a scourge of small cords in his right hand, and another instrument in his left with the most violent gesticulations, whilst a person stood behind to assist in case he should fall from excitement, or from exhaustion. This man, I found to my surprise, was one of the priests, and that the ceremony which I then witnessed, lasted three or four days and nights.

". . . Upon our approach, the priest jumped out, and came towards us with a large palm branch in a threatening manner. I do not suppose that he would have struck me; but Selim, the janissary, probably in order to enhance his own consequence, said that he certainly would, and that the rest of the people would have joined him, unless he had interposed. As soon as he had done so, the priest dropped the stick, and, standing upright, raised his head and muttered a prayer; after which he embraced and kissed Selim the janissary, and then favoured me with the same benediction, no doubt in expectation of receiving a *backshish*. With such instructors, can the savage state of the population be any longer a subject of surprise?"

Two other extracts will suffice to illustrate Vyse's extraordinary deficiency in humour. Visiting a cadet school for Egyptian boys at Bulak, he tells us, without a smile on his face that:

"They have casts of relievos and of ancient sculpture,

and a large collection of prints, after the most eminent
Italian and other masters, and amongst which is a print
of George the Third putting an end to the riots in 1780.
There were also "The Siege of Gibraltar", Wilkie's
"Village Politician", "Opening the Will", etc. . . ."

The other extract, after referring to the fact that Fouath,
an Arab town, "was once famous for its dancing girls", has
the astonishing footnote:

"It is remarkable that both the Crusaders and the
French, in their invasions of Egypt, mistook these people
for a deputation of the most considerable of the inhabitants, coming out to hail their arrival."

Or did the Colonel have his tongue in his cheek? If he did,
he never removes it throughout the whole of this absorbing,
but extremely serious book.

Returning to Cairo, Vyse hurried to Giza to find what
Caviglia had been doing in his absence.

"I set out early in the morning, and went immediately
to the Great, and to the Second Pyramids, where I expected to find M. Caviglia, and his men, but I did not
find a single person, and afterwards I discovered the
people at work on three mummy-pits between the
Sphinx, and the Second Pyramid. M. Caviglia, however,
informed me that parties had been employed by night
and day at the southern side of Davison's Chamber, in
search of the southern air-channel . . . and also at the
excavation of the Third. . . ."

Caviglia, it seems, had been digging for mummies in the
mastabas near the Great Pyramid. However, Vyse persuaded him to assist him in measuring the interior of the
Great Pyramid, and in "copying hieroglyphs inscribed on
the rocks northward of the Second" and in the evening—

"had a long conversation . . . with Mr. Caviglia, in which
he observed that I hurt his feelings by continually urging

him to turn his attention towards the pyramids, instead of employing the people at the mummy pits" (i.e. the *mastaba* tombs). I assured him that I had no such intention, but that as I had undertaken the operations solely with the view to these magnificent structures, particularly the great one, I naturally wished to make some discoveries before I returned to England. . . . He . . . expressed his opinion that the mummy-pits might produce several objects interesting to the scientific world, and, in short, that having begun the excavations, it was necessary to finish them."

Probably the truth was that Caviglia, after twenty years' experience of pyramid excavation, had lost interest in them, that he resented the intrusion of this English amateur, and knowing what an arduous and heart-breaking job it was to hack away at the solid masonry of the Pyramids, had decided to divert the funds so obligingly provided to the easier and more lucrative task of digging in the adjoining *mastabas*.

But Vyse seems rapidly to have got the measure of the Italian, and began to take steps to obtain a more willing and scientific collaborator. There happened to be in Cairo a certain Mr. Galloway, who was a manager of public works for Mohammed Ali, the Khedive of Egypt. He had an able assistant named John Shae Perring, a civil engineer, to whom Vyse was introduced.

"Mr. Hill has assisted me in measuring the Great Pyramid, and also engaged to do the same in mapping the ground, but he observed that a Civil Engineer had arrived with Mr. Galloway, who was furnished with the proper instruments, and who, no doubt, would undertake the survey in the best manner. In consequence of what he said, I took the opportunity of mentioning the subject to Mr. Galloway, who in the handsomest manner acceded to my request, and promised Mr. Perring's able assistance, which that gentleman afterwards most kindly, and disinterestedly continued. . . ."

The result was a most happy collaboration which resulted in the publication of the first comprehensive, scientific survey of not only the Giza group, but the pyramids of Sakkara, Dashur, Lisht, Meidum, Hawara and others. It is still a standard work of reference for students of Egyptology, though it has been superseded by the works of Petrie, Borchardt, Jequier, and later workers in this field.

Having secured the services of John Perring, the Colonel's next problem was to get rid of Caviglia. The opportunity was not long in arriving. Vyse's journal for this period (February 1837) reveals only too clearly the tension which existed between them.

"In returning to the tents in the afternoon, I asked Mr. Caviglia when he would probably have finished at the mummy-pits, and be able to take the bulk of the people to the pyramids. He said in about a fortnight, but that he then intended to begin upon another. I remarked, that in that case it was useless for me to remain any longer, as no discovery could be made before I should be obliged to return to England. . . ."

On February 10th a crisis was imminent. Furious at Caviglia's reluctance to take the Arab workmen from the "mummy-pits" and set them to work on the Pyramids, Vyse engaged more men on his own account. On being informed of this, Caviglia observed—

"that he did not like to employ more men, as the weekly bills were already high. I told him that I thought he was right about the weekly bills, but that, as time was everything to me, I would pay the rest of the people, whom he did not want, and employ them in distinct operations. He then alleged, that he had not leisure to attend any additional works. . . ."

It was shortly after this that the ludicrous scene occurred which I have already described in my Introduction, when

Caviglia stormed into the Colonel's tent, and, after a sharp altercation, flung down Vyse's share of the subscription "wrapped up in an old stocking" which, says the Colonel, "I was careful to return to him with my best compliments, having first extracted the money."

Caviglia was then dismissed. His period of ascendancy was over. No more "curious travellers" employed him on pyramid excavation, and he returned to Europe, a disgruntled man, to live for many years in Paris under the patronage of Lord Elgin.

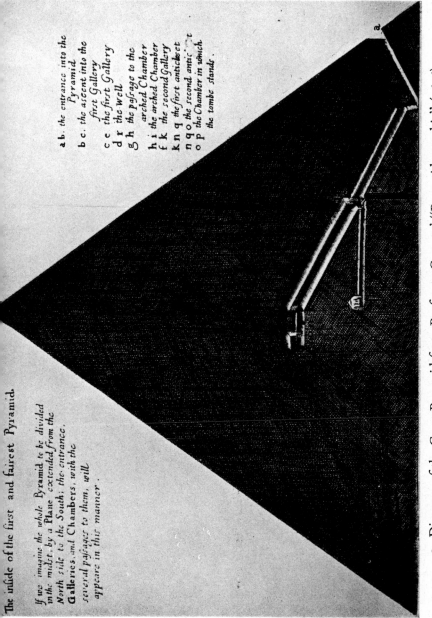

The inside of the first and fairest Pyramid.

If we imagine the whole Pyramid to be divided in the midst by a Plane extended from the North side to the South; the entrance, Galleries, and Chambers, with the several passages to them, will appeare in this manner.

a b. the entrance into the Pyramid
b c. the ascent into the first Gallery
c e the first Gallery
d r the well
g h the passage to the arched Chamber
h i the arched Chamber
f k the second Chamber
k n q the first antichbet
n q o the second antichbet
o p the Chamber in which the tombe stands.

a

9. Diagram of the Great Pyramid from Professor Greaves' "Pyramidographia" (1646)

(By courtesy of the Ashmolean Museum)

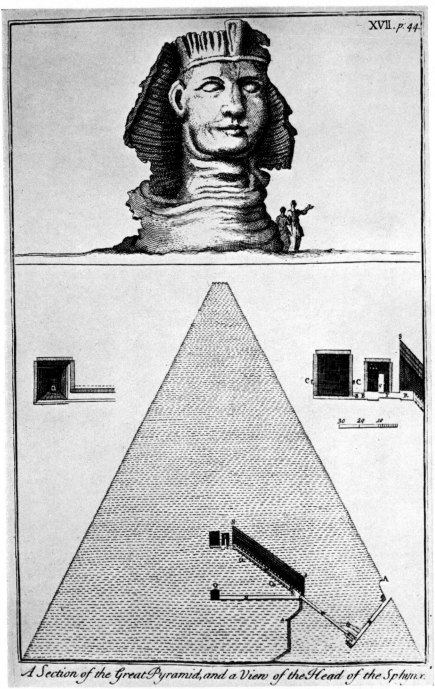

A Section of the Great Pyramid, and a View of the Head of the Sphinx.

10. Plan of the Great Pyramid and view of the Sphinx, as seen by Richard
Pococke (1745)

(By courtesy of the Ashmolean Museum)

11. Self-portrait of Colonel Richard Howard-Vyse, painted in 1816
(By courtesy of General Sir Richard Howard-Vyse, K.C.M.G., D.S.O.)

ENTRANCE to the GREAT PYRAMID.

12. Entrance to the Great Pyramid (reproduced from Vyse's book, 1840)

VIEW OF THE SPHINX DURING THE EXCAVATIONS.

13. View of the Sphinx (reproduced from Vyse's book, 1840)

SEPULCHRAL CHAMBER, THIRD PYRAMID.

14. The burial-chamber of Menkaure (Mycerinus) as seen by Colonel Howard-Vyse and J. S. Perring in 1838

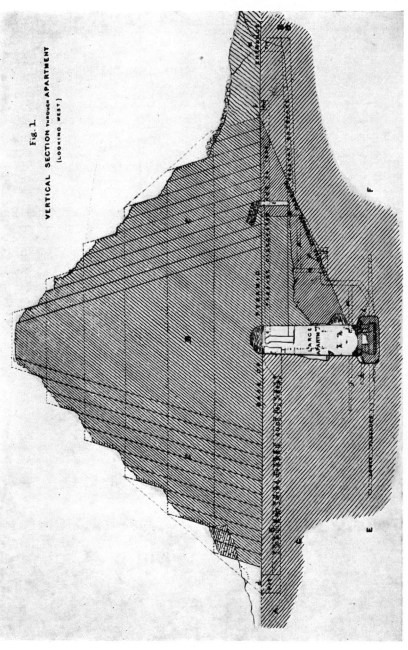

Fig. 1

VERTICAL SECTION THROUGH APARTMENT
(LOOKING WEST)

15. An example of Perring's sectional drawings showing the inner construction of the Step Pyramid, with its "accretion walls" inclining inwards, and the burial pit beneath the Pyramid

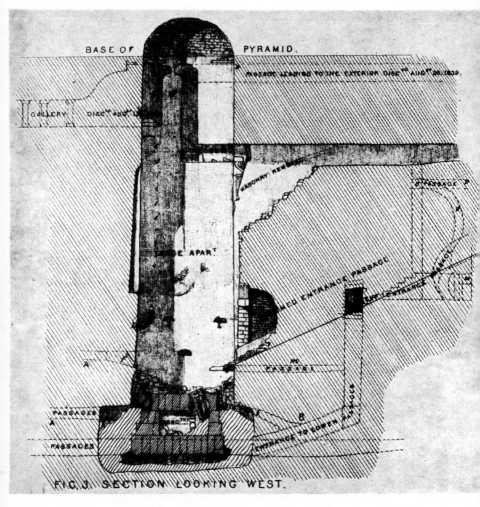

16. The burial pit beneath the Step Pyramid with the granite sepulchral chamber at the bottom (Diagram by J. S. Perring)

CHAPTER EIGHT

EXPLORATION BY GUNPOWDER

Vyse, like many of the explorers who followed him, established his headquarters in a disused tomb near the Great Pyramid, and with his English assistant and reluctant Arab workmen, set about his task. Besides Perring, he had the "able assistance . . . of Mr. Nash, and of Mr. Raven; nor should the valuable services of two other Englishmen (Goodman and Jack) be forgotten, the latter of whom besides being constantly employed during the day, passed every night for nearly five months, in superintending the excavation in the interior of the Third Pyramid."

At this stage, another glance at the Plans of the First and Second Pyramids will be helpful. All the known chambers in the Great Pyramid had been opened, except the upper "relieving chambers" above "Davison's Chamber"—the first room above the King's Chamber. The Second Pyramid was in the state in which Belzoni left it, i.e. it had been entered via the upper Descending Passage which passes through the masonry, and the sarcophagus chamber was accessible. But the other, lower entrance (see Plan opposite page 230) had not then been discovered. As for the Third Pyramid, that was still virgin territory. If an extrance existed its location was unknown.

Vyse's main objects were: (a) to make accurate measurements of the Giza pyramids and draw up plans, (b) by making excavations in the masonry of the Great Pyramid to see if it contained other chambers, (c) to find the second, lower entrance to the Second Pyramid (which was known to exist since its lower end joined the gallery which Belzoni had discovered), and (d) to force an entrance into the Third Pyramid.

Vyse, like Caviglia before him, was intrigued by the "air-channels", the narrow mouths of which entered the King's

129

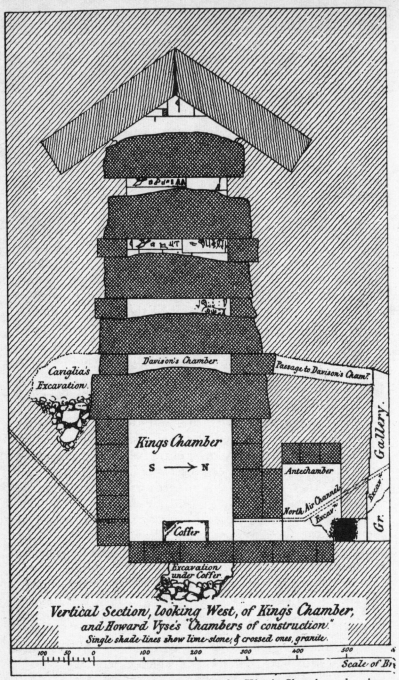

Vertical Section, looking West, of King's Chamber, and Howard Vyse's "Chambers of construction." Single shade-lines show lime-stone, & crossed ones, granite.

4. Vertical section, looking west, of the King's Chamber, showing "Davison's Chamber" and those above it

Chamber on its northern and southern sides. He could not get out of his head that these might lead to other chambers, and he set a Maltese engineer, Paolo, to work with "boring-rods" in the King's Chamber, in an endeavour to force a passage through the granite blocks. Not surprisingly, this attempt was a failure. The granite blocks were too tough for them.

". . . it was found impossible to bore through the blocks of granite, or to remove them on account of the close-ness of the joints. I therefore directed Paolo on the following morning to clear out an old excavation at the north-western corner, and to begin boring at a depth of six feet four inches from the northern, and ten feet nine inches from the western side of the chamber."

Then, one day, Perring accidentally discovered the out-let of the northern air channel on the surface of the pyramid.

"Mr. Galloway, Mr. Perring and myself, measured the exterior of the Great Pyramid; and Mr. Perring, in pass-ing over the centre of the North Front for that purpose, discovered the mouth of the northern air-channel."

At this time the connection between this exterior outlet and the passage in the northern side of the King's Chamber had not been established, "but even if it had," writes the discoverer, "a communication from it to other chambers, was highly probable." So he set men to work to try to enlarge the shaft at its lower end, but the attempt had to be given up.

"The candles would scarcely burn; not more than six inches were cut in twenty-four hours; and I knew, from examination, that at least thirty-six feet remained with-out any opening or apartment." (Presumably he had ascertained this by pushing a long rod into the narrow shaft.)

He encountered similar difficulties when he tried to penetrate through the masonry above the lower relieving
chamber (Davison's Chamber) to establish whether or not
other chambers existed above.

"The place was rather less confined, and more convenient for the object which I had so anxiously in view,
namely, to penetrate over the chamber, yet it was still a
most difficult operation, as the passage was not more
than three feet in height, the stones extremely large and
hard, and the whole over hard work. The Arabs can
stand heat, but are feeble workmen, and have neither the
proper tools, nor skill for such undertakings."

A decision had to be made, as a result of which, in the
spring of 1837, the Pyramids heard a new sound; one which
they had never known in the four thousand years of their
existence, the roar and reverberation of gunpowder ex-
plosions as Vyse's "quarrymen from Mokkatam" blasted
great holes in the ancient masonry above the King's
Chamber.
"They knew their business," says the Colonel. They
certainly did, as any modern traveller can testify who has
examined the interior of the Great Pyramid and its companions. Yet, even with this powerful aid, the explorers
found it hard and dangerous work.

". . . even then the joints were obliged to be cut to get
room for the blasting; and the great fragments, immediately above the workmen, were afterwards drawn out
with much difficulty, and in many instances with considerable danger."

Reading this passage it is almost impossible to reconcile
this ruthless butchery of an ancient monument with the
almost lyrical passage a few pages further on, in which
Vyse describes the Pyramids emerging from the morning
haze. Yet he undoubtedly revered the buildings he was
attacking in the name of science, or how could he have
written:

"The morning was cold and foggy, and at first every object, even the gigantic pyramids, were totally obscured; but as the atmosphere cleared up, the scene from the Sphinx became singularly beautiful. The picturesque forms of the women and children carrying baskets of sand upon their heads near Campbell's Tomb, the finely broken foreground extending to the rocks of the Southern Dyke, and the enormous masses of the ruined temple on the rising ground before the Second Pyramid were in the finest breadth of light and shade. For a time the lofty apex of the Second Pyramid shone alone in the clear blue sky (like the topgallant sails of a ship of war) far above the clouds that shrouded its mighty bulk, which by degrees slowly appeared in all its grandeur; and soon afterwards the southern front of the Great Pyramid, glittering with the morning sunbeams, was displayed in full majesty as the light vapours melted away from its enormous space."

In fact, the Colonel became so absorbed in his pyramid studies that the incidental anecdotes were crowded out of his narrative, though he can still glance aside occasionally to observe a military display by the local Sheikhs:

"Their horses were active, but not particularly well-bred, and they had Turkish saddles and bridles. I went down with them into the plain, when they repeated their exercise on horseback. They then dismounted and advanced, either singly or two at a time, shouting, dancing, and hopping, with a view, it may be supposed, of alarming the enemy, and of exciting their own courage; when suddenly stooping down, they fired, and retired in the same way as they had advanced. It was a ridiculous affair, exactly as might be expected from savages. . . ."

Sometimes he pauses to note the arrival of a distinguished visitor:

"Prince Puckler Muskau arrived, and requested to camp in my enclosure; to this I did not consent, but directed a person to conduct his highness to the Great Tomb in the plain generally occupied by travellers; where he encamped."

And on one occasion he watches an execution.

"In crossing the Nile I saw a crowd of people on the eastern bank, who, I was informed, were assembled to witness the execution of a woman for having married four husbands. The criminal soon made her appearance, completely wrapped up, and concealed in an Arab shawl, and was conducted down the bank to a boat, and seated in the bottom. She was tied round, and probably strangled, with a cord, to the end of which a heavy stone was affixed. The boat was then put off from the shore, and the woman, together with the stone, were suddenly thrown into the deep channel westward of Mekias, on the Island of Rhoda. I never afterwards passed the river without an unpleasant recollection of this event."

Work on the three pyramids seems to have gone on simultaneously. While the "quarrymen from Mokkatam" were busy blasting the interior of the Great Pyramid, others were boring a hole in the side of the Sphinx (to see if it was hollow), and a third group was trying to remove the granite portcullis in the Second Pyramid, in the hope of finding other chambers.

". . . we lowered the portcullis, in order to break it, and in doing so, endeavoured to shut in two of the Arabs, that they might work the harder to effect their escape; but no persuasion could induce them to remain. . . ."

A short, sad, significant passage occurs on the same page.

"I was informed that M. Caviglia had arrived with a janissary to remove his baggage, but I did not see him. . . ."

Vyse's "exploration" of the Third Pyramid was even more ruthless than his attack on the First. Unable to find

the entrance, he gave instructions to his workmen to drive
a passage straight through the side, and also to "bore down
from the top". In this way he was confident that he would
find the burial chamber. While this work was going on,
and the plateau was shaking to the repeated blasts of gunpowder, other men were searching for the lower entrance
to the Second Pyramid. Eventually they found it, in the
pavement a short distance from the northern front of the
pyramid; it was sealed with granite plug-blocks just as
they had been left by the pyramid builders. The interior
of the pyramid was easily accessible through the upper
gallery, as Vyse knew, but this did not deter him from blasting a way through the granite blocks in a vain search for
other chambers.

> "It (the passage) was completely filled up with solid
> masonry, close-joined and cemented; the first stone was
> ten feet long, the others six, or seven. I ordered them to
> be removed so as to admit of a passage, but on account
> of their hardness, confined situation, and the badness of
> the tools, and the unskilfulness of the Arabs, very little
> was effected before the arrival of the men from the
> Mokkatam quarries."

They blew the blocks to pieces.
Meanwhile the gallery forced into the side of the Third
Pyramid had reached within 15 feet of the centre, without
a chamber being found, so the shaft was continued for a
short distance at an angle of 46 degrees, after which a
perpendicular shaft was begun. This, too, was blasted out
with gunpowder.

> "The operation was attended with some trouble, as
> the workmen were obliged to come up from the bottom,
> every time the blasting took place, by means of a rope
> ladder; for those made of wood were destroyed by the
> pieces of stone, and the effects of the powder."

All this effort was entirely wasted; the excavators
reached the foundations without finding a chamber. All

they had done was to damage a perfectly good pyramid. On the other hand it may have had one good effect, in convincing Vyse, and his successors in later years, that, apart from the known chambers, the Pyramids were solid blocks of masonry and that there was nothing further to be gained by blowing holes in them. When at last, Vyse did find the entrance, all he had to do was to remove a few loose blocks from the northern face, and there it was—open. It is difficult to understand why he did not think of this first.

It happened on July 29th, 1837. While the workmen were having their midday meal, Vyse "carefully examined the Third Pyramid, and the result confirmed my opinion as to the position of the entrance". He gave orders for the removal of the loose blocks "under the eastern chasm made by the Mamelucs".

"The stones were removed with great difficulty, particularly a large mass exactly on the spot where I supposed the entrance to be. Its removal proved my conjecture to be right; and I considered that my operations at the Pyramids were at length successfully concluded. I immediately entered the passage which was completely open, and, notwithstanding several large stones, appeared to be accessible for a considerable distance. I then put a guard on the entrance, and went off to the tents to pay off the people.

"As soon as they were dismissed, Mr. Andrews and myself returned full of expectation to the mysterious entrance, impatient to examine what had excited the curiosity, and had hitherto been supposed to have eluded the researches of all explorers, and of which no tradition or account, ancient or modern, was known to exist."

What they found can be seen by consulting Plan 5 opposite this page. The usual sloping corridor passed first through the masonry and then through the rock beneath, until it entered a horizontal gallery which Vyse and his companions found "much encumbered with stones and rubbish, but continued practicable for some distance, as

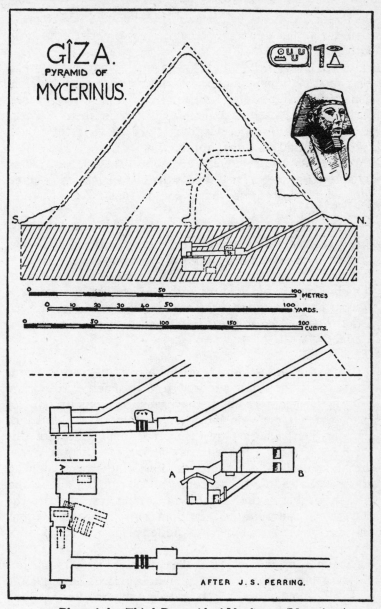

GÎZA.
PYRAMID OF
MYCERINUS.

S.

N.

0   50   100 METRES

0   10   20   30   40   50   100 YARDS.

0   50   100   150   200 CUBITS.

A

B

AFTER J. S. PERRING.

5. Plan of the Third Pyramid of Menkaure (Mycerinus)

the larger fragments had been piled up on one side to make room for a man to pass; further on it was entirely filled up with sand and stones."

On the floor they found "fragments of pottery, a small piece of stick, upon which the bark was still tolerably fresh, some twigs, that would almost bend, Tibni (dried forage), part of an old basket, and a rag of coarse linen". These remains left by earlier visitors indicated that they were unlikely to find an intact tomb.

When they had removed the rubbish they penetrated to an ante-room (see Plan) "the walls of which were covered with white plaster, worked in compartments".

"Directly opposite the entrance into this room a doorway of the same size opened into a narrow chamber, which had been filled up with three portcullises, placed across it from east to west. The middle of the ante-room had also been blocked up with large stones laid across it from north to south, which had completely closed both doorways. Two of them remained in their original position."

From the ante-chamber the horizontal corridor continued for about one hundred feet to emerge in a large rectangular chamber about twenty-six feet long by ten feet wide, the longest axis lying across that of the entrance corridor, i.e. from east to west. A strange feature of this chamber was that, immediately above the entrance from the horizontal gallery there was *another* entrance high up in the wall, leading to a second gallery running above and at first parallel to the first, then inclining upwards into the masonry of the pyramid (see Plan 5). This entrance was only accessible by means of a ladder placed on the floor of the chamber.

On exploring this second gallery, the explorers found that it was a blind alley. After planing upwards through the rock for about fifty feet it entered the masonry of the pyramid, straightened out, then stopped. Another mystery! But Vyse noticed that "this passage had been worked by the chisel from exterior, or north, and ended where the masonry of the pyramid commenced. It must, therefore, have been formed before the other passages or chambers, as the large apartment probably was also."

Previous explorers had excavated great holes in the walls of this chamber and the galleries in a search for other apartments. Though they had not the advantage of blasting-powder, they had done pretty well. At the western end of the Large Apartment just described "a short passage . . . led to a hollow of inconsiderable height, floored by the reverse of the blocks of granite that form the coved roof of the sepulchral chamber immediately beneath it."

This Sepulchral Chamber, the burial place of Mycerinus, was approached by an inclined passage, seventeen feet from the eastern end of the Large Apartment, let into the rock, and originally concealed by a stone pavement, which plunderers had removed.

"It (the passage) contained a quantity of rubbish, and also of black dust, apparently the exuviæ of insects and bats, likewise several large stones . . . when this passage was cleared out, it was found to have been built up with ramps, and with blocks laid upon them after the sarcophagus had been placed in the tomb, and to have been closed at the lower end with a portcullis of granite. The passage entered the eastern side of a sepulchral chamber, which extended north and south, and was composed entirely of granite. . . . No sculpture, or inscription of any kind excepting some rude and unconnected Arabic words and characters scrawled with something like chalk on the walls, and on the inside of the sarcophagus. The only words that could be made out were Mahomet Rasoul over the entrance. . . ."

But there was still another chamber to be discovered in the pyramid. At the bottom of the southern side of the passage leading to the sepulchral chamber a recess had been formed, and on the opposite side a flight of seven steps led into the southern side of a rectangular room, not square of the sepulchral chamber, but at an angle (25 degrees east of north; see Plan 5 opposite page 136). This contained four niches or compartments on the eastern side and two on the northern. It was almost certainly intended to contain the funerary furniture of the king—his beds, chairs, caskets of clothing, arms and equipment—as in the much later tomb of Tutankhamun. Vyse found it full of rubbish and bats' dung.

"The great efforts," wrote Vyse, "which had been made to get into the higher part of the building, were very extraordinary, and the precautions, which had been taken to secure the tomb from violation, were no less remarkable; the ponderous masses of granite, and of calcareous stone, with which the whole of the entrance was filled up as far as the ante-room, the blocks, which secured that apartment, the three portcullises to the smaller chamber, the squared stones, with which the upper returning passage was filled up, the concealment of the immediate entrance to the tomb by the pavement of the large apartment, and the manner in which that passage was closed up with a portcullis of great thickness, with ramps, and finally with solid masonry, indicate the reverence in which the sepulchre was held, and therefore the importance of the personage to whom it belonged."

And what remains of this personage? When Vyse entered the granite chamber he found only an empty sarcophagus —the very same one in which the Saites had probably reburied the remains of Mycerinus some two thousand four hundred years before (see Chapter One). It was of polished basalt, "of a fine brown colour", and its sides were panelled.

"It did not bear any inscription or hieroglyphics. The lid had been fixed by two pins in the usual manner, and also by a dovetail, which was rounded; and the plate of metal had been applied so carefully underneath it, that in order to insert a lever for its removal, it had been found necessary to cut a groove across the rim of the sarcophagus. The lid was not found in the sepulchral chamber, but pieces of it were afterwards discovered."

And what of the body of Mycerinus, the king who "turned nights into days" and tried to cram twelve years of life into six? Did nothing remain after the Arab plunderers (if they were the first) had forced their way into the chamber in the time of the Caliph Ma'mun? When Vyse and his men had cleared out the sepulchral chamber and found nothing, they turned their attention to the entrance descending to it. And there, lying among the debris, they found:

". . . part of a skeleton, consisting of ribs and vertebræ, and the bones of the legs and feet enveloped in a coarse woollen cloth of a yellow colour, to which a small quantity of resinous substance and gum was attached. . . . It would therefore seem that the sarcophagus could not be removed, the wooden case containing the body had been brought to the large apartment for examination. . . ."

Near these remains lay a fragment of the coffin-lid still bearing the hieroglyphic inscription placed there by the Saites twenty-four centuries before:

"*Osiris King of Upper and Lower Egypt, Menkaure, (Mycerinus) living for ever . . .*"

Nothing else remained of the great king within whose ravaged pyramid the excavators stood, a building raised four thousand years before, when four-fifths of the story of civilized mankind had yet to be written. The bones are now in the British Museum, together with the fragment of the coffin-lid. But no human eyes will ever see again the basalt sarcophagus. That lies on the bed of the ocean, among the wreckage of the ship in which Vyse tried to send it back to England.

CHAPTER NINE

THE FIELD WIDENS

W HEN Colonel Howard-Vyse returned to England in 1837 he may have felt that, in his own words, "my operations at the pyramids were at length successfully concluded", but the fact was that the scientific study of the monuments had only begun. He had, admittedly, disclosed the only remaining chambers contained within the Great Pyramid which had still to be discovered. He had forced an entrance into all the remaining "relieving chambers" above the King's Chamber, and named them respectively after Wellington, Nelson and Lady Arbuthnot. In one of these chambers Vyse found the name Cheops in hieroglyphs, which definitely identified the Great Pyramid with that king. He also located the lower entrance to the Second Pyramid, re-opened the galleries and chambers of the Third, and examined most of the smaller subsidiary pyramids of the Queens.

Most important of all, he excavated down to the bedrock on which the Great Pyramid was built and found some of the polished limestone casing-blocks with which the pyramid was once covered. Two of the blocks were in their original position.

"They were quite perfect," he writes, "had been hewn to the required angle before they were built in, and had then been polished down to one uniform surface; the joints were scarcely perceptible, and not wider than the thickness of silver paper; and such is the tenacity of the cement with which they are held together, that a fragment of one that has been destroyed, remained firmly fixed to the original pavement, notwithstanding the lapse of time and the violence to which it had been exposed. The pavement beyond the line of the building was well laid, and beautifully finished; but beneath the edifice it was worked with even greater exactness, and to the most perfect level, in order, probably, to obtain a lasting foundation for the magnificent structure to be built upon it."

These, and other casing-stones discovered later, enabled Petrie and other archæologists to determine precisely the original outer dimensions of the pyramid.

Yet, although the work of Vyse must not be under-estimated, the most valuable scientific results of the Vyse-Perring collaboration were produced by the junior partner, John Shae Perring, the civil engineer whom Vyse engaged to measure and plan the monuments. After Vyse left, Perring remained behind for another season, financed by Vyse, and not only completed his measurements and plans of the Giza pyramids, but visited, examined and measured the Saqqara and Dashur groups, Lisht, Medum, Lahun, Hawara and others.

For by this time political conditions in Egypt had become more stable, travel was easier, and the study of pyramids needed no longer to be confined to the Giza monuments, but embraced a much wider field. In addition, the new-found knowledge of the hieroglyphs enabled the monuments to be studied in relation to the inscriptions found in the nearby *mastabas*, and in some cases within the Pyramids themselves.

From this point, therefore, our survey will take us away from the Giza pyramids, to explore their predecessors and successors. For the pyramids of Cheops, Chephren and Mycerinus were not the first; nor were they the last. Their ready accessibility from Cairo led generation after genera-tion of pyramid explorers to look at these monuments in isolation, disregarding the seventy-odd other pyramids to the south as unimportant; mere imitations of the Big Three. The truth is that they were only three links in a chain, of which the first was forged at Saqqara, ten miles to the south, and the last at Meroe, in the Sudan. If all the cathe-drals of medieval Europe had been destroyed, or were inaccessible, save only Chartres, Rouen and Westminster Abbey, historians might be tempted to believe that these three great monuments were not the product of a steady evolution, but an unique manifestation, the product of divine inspiration. So, to many earnest and devout men, seemed the Giza pyramids. But we know that Chartres was the climax of a long process of architectural development. Similarly, Cheops' great monument was only the supreme expression of an architectural impulse which had started long years before he was born; and even so, his Great Pyramid is only slightly inferior to that built by his father Snofru at Dashur.

Yet, as they were the starting-point of pyramid study, it will be necessary to return to the Giza pyramids from time to time, as we draw nearer to a solution of the many problems which Vyse and Perring left unsolved.

To recapitulate, there was the problem of the inner structure of the Great Pyramid; why did it have three chambers, one below and two inside the pyramid? Why was there an Ascending as well as a Descending Gallery, and how was the former sealed? What was the function of the Grand Gallery? Why are there two truncated shafts in the masonry to the north and south of the Queen's Chamber, similar to the "air-channels" which lead from the King's Chamber, but, unlike them, reaching only a short distance into the masonry? (See Plan opposite page 74.)

Now look at the plan of the Second Pyramid (opposite page 230). Though the layout of the galleries is simpler than that of the Great Pyramid, there is a puzzling feature here, too. Why does it have two entrances, one below the other, the lower gallery having, in the middle of its horizontal section, an unfinished chamber?

Now take the Third Pyramid (Plan 5, page 136), where the galleries and chambers present even more difficult problems. Why does it have two central chambers, the lower one containing a sarcophagus, the upper with an emplacement to receive one? Most puzzling of all, what is the reason for the second sloping gallery above the first, ascending at the same angle, but, unlike the lower gallery, leading nowhere?

Archæologists could only find a satisfactory answer to these questions after they had examined the many other sepulchral monuments of Egypt, and by establishing their chronological sequence, could trace the gradual development of the Ancient Egyptian tomb—from pit-grave to pyramid.

* * *

Many devoted and distinguished men worked on the Pyramids during the latter half of the nineteenth century and they were drawn from many nations; German, French, Swiss, Italian, British and American. Some were primarily explorers and excavators; others, no less important, concentrated on copying and translating inscriptions; others paid little or no attention to the monuments themselves, but devoted a lifetime of work to interpreting the findings of their archæological colleagues from a prolonged and intensive study of the latter's publications. Across the frontiers of Europe, mind grappled with mind; learned gentlemen in London, Paris, Leipzig and Rome exchanged opinions, corresponded, supported the conclusions of their friends, or fired powerful broadsides into those of their opponents. Book after book poured off the presses, and in time a great corpus of works came into existence, by such men as Champollion, Erman, Lepsius, Maspero, Petrie, Borchardt, Hoelscher, Jequier, etc., which provides the firm foundation for present and future study of the Pyramids.

But as this book is concerned primarily with pyramid *exploration*, the scholars who will figure most prominently in our story will be those of the men who worked with theodolite and measuring-rod, *turia* and *maktaf*[1] around, within and under the monuments. This is not to ignore or belittle the work of the copiers of paintings and inscriptions, the philologists who interpreted them, or—equally important—men like Jequier and Lauer who patiently recon-

[1] The two principal tools used by the Arab workmen. The *turia* is a kind of hoe (the Arabs do not use the spade); the *maktaf* is the basket used for carrying away the excavated sand and rock.

structed buildings and sculptured reliefs from scattered fragments—but to do full justice to their work would require many volumes of this size.

There is also the unfortunate fact that, as pyramid exploration became more scientific, the accounts of it became steadily duller. Not that the later explorers did not have dramatic and amusing experiences; it is just that they regarded them as irrelevant, unworthy of inclusion in a serious, scientific work. For example, among workers in this field, none has made a greater and more enduring contribution than the great German scholars, Lepsius, Borchardt, Junker, Hoelscher, etc., yet one will search in vain through their mighty tomes to find a single incident of the type I have quoted from the works of Colonel Howard-Vyse. The French *savants*, Mariette, Maspero, Naville, etc., are almost as disappointing. Among the scientific excavators practically the only exception to the rule is Sir Flinders Petrie, who, fortunately, was among the greatest. But more of Petrie later.

When Vyse returned to England, Perring remained behind, and having measured and surveyed the Giza pyramids, he moved southward and, for the first time since Pococke, who preceded him some eighty years before, visited, explored and surveyed more than thirty pyramids, from Abu Koash in the north to Hawara in the south. Looking through the pages of the book which he and Vyse produced in 1841, one marvels at the patient tenacity of the explorer, who was more than half a century ahead of his time. Each pyramid has been carefully measured and planned. Beside each careful, strictly factual description is a beautifully drawn diagram, not a mere architect's "plan and elevation" but a sectioned drawing which reveals at a glance the inner construction of the monument, its principal dimensions, the layout of its galleries, its original and present dimensions, the "forced" as distinct from the original passages, together with detailed close-ups of individual features, and a copy of any hieroglyphic inscriptions found. (See example opposite page 128.) The translation of the hieroglyphs is entrusted to a Mr. Birch, one of the greatest philologists of his time, who added a short note at the end of each account, such as:

"Although these Pyramids (i.e. those of Abusir) are of less interest than those of Gizeh, the hieroglyphics upon them are of considerable importance, because they contain the dates, prenomens, and royal standards, of two monarchs. . . ."

Then follows a minute description and translation of the inscriptions, of which the following must serve as an example.

"It begins with '*Horus of the two worlds, the hawk of gold*', and then contains in two places the royal standard. . . . Beneath the standard on the right is a date, '*the eighth day of Phamenoth*' and above the one to the left is . . . '*the mighty and the living*' or . . . '*restrainer of the living*'. The name of the king *Shou-re* (actually Nieuserre) and his standard appear, therefore, to be ascertained, and also fragments of the two dates; but whether they relate to the beginning, or to the completion of the pyramid, cannot be positively determined."

These inscriptions, according to Perring and Birch, were quarry-marks painted on the stones by the workmen who hewed the blocks for the Pyramids. Up to this time no inscriptions had been found painted or carved in the galleries of the Pyramids, and it was generally assumed that such galleries were uninscribed, as were the galleries and chambers in the Giza pyramids.

But sometimes, as in this case, the quarrymen who cut the blocks painted on their sides the names and titles of the kings for whose pyramids they were intended. In the past such rough inscriptions were meaningless, but now, thanks to Champollion and his successors, it became possible to translate, though imperfectly, these hitherto undecipherable scrawls, and even to hazard a guess at the name of the king for whom the monument was built. The vital impor-

tance of this lay in the fact that by consulting the lists of
Ancient Egyptian kings set down by Manetho and others,
it was possible to arrive at an approximate date for the
building; to decide whether it was Fourth, Fifth, Sixth, or
even Twelfth Dynasty. Once the builders of the Pyramids
could be identified with approximate certainty it would be
possible to study their evolution and development.

However, it is pleasant to note, even among these
scholarly observations, an occasional human anecdote of
the kind with which earlier travellers used to enliven their
accounts.

"A number of Bedouins came to the works in the course
of the day; this was often the case, as the pyramids may
be considered close to the high road leading from the
Faioum to the Delta, and to Alexandria. . . . Nothing
could exceed the surprise of these savages at hearing
the ticking of a watch, and particularly at the lucifer
matches. After a time, however, the Arab girls found
out the use of the lucifer, and were eager to have
them. . . ."

To me the most interesting part of the book is the
description of Perring's examination of the "Step Pyramid"
at Saqqara, which, as described in my first chapter, was
explored by the Saites in the seventh century B.C. However, he was not the first European to enter these dangerous
galleries in modern times. The German explorer, Baron
von Minutoli, had been there before him in 1821, and had
removed a portion of an ancient skeleton which he found
near the burial chamber, and which may be that of its
owner. These remains are now in the British Museum.

"It . . . differs from the rest (of the pyramids) in many
. . . particulars, namely in the form of the passages, in
having four entrances (one of them on the southern
front) and also a variety of small excavated chambers,
upon the walls of two of which hieroglyphics and peculiar
ornaments are seen; in containing a large apartment

covered in with timber, and furnished with a hidden chamber, and not apparently intended for sepulchral purposes, and likewise a great quantity of fragments of marble, and of alabaster vases and sarcophagi, which give to the building the character of an extensive catacomb, rather than the tomb of a single individual."

The "large apartment covered in with timber" was the eighty-foot pit, cut in the rock beneath the Step Pyramid. Perring apparently approached this pit from both the northern and southern sides. He found three entrances on the northern front, one of which, the largest, was "still closed up with large blocks".

But he found another entrance "at a distance of 52 feet from the building, and eleven feet to the westward of the centre of the northern front . . . generally closed up by the sands of the desert, and often, indeed, by the Arabs, in order to gain money from strangers who wish to visit it. Then it opens into a passage, which is nearly horizontal for about 120 feet, and afterwards descends, in the circuitous and irregular manner shown in the drawings, to the lower part of the large apartment" (i.e. the pit). I have reproduced two of Perring's beautiful drawings (Pls. 15 and 16) to show with what care and artistry this British engineer carried out his work more than a century ago. When one reflects upon the arduous and often dangerous conditions in which the survey was made, one's admiration becomes even greater.

He also found and explored yet another gallery on the northern side of the Step Pyramid "irregularly excavated in the rock. . . . A track had been worn down the middle of it, and a few stones had been piled up on the western side. It communicates in a horizontal, but not quite straight direction, with a recess in the upper part of the western side of the large apartment, where a groove had been cut across the floor, apparently for the insertion of a beam, whence a rope had probably been suspended."

Nor did he miss the horizontal gallery on the southern side, supported by columns—the passage probably made

by the Saites round about 600 B.C. when they were searching for the burial chamber, and along which they removed
the great mass of stone rubble which filled the pit (see
Chapter One).

"These columns have been brought to their bearings
by wedges of wood, inserted both above and below them;
and most of them are cracked by the superincumbent
weight. The southern end of the gallery was stopped up
with sand, but for the length of 160 feet from the interior
it was open, and did not seem to have been previously
visited, as nearly thirty mummies were found in it, apparently undisturbed. They had neither coffins nor sarcophagi. . . . They crumbled to pieces upon being touched,
and could not be removed." (These were probably
"intrusive burials" left by the Saites.)

When, after traversing this gallery, he found himself on
the edge of the great pit, with the mass of the pyramid
poised above him, doubtfully supported by the timber
baulks left by the Saites, Perring calmly observed:

"It (the pit) measures 24 feet by 23, and is 77 feet high
from the floor to the original ceiling, which I examined
by the help of torches made of greased rags, and ascertained it to have been formed with planks, supported by
a platform of timber, consisting of cross-bearers and two
principal beams. One beam remained in its place, but
was broken in the middle; the other, together with the
platform, and about nine feet of the masonry, had fallen
down, and the room was therefore covered in by rubble-
work, which composed the interior of the Pyramid, and
which was retained in its place by the adhesion of the
mortar, and of the materials. The apartment was filled
with rubbish to a height of 25 feet, and the sides of it
were blackened by the smoke of torches. . . ."

He examined the granite burial chamber, originally
sealed by a four-ton granite plug "like the stopper of a

bottle" and wrongly deduced that it was not a burial place but a treasury:

> "because there did not appear any secret entrance, by means of which a man could easily have got into it, and because the ponderous block, by which it was closed, did not seem fitted for mysterious purposes . . . and because it was well adapted for a secure and secret treasury."

Perring also examined the rooms surrounding the burial chamber, which were decorated with blue faience tiles. "The doorway of one of them is bordered with hieroglyphs in relief, and that in another has a similar inscription in black. The characters . . . contain the title, but not the name, of a very early king."

Had the philological knowledge of Birch, Perring's linguistic adviser, been equal to the enterprise and courage of the explorer, a great discovery might have been made. But after careful study of these hieroglyphs, Birch could only state:

> "The inscription over the architrave, and on the lintels of the inner door, have also been published, and have been found to contain the titles and standard of a monarch. The standard is of the usual shape, and is surmounted by the hawk of Hariesi (Horus) crowned with a *pshent*. The two symbols in the standard beneath it express the words . . . 'divine' and . . . 'race' or 'germ', etc. The whole implies 'Horus the divine germ' and is represented four times upon each lintel."

Birch also writes:

> "As a cartouche containing symbols has not been found in this Pyramid, it is at present uncertain whether or not the symbols expressing the sun *resplendent*, etc. . . . are the prenomen of a king. The standard may belong to the founder of the Pyramid."

What Birch did not know was that at the time the Step

Pyramid was built the *cartouche*—the flattened oval in which the royal names were always enclosed after the Fourth Dynasty, had not yet come into use. Before that time the royal name was enclosed in a rectangular frame called the *serekh*. The name of the king who built the pyramid was there for all to see, but in 1839 it was not recognized. Birch could only say, regretfully:

> "The date of the monarch, upon whose standard 'divine germ' is inscribed, has not yet been determined by any inscription, nor has it been ascertained whether he preceded, or was posterior to Cheops."

* * *

Perring's work in the Step Pyramid provides a good example of the way in which the philologist, calmly working in his study a thousand miles from Egypt, could aid and guide his archæological colleague, groping along the perilous underground galleries of the Pyramids in the stifling heat of an Egyptian summer. Birch could not tell Vyse and Perring which king built the Step Pyramid and thus help to establish its date. But he was able to prove the latter wrong in his conjecture that the southern, pillared gallery was contemporary with the rest of the structure.

In describing the southern gallery Perring mentions "twenty two short columns . . . roughly worked *excepting one, which has been inscribed with four rows of hieroglyphs*". (Our italics.) "The characters are badly engraven, and the stone seems to have belonged to some other building, as part of the inscription has been cut away, in order to fit the block for its present purpose."

When Birch came to examine the copy of these hieroglyphs he found that they referred, in the words of his own imperfect translation, to:

> "*the royal scribe, attached to the silver* (white?) *abode of the lord of the world* . . ."

and also to:

"*military chief*", which title, as he points out, "although it occurs under the monarchs of the sixteenth and seventeenth dynasties, was not used during the reign of their Memphite predecessors" (i.e. the pyramid-builders).

Birch suggested, correctly, that this inscribed block had been taken from the tomb of an official of the Eighteenth Dynasty—more than six hundred years after the time of Cheops. On the other hand, Perring, the practical engineer, assumed that if it had been taken from another monument, that building must have ante-dated the pyramid.

Vyse remarks in a cautious footnote:

"Mr. Perring has already observed that, as this stone is a fragment, the hieroglyphics must have belonged to a building more ancient than the Pyramid; but Mr. Birch's opinion of them would seem to induce a belief that the passage in question, had been inserted upon the fragment long after the erection of the building."

In this case the philologist was right and the archæologist was wrong. The columned gallery was most probably made by the Saites more than two thousand years after the Step Pyramid was built. In building it they used a fragment of an Eighteenth-Dynasty tomb to support one of the pillars, and in so doing left a clue by which nineteenth-century scholars could detect and approximately date their intrusion.

CHAPTER TEN

LES PYRAMIDES MUETTES

By the middle of the nineteenth century European interest in Ancient Egypt had grown to such an extent that the Egyptian Government began to have qualms about the way in which its ancient monuments were being despoiled by haphazard excavation, and its valuable antiquities—papyri, tomb furniture, statuary, sculptured reliefs, granite colossi, even obelisks—were being torn from their rightful places and shipped to European museums.

In the words of Mr. E. M. Forster:[1]

"After the Treaty of Vienna every progressive government felt it a duty to amass old objects, and to exhibit a fraction of them in a Museum, which was occasionally open free. 'National possessions' they were now called, and it was important that they should outnumber the objects possessed by other nations, and should be genuine old objects, and not imitations, which looked the same, but were said to be discreditable."

In 1858 the Khedive of Egypt created a new post, "Conservator of Egyptian Monuments" and gave it to a 37-year-old French scholar, Auguste Ferdinand François Mariette. Ever since the French mission sponsored by Napoleon, French culture and scholarship had sunk deep roots into Egypt. The Khedives employed French advisers, French was taught in the schools, French archæologists surveyed and studied the monuments. Mariette's appointment was in keeping with this trend, and when, after a few years, the Service des Antiquités was founded he became its first Director, a post which was monopolized almost exclusively by his countrymen until quite recent times.[2]

[1] From *Abinger Harvest* published by Edward Arnold.

[2] The last Frenchman to hold the post was the Abbé Drioton, who resigned in 1952. It is now held by an Egyptian, Dr. Mustapha Amer.

Mariette, born in Boulogne in 1821, became interested in Egyptology and in 1849 obtained a minor post in the Louvre. In 1850 he visited Egypt, nominally to collect Coptic manuscripts, but managed to raise funds and conduct excavations for several years, before receiving his appointment as Conservator of monuments. After that he settled in Egypt and started numerous rather superficial excavations at various points throughout the country and his many finds provided the nucleus of the collection in the Bulak Museum, later transferred to the present Egyptian Museum in Cairo. It was he who discovered the magnificent diorite statue of Chephren, builder of the Second Pyramid, one of the finest works of art in the world (see frontispiece). He made this discovery while working in 1853 on the famous Valley Temple of Chephren, although he did not clear it completely. He also examined the Mastabat Faraun, the peculiar, sarcophagus-shaped tomb of King Shepseskaf, of the Fourth Dynasty, at Saqqara, although he wrongly attributed it to Unas, last king of the Fifth Dynasty. His most famous discovery was the Serapeum, the subterranean galleries near Saqqara in which were buried the sacred Apis bulls. He had read in Strabo that at Memphis there was "a temple of Serapis in a spot so sandy that the wind causes the sand to accumulate in heaps, under which we could see many Sphinxes, some of them almost entirely buried, others only partly covered".

In 1850, when Mariette was searching for Coptic manuscripts on behalf of the French Government, he noticed, in the garden of a M. Zizinia, at Alexandria, several sphinxes, of which similar examples existed in another garden which he had visited in Cairo.

"One day," he writes in *Monuments of Ancient Egypt*, "attracted to Sakkarah by my Egyptological studies, I perceived the head of one of these same sphinxes obtruding itself from the sand. The one had never been touched, and was certainly in its original position. Close by lay a libation table on which was engraved in hieroglyphs an inscription to Osiris-Apis. The passage in Strabo suddenly occurred to my mind. The avenue which lay at my feet must be the one which led up to that Serapeum so long and so vainly sought for. But I had been sent to Egypt to make an inventory of manuscripts, not to search for temples. My mind, however, was soon made up. Regardless of all risks, without saying a word, and almost furtively, I gathered together a few workmen, and the excavation began! The first of the Grecian statues of the *dromos*, together with the monumental tables or stelæ of the temple of Nectabeno, were drawn out of the sand, and I was able to announce my success to the French Government, informing them, at the same time, that the funds placed at my disposal for the researches after the manuscripts were entirely exhausted and that a further grant was indispensable. Thus was begun the discovery of the Serapeum."

The work took four years. Eventually Mariette uncovered the entrance to a series of long underground galleries from which branched huge sepulchral chambers, each containing an enormous granite coffin which had once contained the mummified bodies of the black Apis bulls, adorned, no doubt, with rich regalia. All the sarcophagi were empty, and one still blocked a passage where the workmen had left it. The Serapeum is one of the showplaces of Saqqara and thousands of tourists visit it each year, although, unlike Mariette's distinguished visitors, they are not entertained to a champagne party in the largest sarcophagus at the end of their trip!

Herodotus mentions the cult of Apis in his *History*.

"Now this Apis, or Epaphus, is the calf of a cow which is never afterwards able to bear young. The Egyptians say that fire comes down from heaven upon the cow, which thereupon conceives Apis. The calf which is so called has the following marks—he is black, with a square spot of white upon his forehead, and on his back the figure of an eagle; the hairs in his tail are double, and there is a beetle on his tongue."

After its death, the sacred animal was buried in the Serapeum, and the priests would then search the country for another animal bearing the same marks. When found, he became the new Apis, or Apis reborn. Although the cult had no direct connection with the Pyramids, it was practised by the same Memphite priesthood which exerted such a powerful influence on the builders of the Old Kingdom.

A contemporary and friend of Mariette was Karl Heinrich Brugsch, a German scholar, who came to Egypt in 1853, and in 1870 started a school of Egyptology in Cairo which was closed nine years later. Although Brugsch was not an excavator, his contributions to Egyptology were very great; he was a pioneer of "demotic"—a cursive form of the hieroglyphic writing—published a Demotic Grammar and a hieroglyphic dictionary. His younger brother, Emile Brugsch, later became assistant to Mariette and assistant conservator of the Bulak and Cairo Museums under his successor, Maspero.

Another great German Egyptologist of this period was Karl Richard Lepsius (1810–84), who came to Egypt a few years after Vyse left it. He led the Prussian expedition to Egypt and Nubia, and collected an enormous mass of epigraphic material which formed the basis of one of the greatest works of Egyptian philology ever written—the *Denkmaler*. None the less, he was more interested in archæology than in philology and most of his writings are concerned with these subjects. The Pyramids fascinated him. He explored many of them, including the Step Pyramid at Saqqara, from which he removed one of the doorways near the south-east corner of the tomb chamber, together with some of the blue tiles, and presented them to the Berlin Museum. He also formed the now discredited "accretion theory", the basis of which was that the size of a pyramid was governed by the length of its builder's reign. Thus Cheops, who is believed to have reigned for twenty-three years, built a larger pyramid than either Chephren or Mycerinus, who were presumed to have reigned for shorter periods. His theory has been summed up as follows:

"At the commencement of each reign, the rock chamber, destined for the monarch's grave, was excavated, and one course of masonry erected above it. If the King died in the first year of his reign, a casing was put upon it, and a pyramid formed; but if the King did not die, another course of stone was added above and two of the same height and thickness on each side; thus in process of time the building assumed the form of *a series of regular steps* (our italics). These were encased over with stone, all the angles filled up and stones placed for steps. Then, as Herodotus long since informed us, the pyramid was finished from the top downward, by all the edges being cut away, and a perfect triangle left."[1]

In the middle of the century were born two men, one French, one German, who became rivals for the foremost place in Egyptology in their generation. The German, Johann Erman (1854–1937) became the Director of the Egyptian Department of the Berlin Museum and Professor of Egyptology; his studies, in the words of Warren Dawson, "led to a completely new conception of the ancient Egyptian language, which his own numerous works, and those of his pupils and successors, have established as the basis of all modern philological study." Although not an excavator, his work on the Ancient Egyptian language played a great part in the interpretation of the monuments, including, of course, the Pyramids.

The Frenchman was the great Sir Gaston Maspero (1846–1916) who, after holding the post of Professor of Egyptology, Collège de France, in 1874, went out to Egypt in 1880 as the Director of the Mission Archéologique. Mariette, the Director of the Antiquities Service, was then nearly sixty, and a sick man. It was thirty years since he had first come to Egypt, and he had long passed those eager, youthful days when he had conducted an unauthorized excavation of the Serapeum with funds intended for the purchase of Coptic manuscripts.

In fact, he had become rather set in his ideas, one of which was that the Pyramids were "muettes" (dumb), by which he meant that, as not a single example opened up to

---

[1] Karl Richard Lepsius, *Discoveries in Egypt and Ethiopia*, 1842–45.

his time had contained inscriptions, except that of Djoser (and the quarry-mark discovered by Vyse in one of the "relieving chambers" of the Great Pyramid), the rest were also "dumb".

In his *Recueil de travaux en Egypt et Assyrie*, Vol. 5, Maspero remarks:

"One knew what was Mariette's opinion on the subject of the pyramids; in the preface to his unfinished work on the *mastabas* he again endeavoured to demonstrate that not only did they not enclose a single inscription (*ne renfermaient aucune inscription*) but that they had never enclosed such (. . . *elles n'avaient jamais du renfermer*) and that it would be a waste of time and money to try to open them" (i.e. those that remained unexplored).

But, as the younger man remarked, not all the world was of this opinion, and in the spring of 1879 rumours began to circulate among archæological circles in Cairo that an inscribed pyramid had been found at Saqqara. According to de Morgan, in his *Fouilles à Dachour* (1894)—

"a fox managed to penetrate into a cavity situated in the rubbish surrounding a ruined pyramid, and the animal was followed by an Arab head-workman (*reis*) who, passing into the cavern, arrived at the funerary chamber of King Pepi I." (The third king of the Sixth Dynasty (2420–2270 B.C.)). "The walls of this tomb were covered with hieroglyphic texts."

"Mariette did not hear of this till a long time afterwards, when he was on his death-bed. He authorized excavations to be carried out near to this pyramid, and on January 4th, 1881, sent Heinrich Brugsch and his brother Emile—his two German assistants—to verify the Arab's statement. It is doubtful whether, before he drew his last breath, the illustrious archæologist wished to credit the statement of his assistants. (*C'est à peine si, avant de rendre le dernier soupir, l'illustre archæologue voulut croire au récit de ses mandataires.*)

Mariette died in January 1881. A short time afterwards Maspero, the newly appointed Director of the Service des Antiquités, opened the pyramid of Pepi I. "He had only," wrote de Morgan, "to follow the information which he had been given by his predecessor to begin his great field of excavation following which he published the funerary texts of Unas, Teti, Pepi I and II, and Merenre."

Maspero himself, in a lecture printed in the *Bulletin of Egyptology* (Ser. II, No. 6), described what followed.

"The excavations, interrupted by the death of Mariette, were resumed with a new vigour during the early days of February. Beside the hope of finding texts of great value for the history of religion, I hoped to verify, in the same places, an idea which was not that of Egyptologists in general, but which I had held for many years. The discovery of the Pyramids of Pepi I and of Merenre at the place where the theory affirmed that they would be found, decided me to direct the attack on the entire front of the Memphite Necropolis, from Abu Roash to Lisht. Rapid success followed. Unas was opened on the 28th of February, Pepi II, Neferirkera on April 13th, and that of Teti on the 29th of May. In less than a year, five of the so-called 'dumb' pyramids of Saqqara had spoken . . . four pyramids in the neighbourhood did not yield a single inscription, and the other groups vigorously cut into (*entamés vigoureusement*) in December 1881 have not given anything up to the moment. The result is considerable. The inscribed Pyramids of Saqqara have given us almost 4,000 lines of hymns and formulas, of which the greater part were written originally during the prehistoric period of Egyptian history."

The Pyramids, once thought to be mute, could speak.

*   *   *

The inscriptions were religious texts, now known as the Pyramid Texts. "They do not form," says Edwards,[1] "a

[1] I. E. S. Edwards, *The Pyramids of Egypt*, London, 1947.

continuous narrative, but consist of a collection of spells assembled with little regard to content and in no fixed order. . . . The purpose of the Pyramid Texts, like that of every other element in the Pyramid complex, was to secure for the king or queen a happy after-life. So powerful was the magic of the written word that its presence alone provided a sufficient guarantee that the thought expressed would be realized."

We have mentioned the offering-chambers in the temples which usually adjoined the Pyramids. A regular supply of food and other offerings was essential for the sustenance of the dead king in the after-life, and in Old Kingdom tombs and pyramids one finds so-called "false doors" which were intended to allow the spirit to come out of the tomb and partake of the offerings. But if the offerings were not kept up, or the appropriate spells not recited by the priests, it would still be possible for the dead to receive their due offerings if the necessary words were represented in writing on the walls of the tomb.

"For instance," says Edwards, "a text which is generally inscribed on the north wall of the burial chamber reproduces the ritual which the priests used to recite every day in the Mortuary Temple when laying the provision on the altar in front of the false door. . . . For the most part, the Pyramid Texts were certainly not inventions of the Vth or VIth dynasties, but had originated in extreme antiquity." And he goes on to cite the three which I have quoted in Chapter One—"Twilight of the Gods"—in which one spell includes the words "cast the sand from thy face", which could only refer to the primitive practice of burial in the sand, which the ancestors of the Ancient Egyptians had used perhaps a thousand years before the invention of the pyramids. Another puzzling text contained the words: *"the bricks are removed for thee from the great tomb"*, which seemed to have no logical connection with the Sixth Dynasty pyramids, which were built not of brick but of stone. The explanation of this was only found much later, when archæologists had traced the development of the pyramid from earlier and more primitive structures.

But the main purpose of these magical texts was to enable the king to gain admittance to the other world, which, in the Old Kingdom period, was regarded as existing in a celestial region to the east, approached across a lake, known as the "Lily Lake", beyond which lay *the fields where the gods were begotten, over which the gods rejoiced on their New Year's Days*". These were the original "Elysian Fields" which the Greeks adapted to the purposes of their own religion. It is an interesting commentary on the deep roots of our civilization that when we hail a Paris taxi and ask to be driven to the Champs-Élysées, we are repeating an Ancient Egyptian religious text.

But what happened when the king, ferried by the austere boatman named "*he who looks behind*", arrived on the opposite shore of the lake? The texts assure him of a welcome by the gods. "*This king Pepi,*" says one of the texts, "*found the gods standing, wrapped in their garments, their white sandals on their feet. They cast off their white sandals to the earth; they threw off their garments. 'Our heart was not glad till thy coming', they say.*"

But the texts are very inconsistent in other ways. The Ancient Egyptians, an intensely conservative race, never discarded anything, even when new religious ideas made older ones redundant. I. E. S. Edwards, to whom I am indebted for most of the material of this chapter, points out that whereas, in the earliest Pyramid Texts it is asserted that the king becomes the Sun-God's secretary—

"*King Unas sits before him (Re); King Unas opens his chest (of papers); King Unas breaks open his edicts; King Unas signs his decrees*", etc.

—in others he is presented as ruling in splendour, as he had done on earth; with his courtiers around him and his subjects prostrate before him. In other texts the king is shown accompanying the Sun-God, Re, on his daily journey across the sky:

"*King Pepi receives to himself his oar; he takes his seat; he sits in the bow of the ship; he rows Re to the west*", etc.

It was this cult of the solar barque which, as we shall see in a later chapter, sometimes led the Ancient Egyptian kings to have actual timber boats buried in pits beside their pyramids, one example of which was discovered quite recently.

Previous to the finding of the Pyramid Texts, the exploration of the Pyramids had been directed mainly to discovering the secrets of their construction. Maspero's discovery, and of his successors', provided first-hand, tangible evidence of the religious beliefs of their builders.

CHAPTER ELEVEN

THE GREAT PYRAMIDIOT

This chapter could be described as a digression, because it deals with a form of pyramid study which is outside the main stream which we have been following. When I mentioned to some of my archæological advisers that I proposed to include a chapter on the Great Pyramid Theorists an unhappy look came into their eyes, like that seen on the faces of friends who think one is about to commit some irretrievable folly.

"I wouldn't do that if I were you," said one Egyptologist. "Personally I wouldn't touch that subject with a hundred-foot pole," said another. "Once you get tangled up with *those* people . . ." and he shook his head.

In one way the Egyptologists are right. The Great Pyramid Theorists have nothing to do with pure archæology or with science in the usually accepted meaning of the word. You will look in vain through most standard works of reference on Ancient Egypt for the names of John Taylor, Charles Piazzi Smyth, Edgar Stewart, the Rev. John Davidson and the other "pyramidologists". Yet they have produced enormous and weighty books on the Pyramids, with charts, diagrams, tables of measurement and elaborate mathematical calculations (which are probably above the heads of ninety per cent of their readers). Moreover, these books have been read and quoted by scores of thousands in Great Britain and in America (not in Europe —for "pyramidology" seems to have been mainly an Anglo-Saxon pursuit) and although their prophecies have often been proved wrong, their calculations inaccurate, their theories unacceptable by any unprejudiced mind, they still have their followers, though it is nearly a century since their arch-priest, Mr. Charles Piazzi Smyth, Astronomer

Royal for Scotland, published his *Life and Work at the Great Pyramid*.

Egyptologists, having done battle with the Pyramid Theorists in the early days, now prefer to ignore them, and certainly their influence is small compared with what it was in the latter half of the last century, when the uneasy Victorian conscience, faced with the disturbing facts which science was revealing with relation to the age of the earth and the development of the human species, tried desperately to find some way by which it could reconcile demonstrable truth with the dogmas of revealed religion.

However, I have decided to give the theorists a chapter, if only for one reason. There may be among my readers some who have come fresh to the study of Egyptology, and who, from lack of a wider knowledge of the subject, may be tempted by the siren strains of the "pyramidologists" such as Piazzi Smyth and his followers on to the barren rocks of quasi-scientific, quasi-religious speculation. It is important for them to recognize the song which this Neapolitan siren sang. To others it may be interesting as an historical curiosity.

I wrote "siren strains" advisedly, because, although the works of most of his successors are of a monumental dullness, Piazzi Smyth, the high-priest (though not the founder) of the cult, was an insidiously fluent and engaging writer, as well as a brilliant astronomer and mathematician. In fact, provided one does not take them seriously, his books are well worth studying by anyone interested in the springs and motives of human behaviour. There is an inspired lunacy in his arguments, which compels admiration, even while one regrets that such a first-class mathematical brain should have wasted its energies in so unprofitable a field.

As all subsequent writers on the Great Pyramid Theory are disciples of Smyth, I shall deal only with his own major works, *Life and Work at the Great Pyramid* and *Our Inheritance in the Great Pyramid*, both published in the sixties of the last century.

Charles Piazzi Smyth, born in Naples in 1819, was the son of Admiral William Henry Smyth, F.R.S. In 1845 he was Astronomer Royal of Scotland, and Professor of Astronomy, Edinburgh University. He became a Fellow of the Royal Society in 1854, but resigned twenty years later when the Society refused to accept from him a paper on his interpretation of the design of the Great Pyramid.

He was not an Egyptologist; in fact he hated Ancient Egypt. This should always be borne in mind by anyone thinking of embracing the "Great Pyramid Theory". If you are interested in Ancient Egypt for its own sake, if you admire the art and culture of the Ancient Egyptians, then you can never be a true disciple of Charles Piazzi Smyth. Here are a few random extracts from his book *Our Inheritance in the Great Pyramid* which illustrate this point.

> "With many of the smaller and later pyramids there is little doubt about their object; for, built by the Egyptians as sepulchres for the great Egyptian dead, such dead are buried in them, and *with all the written particulars, pictorial accompaniments, and strange sepulchral adornments of that too graphic religion, which the fictile nation on the Nile ever delighted in. . . ."* (Our italics.)

And on the next page he declaims against

> ". . . all those hieratic emblems . . . which from the first have utterly overlaid every Egyptian temple proper, as well as all their obelisks, sphinxes, statues, tombs, and whatever other monuments they, the Egyptians, did build up . . . in connection with their peculiar, and alas! degrading religion."

The beautiful inscription on the coffin lid of Mycerinus, quoted on page 30 (Chapter One) becomes in Smyth's words:

> "an idolatrous dedication in Mizraite hieroglyphics on the coffin-board."

At the very mention of the Sphinx he becomes almost hysterical:

". . . that monster, an idol in itself, with symptoms typifying the lowest mental organization, positively reeks with anti-Great Pyramid idolatry throughout its substance; for when the fragments of its colossal stone beard were discovered in the sand excavations of 1817, it was perceived that all the internally joining surfaces of the blocks had been figured full of the animal-headed gods of the most profane Egypt. . . ."

And he compares the "monster" with the Great Pyramid "whose pure and perfect surface of blameless stone, eschews every thought of idolatry and sin".

This obsession with "sin" and its opposite "purity" may seem strange to most of us, when applied to a mass of masonry, but it was not so to the Astronomer Royal for Scotland. When he is making his mathematical calculations, measuring, dividing, multiplying, establishing, for instance, that one three hundred and sixtieth part of his estimated base-length of the Great Pyramid is equal to "one ten-millionth of half the earth's axis of rotation" he is calm, and within the framework of his theory, logical. But the moment he has to touch on Ancient Egyptian monuments which are *not* his beloved Great Pyramid, his voice rises to a scream of rage, which is directed also at the Egyptologists who have dared to unearth these idolatrous, Mizraite monuments. Poor Mariette is trounced for having re-discovered the Serapeum—"recently brought once more to the notice of man by Mariette Bey's too successful excavations of ancient idolatries."

When the same archæologist published a hieroglyphic inscription found in one of the pyramid temples, Smyth comments bitterly:

"There is good news in it for almost every one of the Mizraite false gods; so that all profoundly devout readers may learn with thrilling interest that the images of the

hawk of Horus and the ibis of Thoth, in that problematical temple, of which this single stone is supposed to have
once formed a part, were of wood gilt; the boat of the
'three times beautiful Isis' was in gilt wood with in-
crustations of jewels; that the principal statue of Isis
was in gold and silver . . ." etc., etc.

One can almost feel his shudder of pious horror as he
writes this, adding that, "*as a rule, it is Frenchmen and
Roman Catholics who get up the most outrageous enthusiasm
for the Sphinx.*" There is a frightening intensity in Smyth's
Scottish puritanism which takes us much further back than
the nineteenth century. It partakes more of Cromwell and
the Covenanters, or of the cathedral-wrecking fanatics of
the sixteenth century. Yet, I suspect that even this was
only the outer mask which covered a deep psychological
conflict to which a clue may be found in his continual
references to the "purity" of the Great Pyramid, and its
"soft, fair, limestone". His fury at the tourists who make
merry within the King's Chamber, though understandable,
almost suggests that an outrage has been perpetrated on a
human mistress: in fact his agony becomes comical, like
that of a cuckold.

While he was measuring the temperature of the galleries
within the Great Pyramid, he noticed a perceptible increase in temperature:

"after a large party from some vulgar steamer, had had
their whirling dances over King Cheops' tomb-stone and
their ignorant cursing of his ancient name, in the vocal
music of passionate shouting and the painful thunder of
the coffer being banged, to close upon breaking, with a
big stone swung by their Arab helps . . ."

—and he goes on to inveigh against—

"those mad and multitudinous scenes of lurid-lighted
revelry, indulged in by many smoking, tobacco-stinking
gentlemen, a few ladies, and imp-like Arabs of every
degree, black, brown and grey. Lamentable scenes to be

beheld in the present educated age of the world; yet scenes which both disturbed my quiet days of measuring and photographing by magnesium light, there, at intervals of about three or four hours. . . ."

It is interesting to notice that for this one moment, Smyth's sense of outrage done to the Great Pyramid even outweighs his hatred of the Ancient Egyptians and all their works, for he had convinced himself that the Egyptians were not the designers of the Great Pyramid, though they may have laboured on it; and also that it was not a tomb but a mysterious, divinely inspired compendium of weights and measures, and a chronicle of man's history, past and future, which could be interpreted by mathematical calculations based on the dimensions, capacities and proportions of its outer structure and inner galleries and chambers.

He did not invent this theory, which was first set down by a certain John Taylor, who, in 1859, published a book called *The Great Pyramid; why was it built, and who built it?* But it so fired the imagination of the Astronomer Royal for Scotland that the disciple soon outshone his master, who, at his own expense, as he informs us in his preface, "determined to set sail for Egypt" (with his wife) "and did, very soon after Mr. Taylor's death, through four months of residence on the Pyramid hill itself, employ a large variety of scientific instruments, in obtaining many measurements of the mighty monument, some of them with far more accuracy than had ever been attempted before. . . ."

It would not be fair either to Smyth or my readers to try to explain, in a couple of thousand words, a theory which he expounded in three large volumes crammed with mathematical formulæ. I shall, therefore, simply quote a few of his principal beliefs, without attempting to unfold the process of reasoning that led to them.

First, he states that "the vertical height of the pyramid, is to . . . the side or breadth of its base, when multiplied by two, as the diameter to the circumference of a circle; or A C: 2 B D :: 1 : 3.14159 + etc.; this last number, 3.14159 etc., being the quantity known amongst modern mathematicians under the convenient, to us now doubly convenient designation π."

This is his first argument for the "divinely-inspired" origin of the Great Pyramid, since the value of π was "a quantity which men in general, and all human science too, did not begin to trouble themselves about until long, long ages, languages, and nations had passed away after the building of the Great Pyramid; and after the sealing up, too, of that grand primeval and prehistoric monument of the patriarchal age of the earth according to Scripture".

But measuring the "grand primeval monument" in English feet and inches results in inconvenient fractions, so in order to make his calculations easier, he decides that the unit of measurement used by its builders was the so-called "Pyramid Inch" which he states to be .999 of a British inch. This, incidentally, gives a certain clue to his working methods. If his calculations do not work out exactly then he invents a unit of measurement which makes things easier for him, and immediately adopts it as his standard measurement, ignoring the fact that he invented it himself.

Next he takes his measurement of the base line of the pyramid, subsequently shown by Petrie to be inaccurate, and, after dividing it by 366 (almost, but not exactly, the number of days in a natural year) he finds that the resultant length—close upon 24 British inches—is "a length approaching nearly one ten-millionth of the earth's semi-axis of rotation". From this he calmly deduces that the architect of the Great Pyramid had "laid out the size of the Great Pyramid's base with a measuring rod 25 inches long in his hand; and in his head, the number of days and parts of a day in a year, coupled with the intention to represent that number of days in terms of that rod on each base side of the building." Later in the book he goes to great lengths to convince us that this standard measure used by the builders was not the "ancient profane cubit of idolatrous Egypt, 20.7 British inches long" but the Hebrew or "sacred cubit" of 25.025 British inches "which the profane Egyptians, and the Jupiter and Juno and Venus-worshipping

Greeks, when in Egypt, knew nothing of". And he devotes a long and wearisome chapter to an analysis of the measurements of the Ark of the Covenant which the Israelites carried during their sojourn in the desert.

Incidentally, when considering Smyth's theory that the designers of the Great Pyramid were not the idolatrous Egyptians but the divinely-inspired "Sethic" ancestors of the Chosen People, it is worth recollecting that, according to the Old Testament, the ancient Hebrews were so far from being capable of building even their own little Temple of Solomon that they had to employ Phœnician workmen to do it for them.

But to return to Piazzi Smyth, groping about in the Grand Gallery with his "clinometers" etc. Having established to his own satisfaction that the Great Pyramid incorporated within its mysterious structure a unit of linear measurement, viz. the "pyramid inch", he now sought for a *capacity* measure. And, sure enough, he found it. And in what more likely place than the Holy of Holies itself, the King's Chamber? And, within that chamber, in what place could this sacred unit be found except in that solitary, lidless box of granite which "profane" Egyptologists had identified as a sarcophagus, but which was, of course, not a sarcophagus at all, but a "coffer"? Carefully the *savant* measures it, again and again, inside and out, takes out his pencil and makes his elaborate mathematical calculations. He finds that the capacity of the interior is 71.214 cubic inches.

John Taylor had stated that:

"The coffer in the King's Chamber of the Great Pyramid was intended to be a standard measure of capacity and weight for all nations; and certain nations did originally receive their weights and measures from thence. . . ."

Smyth then elaborates on this theme.

"Take, for instance, our own case. When the British

farmer measures the wheat which the bounty of Providence has afforded him as the increase of his land, in what terms does he measure it? In *quarters*."

Quarters! Quarters of what?

Can one doubt what the answer is going to be? Why, in quarters of the cubic capacity of the "coffer" in the Great Pyramid! When Smyth looks up from his calculations, interrupted perhaps by another contingent of "tobacco-stinking" English gentlemen and their ladies, he finds that his mentor's statement is true—that the English "quarter" *is* one quarter of the 71.214 cubic inches internal capacity of the "coffer" in the King's Chamber—well, more or less. . . .

After this, need we have any doubt that Smyth will discover that "the immense superiority in height of the Grand Gallery over every other passage in the Great Pyramid arose from its representing the Christian Dispensation while the passages typified only human-devised religions, human histories or little else—though it was built some two thousand years before the birth of Christ"?

Surely, there is nothing more to do but to raise our hats and tiptoe reverently away?

*   *   *

Perhaps some of my more tender-hearted readers will accuse me of malice in spotlighting in this way the follies of this devout but misguided man. Nothing is further from the truth. There was much that was extremely likeable about the Astronomer Royal for Scotland. He had a vivid descriptive style, and a fiery enthusiasm which grips one's imagination—in contrast to many of the dull Egyptological pedants who reduced the Great Pyramid and all its wonders to a mere list of dimensions, although they happened to be right in their facts. In my view he was essentially a poet who had his wings clipped by Heaven knows what dour, inhibiting Presbyterian background, coupled with the cruel twist of Fate which made him a scientist and a mathematician.

Unfortunately, his influence, extending even down to our own day, has been to darken counsel because, instead of being accepted as a poet and a fantasist, as he was, he tried, with considerable success, to pass himself off as a scientist. In the field of astronomy he undoubtedly was, but his incursion into the field of Egyptology has been disastrous, leading scores of thousands of innocent seekers after truth away from the true facts of pyramid construction—wonderful enough in themselves—into those arid fields of pseudo-religious speculation which he shares with the "Flat-earthites" and the people who have bought plots of land on the Mount of Olives in preparation for the Second Coming.

To conclude, I will quote one or two comments by some of the leading Egyptologists who have examined the Great Pyramid theories.

Petrie: *Seventy Years in Archæology*:

"The fantastic theories, however, are still poured out, and the theorists still assert that the facts correspond to their requirements. It is useless to state the real truth of the matter, as it has no effect on those who are subject to this kind of hallucination."

Sir Wallis Budge: *The Mummy* (1925):

"According to some distinguished thinkers, the arrangement of the chambers, the lengths and angles of the inclination of the corridors, etc. represented mysteries the knowledge of which was of the highest importance to the human race, and every measurement had its esoteric meaning and symbolism. The present writer is convinced that the Great Pyramid was built not to serve as an astronomical instrument or as a standard of measurement for the world, but as a *tomb*, and as nothing but a tomb."

And finally, Lieutenant-Commander N. F. Wheeler, who worked under Reisner at Giza for many years:

". . . There is really no particular reason why these

mystics should have chosen or limited themselves to the Pyramid of Khufu. Borchardt, in the publication previously referred to, makes a present of the fact that the pyramid of Sahure's queen at Abusir the proportion of half the base perimeter to the height of which is equal to Napier's logarithmic base 'e' (2.71828). We might go further and suggest that if the Crystal Palace were substituted for Khufu's pyramid an enormous increase in the possible number of measurements would be found, and undoubtedly a great many of them would yield the exact values of a number of things. If a suitable unit of measurement is found—say versts, hanks or cables—an exact equivalent to the distance to Timbuctu is certain to be found in the roof girder work, or in the number of street lamps in Bond Street, or the Specific Gravity of mud, or the mean weight of an adult goldfish.

"To those who are familiar with Wilde's 'Portrait of Mr. W.H.' that tale will present a good parallel to the mentality which has invented and maintained these astounding theories. It has been customary in some circles to dub them 'Pyramid-ites', but after all 'Smyrniot and 'Cypriot' are used for 'those of Smyrna' and 'those of Cyprus'; so why not *Pyramidiot*?"

CHAPTER TWELVE

THE YOUNG PETRIE

A FEW weeks before the death of Mariette a dark, bearded
and extremely good-looking young Englishman of twenty-
six arrived in Cairo. His name was William Matthew
Flinders Petrie, a name at that time almost unknown to the
archæological world, but destined to become one of the
greatest.

To do full justice to Petrie's work in Egypt would need
several books of this size, and the difficulty is to select such
passages from his many works (he wrote over one hundred
books) which will give readers a sufficient taste of his
quality to induce them to read more. For there was an
heroic quality about Petrie as a young man—something of
knight-errantry and derring-do—which has vanished from
modern works on Egyptian exploration and will probably
never recur again.

Petrie's first visit to Egypt was the result of one of those
ironical little tricks which Fate sometimes plays upon
gifted men. Petrie was to make his name as a scientific
investigator, but the impulse which first sent him to Egypt
began in a totally different way; it arose from the irrational
religious beliefs of his father, who was a follower of Charles
Piazzi Smyth and his "Pyramid Theories". William Petrie
the elder was another of those strange, tortured personali-
ties, typical of the intelligentsia of his period, who tried to
reconcile scientific fact with a literal interpretation of the
Old Testament. He was a chemical engineer and a man of
considerable attainments, who, as his son explained,
started studying medicine but "methods in 1844 seemed so
irrational that he dropped it". He studied chemistry at
King's College, and, during the railway mania of 1847
turned to surveying.

When that fever was over he turned to electric lighting,

and developed a system of generating current by rotating magnets "which reached the practical stage of a brilliant arc light on the steps of the National Gallery, lighting all down Whitehall, and also on Hungerford Bridge".[1] But business mismanagement ruined that project and William Petrie left it in disgust, and turned to chemical engineering. "From this," wrote his son, "I gleaned much in long talks with him on all kinds of chemical and physical questions, schemes and speculations, and for twenty years soaked in all he had to tell. He was a literalist in his beliefs, and sought his longed-for-perfection in primitive Christianity."

Flinders Petrie was a prodigy from childhood; his mother, the daughter of Matthew Flinders, the great explorer, was also highly gifted; and from her, and from his maternal grandfather, he inherited a passionate interest in mathematics, especially geometry, and from his father an interest in mechanical and technical processes and in surveying and measurement. As a boy he helped to excavate an earthwork on Blackheath Common, and "made myself a working sextant with cardboard and a looking-glass, and then my father let me have his sextant, and I began plotting earthworks".

As a child he was "fascinated with scales and weights, and whenever they were brought out, I weighed everything available". Prevented by delicate health from going to school, he gained his education through his gifted parents, and his own omnivorous reading. He taught himself geometry and trigonometry, which fascinated him, and in his early twenties became interested in the standards of measurement which had been used in different parts of the world in the construction of ancient buildings. He tramped around Great Britain measuring churches, read all he could on the subject, and, at the age of twenty-four, published, with his father's help, a book on the subject called *Inductive Metrology*.

His father, having read Smyth's *Our Inheritance in the Great Pyramid*, decided to go to Egypt with his son and conduct a scientific survey of the Great Pyramid with more

---

[1] W. M. F. Petrie, *Seventy Years in Archæology*, London, 1931.

17. Sir William Flinders Petrie, in his early forties

18. Gold crown of the Princess Sat-Hathor-Unet
(*By courtesy of the New York Metropolitan Museum of Art*)

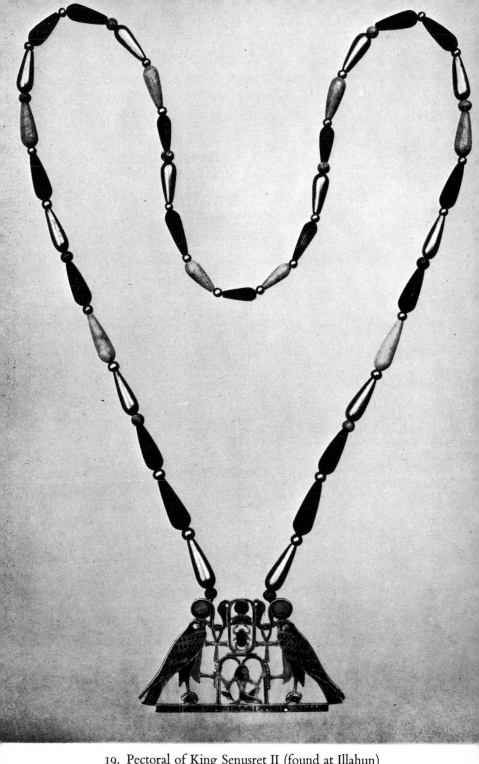

19. Pectoral of King Senusret II (found at Illahun)
(*By courtesy of the New York Metropolitan Museum of Art*)

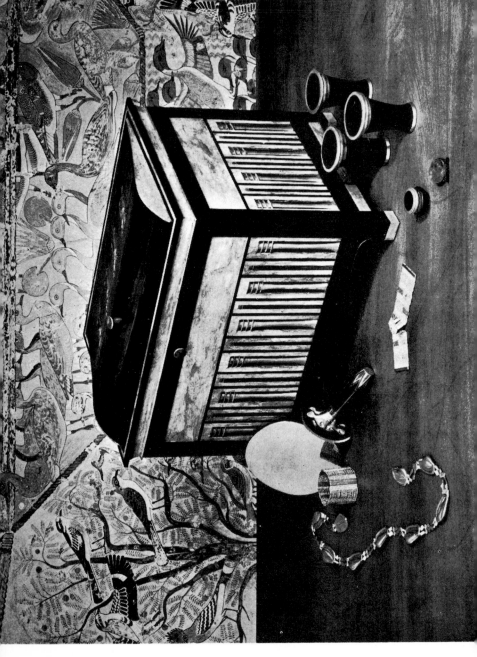

20. Some of the jewellery of Princess Sat-Hathor-Unet, including her golden girdle, anklets, mirror, mascara pot, rouge dish and toilet jars, with the inlaid casket which contained them

(By courtesy of the New York Metropolitan Museum of Art)

21. Golden girdle of Princess Sat-Hathor-Unet
(*By courtesy of the New York Metropolitan Museum of Art*)

22. Pre-dynastic grave with skeleton
(*By courtesy of Rex Keating, Esq.*)

(*Photo: Exclusive Photo Agency*)
23. The Pyramid of Medum from the air

24. The "Bent" or "Blunted" Pyramid at Dashur, ascribed to Snofru

25. The funerary furniture of Queen Hetepheres
(By courtesy of University College, Chicago)

26. Ancient Egyptian quarry showing method of cutting the stone blocks

(Photo: Cottrell)

(Photo: Cottrell)

27. The boat-pit at Giza showing the funerary boat of Cheops

accurate instruments than Smyth commanded. Father and
son spent two years in designing and making these instruments, but the elder Petrie was an incorrigible procrasti-
nator; he was never ready and finally, in the winter of 1880,
the young man went out to Egypt by himself; his father
intended to follow him but never did.

I am indebted to Lady Petrie for permission to reproduce
some of her husband's journals of the period, which have
never previously been published. From these it is fairly
clear that the young Petrie had, from the very beginning,
the strongest doubts concerning the validity of Smyth's
theories, though he never attacked them openly, out of
respect for his father's opinions.

"I had a talk with Dr. Grant (a friend of Smyth's) on
various pyramid matters for about an hour. He strongly
advises clearing the entrance passage for reaching the
subterranean gallery. He has done a quantity of measuring, which Smyth will not say anything about, though
sent to him, because it will not fit some very minor points
which he has taken up. Dr. Grant is evidently provoked
and rather vexed and annoyed . . . by this suppression of
inconvenient facts. . . ."

There was the question of the so-called "boss"—a small
projection of stone in the anti-chamber to the King's
Chamber which Smyth had adopted as the measure of his
so-called "pyramid inch".

"Mrs. Grant told with zest how Mr. Glover (a disciple
of Smyth) was eaten of mosquitoes, and sat with his eyes
closed on their sofa, gently rubbing his hands with a hair-
brush, and meandering on about the Pyramid all day
long. The doctor told how on taking some measures of
the 'boss' Mr. Glover pulled out a saw file and tried to
reduce the granite to the exact size which he wanted for
his Divine Inspiration Theories!"

For months Petrie, then twenty-six years of age, lived in
a tomb near the Great Pyramid, and, with the assistance

of an Arab named Ali Gabri, subjected the Great Pyramid to a survey of such accuracy as it had probably never known since its builders planned it more than four thousand years previously. His enthusiasm is infectious.

"After getting up and breakfast, I went off with Ali to the Pyramid. There had been a good deal of rain in the night, and it lay on rocky parts and in pools in the plain, it had also run in and filled the footholes cut in the descending passage . . . went into the Queen's Chamber and then up the Grand Gallery to the King's Chamber. Crawled into all the length of Vyse's cut by the air channel, and saw that the bottom end of it is clear, but there was no draught in it. Then in the King's Chamber I measured the joints of the bottom course of the north wall . . . and then took sundry measures in the ante-chamber. Three parties of travellers came in, and for one some fires were burnt, which obliged me to beat a retreat from the sulphurous gas . . . which filled the air and set Ali coughing. I found the smell of bats very unpleasant but got used to it. The heat was too much for working in, and I took off hat and coat at first; when Ali went off to mid-day devotions, I also dispensed with boots, shirt, and trousers and found I could then get on comfortably, so I shall work by night (as Dr. Grant recommended) to avoid travellers, and dispense with Ali, to avoid clothes, for I can work twice as quick without. . . ."

While working at night in the Great Pyramid he had more than one alarming experience. Perhaps the worst was when his friend, Dr. Grant, who was helping in the survey, fainted when they were both half-way down the "well". ". . . to raise a heavy man, barely conscious, up a shaft of seventy feet with scanty foothold, when at any moment he might sweep me away to the bottom was a risk not to be forgotten."

Practical man though he was, he had an artist's eye for the beauty of the Egyptian landscape, especially at dawn and sunset.

". . . The sunset was very fine; before it the hills far away at Helwan and beyond, on the other side of the Nile, were lovely in pink warm tints on the sunny slopes of rock, and blue in the shadows, then where the sun went down a soft pink purple shade up in the east, with blue beneath it, and over the sun a delicately flecked cloud of crimson hung in a tawny sky. . . ."

He had scant respect for the methods of earlier archæologists.

"Mariette is having some excavations made near the Sphinx and they are filling up all the clearing which cost so much to make on both sides of the Sphinx, in fact covering it up again; this, absurd as it seems, is all of a piece with the style of excavating here; rubbish is always thrown over the nearest handy place quite irrespective of whether it may be in the way or not, or what it may cover. I should like £100,000 to shoot all the sand and stuff off the hill by steam excavation down a tramway into the plain below, and leave the thousands of tombs all clear and bare, instead of having 10 to 20 feet of rubbish over all the surface to be dug and cut every time a hole is made. I hear that some Pasha most rascally blasted to pieces all the fallen parts of the granite temple by a large gang of soldiers to clear it out, instead of lifting the stones up and replacing them with tackle. "I should like to put a hundredth of the powder in his inside with a fuse. . . ."

All the enthusiasm and intolerance of the young archæologist of genius is in that passage; he saw clearly how the work of excavation should be done, and he is full of contempt and anger for the selfish amateur methods which, up to his day, had sufficed.

"Nothing seems to be done with any uniform or regular plan. Work is begun and left unfinished, no regard is paid to future requirements of exploration; and no civilized or labour-saving appliances are used, nothing but what the natives have; all the sand being carried in small baskets on the heads of children. . . . It is sickening to see the rate at which everything is being destroyed, and the little regard paid to its preservation. . . . Anything would be better than leaving things to be destroyed wholesale; better spoil half in preserving the other half, than leave the whole to be smashed. After supper, writing and looking over measures, 20.70 is about the granite temple cubit. Then wrote this up and to bed. . . ."

Fifty years later, knighted, and heaped with honours awarded by the Universities of the world, he recalled, in his autobiography, this youthful period of his life:

"The science of observation, of registration, of recording, was as yet unthought of; nothing had a meaning unless it were an inscription or a sculpture. A year's work in Egypt made me feel it was like a house on fire, so rapid was the destruction going on. My duty was that of a salvage man, to get all I could, quickly gathered in, and then when I was sixty I would sit down and write it up. That was a true forecast. Two months after I was that age the (First World) War broke out, I was not allowed to take my part abroad, but was ordered to stick to my post at the University. Until then I could only write up the annual volumes of discoveries. During the (1914–18) War however, I could do as I had planned, and begin to write up the results of observing and collecting. . . ."

*　　*　　*

Petrie's survey, carried out with such care and thoroughness during the years 1880–81, revealed a phenomenal accuracy of construction which, in the writer's opinion, is far more impressive than any of Piazzi Smyth's theories. For example, he showed that the orientation of the Great Pyramid is so incredibly precise that compass errors can be checked against it. The estimated errors of each side are as follows:

North side . 0° 2' 28" south of west
East side   . 0° 5' 30" west of north
South side . 0° 1' 57" north of west
West side   . 0° 2' 30" west of north

The maximum error was therefore only 5' 30" or a little over *one-twelfth of a degree*. On the south side the error was *one-thirtieth of a degree*. Who, one wonders, was the master engineer who planned and laid out this great building with such precision? And how was it done?

Then, as another example, take the outer casing stones, which originally covered the whole pyramid. The fineness of their workmanship is almost beyond belief. Petrie wrote:

". . . the mean thickness of the eastern joint of the northern casing stones is .020" (1/50th of an inch) therefore, the mean variation of the cutting of the stone from a straight line is but .01" (1/100th part of an inch) of 75 inches up the face . . . these joints, with an area of 35 square feet each, were not only worked as finely as this, but cemented throughout. Though the stones were brought as close as 1/500th of an inch, or, in fact, into contact, the mean opening of the joint was 1/50th of an inch, yet the builders managed to fill the joint with cement, despite the great area of it, and the weight of the stones, some 16 tons."

Petrie also proved, by careful measurement of the sarcophagus in the King's Chamber, that it could not have been admitted through the Ascending Gallery after the pyramid was built, but must have been placed in the chamber before its roof was erected. He also noticed, though without endeavouring to explain them, the so-called "girdle-stones" in the Ascending Gallery, stone blocks placed at regular intervals through which the corridor had been driven. (It was, however, the German archæologist Borchardt who showed the purpose of these "girdle-stones".) Petrie was also able to demonstrate that the granite plug-blocks which sealed the Ascending Gallery were too large to have been stored either in the Horizontal Gallery leading to the Queen's Chamber or within the Queen's Chamber itself. The only place in which they could have been stored before the interment of the king was the Grand Gallery, from which they were slid down into the Ascending Gallery, after the funeral ceremony was concluded. But this still left a mystery unsolved. As Petrie says:

"... we are met then by an extraordinary idea, that all access to the King's Chamber after its completion must have been made by climbing over the plug-blocks, as they lay in the gallery, or by walking up the ramps on either side of them. Yet, as it is a physical impossibility for the blocks to have been lying in any other place before they were let down, we shut up to this view."

Did the funeral cortege of Cheops have to climb over enormous blocking stones on their way to the King's Chamber? Petrie thought that there was no alternative, but he was wrong. It was left to Borchardt to demonstrate what is most likely to have happened; his theory will be explained in another chapter.

Incidentally, the names "King's Chamber" and "Queen's Chamber" have no basis in reality. They were given by the Arabs, in conformity with their custom of making the tombs or niches for men flat-topped, and those of women with a sloping gable-roof. In actual fact, the so-called "Queen's Chamber" could have been the *serdab* of the pyramid, the repository of the *ka*-statue of the king, which may have been placed in the niche on one side of the chamber. Petrie found, on the hill opposite the entrance to the Great Pyramid, a mass of tiny diorite fragments, which led him to form the opinion that the niche in the Queen's Chamber may have contained a statue of Cheops in diorite like the famous one of Chephren in the Cairo Museum (see frontispiece) and that this was ruthlessly smashed by the same people who destroyed the sarcophagi and statues of other Fourth Dynasty kings during the troubled period of the Seventh to the Tenth Dynasties.

"When, then was the Pyramid first violated?" he asks.[1] "Probably by the same hands that so ruthlessly violated the statues and temples of Khafra (Chephren) and the Pyramids of Abu Roash, Abusir, and Saqqara. That is to say, probably during the civil wars of the seventh to tenth Dynasties. At that time the secret opening of the Pyramid, by which the workmen retired (i.e. the "well") would still be known; and while that was the case, and before any forced openings had been made, the coffer was lifted up to see if any hidden passage existed beneath it; then probably its lid was broken off, and the body of the great builder treated to the spite of his enemies. Then also the Queen's Chamber—the *serdab* of the Pyramid—may have been forced open, and the diorite statue torn from its grand niche, broken up, pedestal and all, and carried out to be smashed to chips, and scattered on the hill opposite the pyramid door, so that no one should ever restore it. . . ."

"The history of the destruction of the Pyramids really begins with the Arabs. They first, under the Caliph Ma'mun, forced the great hole through the masonry, from the outside to the part commonly called Ma'mun's Hole, at the beginning of the ascending passage. Had it not been for their shaking of the masonry, which let fall the stone which concealed the plug-blocks, perhaps the upper chambers would have remained yet unknown. Hearing the stone drop, they turned aside their southward progress and burrowing twenty feet eastwards they broke into the entrance passage, and found the fallen stone; here they saw that it had covered the beginning of another passage, and so they forced out of their hole a continuation southward and upward to get behind the granite plug; finding they only hit the side of the plug-blocks, they tracked along them in the softer limestone,

[1] In *The Pyramids of Gizeh*, by W. M. F. Petrie, Field and Tuer, the Leadenhall Press; Simpkin Marshall & Co., London, 1885.

until they reached the upper end, and then they rushed freely up the hitherto unused passage.

"Probably they found the plug at the top of the well not replaced, after the earlier destroyers; and so got down the well and forced its lower closing, which must have been in position, for the Greeks and Romans not to have been aware of the passage. Such, from the statements of the historians, and the details of the place, seems to have been the history of the attack on the interior of the Great Pyramid."

Petrie also recognized that there had been several changes of plan in the construction of the Great Pyramid.

"The plan of the passages was certainly altered once, and perhaps oftener, during the course of the building. The shaft, or 'well' leading from the N. end of the gallery down to the subterranean parts, was either not contemplated at first, or else was forgotten in the course of building; the proof of this is that it has been cut through the masonry after the courses were completed. . . . Another evidence of altered plans is the Queen's Chamber floor. This is not merely left in the rough core, but it has actually had another course of the rough core masonry built, or at least fitted, on to it; and this upper course has been removed, or omitted, in order to build the chamber there. Of the Subterranean Chamber, all that can be said is that it is wholly unfinished and hardly more than sketched out; so that a change of plan with regard to that also seems proved, since it was the first part begun."

Where Petrie went wrong was in believing that the entrance to the Descending Gallery had always been accessible. He adopted this view on finding, at the entrance to the Southern Pyramid of Snofru at Dashur, holes which seem to have been intended to receive the pivots of a "flap-door" of a type mentioned by Strabo when describing the entrance to the Great Pyramid.

". . . the one slightly larger than the other . . . has, about half-way up its sides, a removeable stone. On taking this away there is a winding gallery to the vault."

No doubt in the time of Strabo the Descending Gallery of the Great Pyramid was accessible in this way (though the upper galleries and chambers were probably still a secret) but, according to modern archæologists such as Mr. I. E. S. Edwards, what had probably happened was this. Originally the Descending Gallery was sealed by plug-blocks, as was the lower descending gallery of the Second Pyramid discovered by Vyse (see Diagram 10, page 231). During the troubled period of the Seventh to the Tenth Dynasties this passage was probably forced, and still later, under the Saites, re-sealed again by means of a stone flap-door which gave access to the Descending Gallery in Greek and Roman times. Later the secret of the door was lost, and when the Arabs came to make their attack they were unaware of the existence of the door, and therefore forced an entry through the masonry below it.

Petrie was also able to demonstrate, by careful measurement and planning of the three main pyramids of Giza, that although they had been subject to alterations in their internal layout during construction, *they had been planned from the start to occupy their present area.* He drew a sectioned diagram of the Great Pyramid with its entrance passage and galleries, and then drew two small, hypothetical pyramids inside it, to test the truth of the "accretion theory" advanced by Lepsius. In the case of the smallest possible pyramid, he was able to prove that "if a Pyramid had existed of this size, it would be completely anomalous, and unlike any type known; it would have (1) a horizontal passage, (2) an opening near the top of it, (3) a chamber close to the top of it, and (4) an entrance to the lower chamber far outside the Pyramid. Each of these peculiarities condemns it as impossible. The next larger size which would leave chambers half exposed on the outside of the building, would have (1) two entrances on one face, (2) one sloping upwards, (3) a great chamber close to the outside and near the top of the Pyramid. . . . Thus it is plain that the 'accretion theory' breaks down in its application to any size under six hundred feet for the Great Pyramid; and if we are thus compelled by its arrangements to acknowledge a primary design of a base of 600 feet (which is larger than nineteen-twentieths of the other pyramids) what need is there for a theory of accretion to account for its being 750 feet?"

As for the "Great Pyramidiot" and his Divine Inspiration Theories:

"The principal result of the survey was to show that the casing did not slope down to the pavement above the corner sockets, but sloped down to the floors of the sockets, and the pavement laid over it there. The base of the pyramid at the pavement was therefore much less than the distances between the outer sides of the rock sockets. *Therefore, instead of a pyramid measuring 9,140 inches, as was supposed, it measured only 9,069 inches. Hence all theorizing about the days in the year being represented was entirely erroneous. . . .*[1] The theories as to the size of the pyramid are thus proved entirely impossible. . . . The fantastic theories, however, are still poured out, and the theorists still assert that the facts correspond to their requirements. It is useless to state the real truth of the matter, as it has no effect on those who are subject to this type of hallucination. They can but be left with the flat earth believers and other such people to whom a theory is dearer than a fact. . . ."

[1] Our italics.

CHAPTER THIRTEEN

EGYPTOLOGY UNDER WATER

THE forty years which followed Petrie's arrival in Egypt in 1880 could be described as the flood-tide of Egyptology, though valuable and important work has been done during the period between the two World Wars. But from 1880 to 1920 problem after problem was fully or partially solved, and most of our modern knowledge of the Pyramids is derived from the work carried out during those forty years. It can be divided roughly into two categories, (a) exploration of pyramids hitherto unexcavated or at least only superficially explored, and (b) the more careful, scientific examination and dating of known pyramids, such as those at Giza and Saqqara. Allied to this work was the investigation of tombs of the pre-pyramid ages, which enabled archæologists like Professor Reisner, the American scholar and excavator, to trace the development of the Egyptian tomb, and to prove that these great monuments were not the product of spontaneous generation but grew logically from earlier and simpler forms of tombs.

In fact, the most fruitful field for future excavation and study will probably be among the monuments of the First and Second Dynasties. Already Professor Walter Emery, working for the Egypt Exploration Society of London, has uncovered royal tombs at Saqqara of the First Dynasty which indicate that even at this remote period, the Ancient Egyptians had attained a degree of civilization almost equal to that of the builders of the pyramid age. The tendency to-day is to push the frontier of Ancient Egyptian civilization further and further back in time.

Inevitably, as work becomes more scientific, and conditions of work more stable and regular, it has also become less adventurous, and it is doubtful if any future accounts of pyramid excavation will be written in the rich anecdotal style of Sir Flinders Petrie. Let us therefore take one or two more glimpses of him during the period 1880–90, when, after dealing with the Giza pyramids, he moved southward to attack some of the unexplored pyramids at Dashur, Medum, Hawara and Lahun.

He worked under difficulties which would have driven some modern Egyptologists prematurely grey, and only his burning faith in his work, coupled with a supple diplomatic sense, great physical courage and capacity for endurance, enabled him to carry on. Among these difficulties two loom largest. The first—which probably worried him least—was the unstable condition of the country; the Bedouin on the desert fringes were suspicious of foreigners, and sometimes terrorized the Egyptian villagers from whom Petrie drew his workmen. Police protection was inadequate and often more of a liability than an asset. Petrie carried a revolver and sometimes had to use it.

"I pitched my tent at the edge of the cultivated land (near Dashur) some half mile from the village, beneath a small grove of palms on a sandy rise, with several fairly good wells around it. The only trouble was the need of having guards, owing to the distance from the village. Happily I got two very quiet men, whom by many injunctions I restrained from talking at night, for when living in a tent one is one's own policeman, and the slightest whisper outside is enough to break a sound sleep. Those guards slept in an enviable manner; one night I was awoke by a whine, and leaning forward to my man Muhammed, who was also awake, he said that a hyena had been smelling the guards' feet, but thought they were alive, so hesitated to begin on them. On Muhammed's moving, the hyena had slipped into the shadow of a palm and stood whining at a distance from the prospect of supper. The guards were snoring quite steadily, when I just sent a shot towards the beast to scare it off; as the crack of the revolver died away, I heard the same snore continuing without the least break or change. Happy sleepers who can ignore such a sound over their heads!"

On another occasion his pyramid studies were interrupted by a murder investigation.

"The first day that I was going to the pyramids I smelt a smell; and following my nose I came to some uncanny legs, off which the hyenas had eaten the flesh, sticking out of a hollow behind some stones. I thought they looked suspicious, so when I had Muhammed up there the next day I told him about them. He came to me and said it was a man, he was sure of it, for he felt his hair stand on end, and moreover there were clothes about. . . ."

Petrie then sent for the police, who were not much help.

"Finally a guard was appointed to watch the remains while a doctor should arrive. These unlucky guards were levied from the neighbouring villages, twelve in all, with four policemen; they passed the night lying about the corner of the pyramid, hearing the 'afrit' (spirit) of the murdered man by night, and baked by day in the barren desert. Then a full examination took place, and the two bodies of men were overhauled and reported on. While the police were waiting about at the pyramid, a party of three thieves, driving five buffaloes over from the Fayum, ran right across them; a challenge followed then an exchange of fourteen bullets, and then the thieves bolted."

The second problem which beset the young archæologist was corruption and intrigue among high officials, coupled, sometimes, with a cynical indifference to the fate of the monuments placed in their care. The Egyptians themselves had little if anything to do with this; since the foundation of the Department of Antiquities, of which Mariette had been the first Director, the leading officials of the Department had been mainly French. The memoirs of this time often contain bitter attacks on the administration of the Department, many of them unfair. There was certainly rivalry, sometimes breaking into open hostility, between the French officials in charge of the Department and the British civil administration. There was also the fact that dealing in antiquities had become a highly profitable business, and some Egyptian and foreign dealers were not above greasing the palms of officialdom in order to gain the much-coveted *firman* (permit) to excavate.

It is futile to try to pin the guilt on any one nation; none came out of the business with entirely clean hands; British, French, German, Egyptian—each can point with pride to their distinguished and disinterested scholars—a Petrie for a Borchardt, a Lepsius for a Maspero. Equally each has produced its quota of less estimable people; nor were the scholars themselves always above reproach. Nationalist suspicions, the bitter rivalry of scholars working in the same field—and none can be more bitter than Egyptologists when they wish to be—combined with the corrupting influence of unscrupulous dealers; these provided the background against which nineteenth-century archæologists like Petrie had to work.

Petrie, according to the testimony of all who knew him well, had many of the qualities of the saint. But he was no cloistered innocent, and when he knew that dirty business was afoot he had his own ways of circumventing it, which often succeeded; for example, when commencing work at Hawara in 1888:

"On first going out I at once resumed the attack on the pyramid of Hawara, and while thus engaged I also cleared a large tomb of the XXVIth Dynasty, and found a few more portraits and cartonnage busts of the Roman age. . . . But within a fortnight of beginning I heard that (a certain individual) was intending to occupy Illahun, where I was going myself. As this person was quite ignorant of archæology, and was allowed to dig simply for the sake of plunder, I could not tolerate his ruining the results of such an important site. And as his power of working in the Fayum was exactly the same as mine —a permission from the Government—I had to occupy

the ground if it was to be saved. So for eleven weeks work
was just kept alive by a few men at Medinet Gurob and
at Illahun, while I was finishing at Hawara. It was quite
contrary to my wishes to carry on excavations without
proper supervision, as I could only go to these places
about once a week, and that entailed a walk of seventeen
miles; but it was the only means of saving places which
proved, when I worked them, to be of the greatest
historical value."

All the best of Petrie is in that passage; his cool, almost
arrogant self-confidence; his devotion to his chosen task of
scientific exploration as distinct from plunder; his tenacity,
his endurance, and his racy narrative style. His account, in
the same archæological report, of his tunnelling operations
under the Hawara pyramid reads like an adventure story,
as indeed it was.

The Hawara pyramid was built by the great Twelfth
Dynasty king, Amenemhat III, the king who, under the
name of Moeris, is described by Herodotus as the creator
of the great lake in the Fayum which bore his name.

"Moeris . . . dug a lake of remarkable usefulness,
though at the cost of incredible toil. Its circumference,
they say, is 3,600 stades, its depths at most points fifty
fathoms. . . . No-one can adequately commend the king's
design, which brings such usefulness and advantage to
the dwellers in Egypt."
"Since the Nile kept no definite bounds in its rising,
and the fruitfulness of the country depended upon the
river's regularity, the king dug the lake to accommodate
the superfluous water, so that the river should neither
by its strong current, flood the land unseasonably and
form swamps and fens, nor, by rising less than was
advantageous, damage the crops by lack of water. Between the river and the lake he constructed a canal,
80 stades in length and 300 feet in breadth. Through
this canal, at times he admitted the water from the river,
at other times he excluded it, thus providing the farmers

with water at fitting times by opening the inlet and closing it scientifically and at great expense. . . ."[1]

Amenemhat built two pyramids, one at Dashur, which was probably a cenotaph, and another at Hawara, in the Fayum, not far from the above-mentioned canal. The Hawara pyramid almost certainly at one time contained his body. During the Twelfth, Thirteenth and Fourteenth Dynasties the kings no longer built their pyramids entirely of stone, as had their predecessors of the Fourth to the Sixth Dynasties, but of mud-brick. On the other hand, they took far more elaborate precautions for the conceal-ment and protection of their burial-chambers, which were hewn out of the rock beneath the pyramid, and protected by enormous granite blocks arranged in pent-house fashion above the sepulchral chamber. They also relied on "puzzle-passages", blind alleys and other devices to conceal from intending robbers the true location of their tombs.

Profiting, as they hoped, by the experience of their pre-decessors, whose pyramids had been entered and robbed, they also took great pains to conceal the entrance, which was no longer placed in the north side of the pyramid, as in the time of Cheops, Chephren and Mycerinus. This fact gave Petrie infinite trouble. He already had a skeleton force working at Illahun "in order to occupy the ground" and prevent the plundering dealers getting in. With the rest of his scanty band of Arab helpers he worked around the faces of Hawara pyramid, clearing the areas in front of the northern, western and eastern faces in the hope of find-ing the entrance, but without success.

"The opening of the pyramid of Hawara proved a far longer and more troublesome affair than seemed probable at first sight. When we knew that every pyramid yet examined opened from the north side, and not far from the base, nothing seemed simpler than just to clear the north side, as Belzoni, Perring and Mariette had done on

[1] "Although Amenemhat III may well have undertaken some irrigation or land reclama-tion schemes in the neighbourhood of the lake . . . it was almost certainly in existence before his time." I. E. S. Edwards, *The Pyramids of Egypt.*

other pyramids. I accordingly began to clear this side the first thing when I went to Hawara in January 1888. But I saw that some previous excavator (Lepsius or Vassali) had already made desperate attempts, having cut away all the middle of the north face for some yards in; and had moreover begun the appalling task of destroying the pyramid, by cutting an open trench down the middle. . . . This open trench affair was however far too much to carry out, and was abandoned after hopelessly disfiguring the brickwork."

Nonetheless, after searching vainly for the entrance on the south, east and north sides, Petrie reluctantly had to begin tunnelling under the north face.

"The pyramid being built of mud-bricks laid in sand did not offer any serious difficulty, but yet the tunnel was not so simple as it seemed. The sand between the bricks was in very thick layers, usually half to one inch; and being quite dry and clean, it ran out interminably in some parts, coming down as in an hour-glass from the joints. It was needful therefore to board up the roof of the tunnel all along, and as no native would treat the place with sufficient tenderness to avoid loosening the bricks overhead, I had to fix every board myself as the tunnel advanced. The bricks moreover were so large and heavy, being double the size each way of an English brick, and weighing 40 or 50 lbs, that a single one dropped on a person would have settled his moving powers for some time to come."

Occasionally, falls of the side occurred, and the false roof of timber would break away, or hang so that a touch would bring it crashing down. Petrie had brought in masons from Cairo to chip a way through the stone walls of the galleries and chambers when he found them, but he had to conceal them from the dangerous state of the tunnel lest they should refuse to work there.

"In the second season the state of matters was still

more dangerous; falls of the sides and roof continually took place, even three times in twenty-four hours. As masons from Cairo were working inside it was needful to clear away all signs of the falls, and re-strut the sides, as quickly as possible; and as happily nothing much fell while they were inside they never knew anything about the true state of affairs. One of these falls would bring down tons of bricks from the sides and roof, along perhaps 20 feet in length. I then at once began clearing the stuff out with some lads, needing to pass all along the unsupported tunnel to get it clear; and then turning everyone out—sometimes at night—I used to re-prop the sides without any interference. The need of listening acutely all the time to detect any sand running down— the prelude to a fall—and the need of having the narrow way quite clear to retreat in half a second if need be, made it necessary to work quite alone. . . ."

For more than seven weeks Petrie toiled away at the tunnel without finding any indication of a burial chamber. And then "we found the rock drop straight down, and knew that the pit and chamber were before us". It was half past one on a dark night, when one of the Arab boys came running up to Petrie with the words: "The stone is found! The stone is found!"

"I went up at once," he wrote, "and saw that we had reached the sloping roof stone of the chamber." But still a great problem now faced him. How was he to get through the massive blocks into the chamber itself? "I . . . got over some masons on the 16th April from Medinet, but they were quite helpless in the face of such a job. As no good ones were then to be had, and the season was late to begin such a task (owing to the heat) I reluctantly left it after earthing over the mouth of the tunnel."

Petrie then returned to England, as he did every year to arrange an exhibition of the antiquities which he had found, and only returned to Hawara in November. He employed stone-masons from the Fayum to attack the stone roof, but without success, so he brought over two more from Cairo. But it was a long, slow, heartbreaking job.

"On the twenty-first day, however, a boy ran down with the welcome news of a hole found. I had just been all the morning at work in the water of Horuta's tomb, and had come out for a wash and breakfast; but I went up, as I was, to see to the matter. There was a black hole in the floor of the mason's cutting, and they were chipping away the edges scrap by scrap. Soon I managed to squeeze through, and found that I was in a little forced passage cut by ancient treasure-seekers, which led to the super-chamber. Searching around it I saw the top of the entrance passage on the north side, on a level with the floor I was on. Jumping down, I found the passage was blocked; but there was a hole under the stone I had been standing on. Into this I squeezed, sloping head downwards, on the mud which partly filled it, and managed to see that there was a chamber beneath with something in it, and a great deal of water."

The reason for this was that the Nile had risen considerably since Amenemhat III built his pyramid, and the level of the subsoil water had now risen to well above the floor of the sarcophagus chamber. Jammed tightly in the hole, Petrie looked down into the black depths, and could not see the bottom. "Get back I could not, for I was jammed tight to the shoulders; and the masons had to drag me up out of the hole by my legs."

"Then, clearing the mud away, I asked a thin and active lad if he would undertake to go in; and having sounded the depth of water, and found it not more than chest deep, he slid through feet foremost with a rope ladder to hold by, and I watched him through the hole, which would not let my shoulders pass. I then saw the sarcophagi, the large one in the middle, and the curious added one at the side."

The sarcophagus, as expected, had been robbed in

antiquity; but Petrie was looking for facts, not treasure. Was the pyramid really that of Amenemhat? He and his Arab boys spent days chest deep in water, carefully removing every fragment which might yield a clue.

"The chamber floor was covered with blocks, chips and earth, which had fallen in; but the water was too deep to reach anything by hand, and too salt and acrid to put eyes or nose beneath it. I therefore first cleared out the sarcophagi thoroughly, as they were shallower, and could

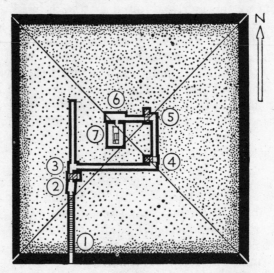

6. Plan of the Pyramid of Amenemhat III
at Hawara

pick out everything by hand. And then the lads gradually picked up the stuff from the chamber, by shuffling it on the broad blade of a native hoe with a foot. . . . I promised half a piastre for every hieroglyph found, and a dollar for a cartouche. Within a day the cartouche was found on a bit of alabaster vase, Amenemhat III as I had expected. . . ."

The second sarcophagus was apparently that of one of the king's daughters, Ptahneferu, who seems to have died

young, before her father, and to have been buried side by
side with him in his pyramid, indicating that customs had
changed since the days of the Old Kingdom, when wives
and daughters were buried in separate pyramids.

Next came the problem of finding the entrance by following the passages leading outward from the sarcophagus
chamber. This was even more hazardous than the initial
tunnelling in, for the passages were devious, and half under
water, half-blocked by trap-doors of stone, past which the
archæologist had to squeeze as best he could.

"Up the east passage the muddy earth rose nearly to
the roof, and we had to crawl through. At the south end
of this there seemed to be no exit, but a slight gap under

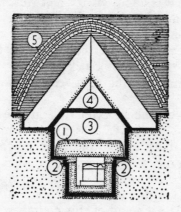

7. Plan of the Burial-chamber of
Amenemhat III at Hawara

the S.E. trap-door showed that there was a way; and
clearing out some earth I got in far enough to stick tight,
and knocked the candle out. Matches had to be fetched,
as we were streaming with the heat, so that nothing could
be kept dry in the only garment I had on. Under the
stone I got into the S.E. chamber, and then the south
passage was so nearly filled with mud that we had to lie
flat and slide along it propelled by fingers and toes.

"At last I reached the S.W. chamber. The blind

passage being level did not promise a way out; the lean
lad got up on the top of the first trap-door in an incredibly shallow space but found no exit; then I slid
down the narrow forced hole beneath the trap-door, and
waded through the water to the ante-chamber. There at
last I found a passage sloping considerably upward, and
knew that we were in the entrance passage."

To understand the complexity of these passages I refer
the reader to Plan 6 on page 196 (for which I am indebted to Mr. I. E. S. Edwards). The architect of Amenemhat had employed every cunning device to outwit the
robbers who he knew would one day attempt to force the
pyramid.

The entrance was about eighty feet west of the middle of
the south face, and began as a flight of steps (1) descending
to a small chamber (2). Beyond this lay a short passage
leading to a dead end. But concealed in the roof of this
passage was a twenty-ton block of stone which could be
slid sideways, and leading to a second chamber *above* the
first (3).

Beyond this chamber, extending in the same direction
(north-south) as the lower passage, was another long passage, carefully blocked, but leading nowhere. It was a
blind. Leading off to the right was another passage, closed
by a wooden door, which, by way of two right-angled turns
(see Plan) and two further trap-doors, led to a large ante-
chamber (6). At each end of this chamber a deep well had
been sunk into the floor and carefully blocked with stone.
These, too, were blinds, intended to delude the tomb-
robbers, who might be led to waste their time in removing
the filling in a vain search for the burial chamber. Time
was important. The longer it took for the tomb-robbers to
find the real chamber, the greater would be the chance that
they would be discovered and prevented. Nor was this the
only trick which the cunning architect had up his sleeve.
The entire northern half of the ante-chamber was blocked
with stone, but there was nothing behind but the rock.

Where was the real burial-chamber? To understand this

it is necessary to examine the other diagram on page 197, which shows its construction. First the builders sunk a pit or shaft in the rock—not exactly under the peak of the pyramid but a little to the west. The burial chamber, which was sunk into this pit, consisted of a single block of quartzite, about 22 feet long and 8 feet broad, and 6 feet high. Its weight must have been about 110 tons. The corners were so exquisitely cut that at first Petrie did not realize that he was looking at a solid stone box, but thought that it was jointed.

Above this chamber lay three slabs of quartzite—an extremely hard stone—each four feet thick and lying side by side. These formed the roof of the burial chamber, but before the tomb was finally closed the roof slab nearest the ante-chamber was propped up, leaving a gap towards which a cross-trench in the floor of the ante-chamber led.

When they came to bury the king, the Ancient Egyptians slid his mummy through the gap and lowered it into a large quartzite sarcophagus which had already been placed in position, together with that of the king's daughter. (Probably she was buried first and the gap left open until the king died.) When the funeral ceremony was over, the 45-ton quartzite slab would be lowered into position, sealing the chamber. Then the trench in the ante-chamber would be filled in and covered with a pavement of stone, so that there was no indication of where the burial chamber lay.

Nor was this all. Above the burial chamber were two relieving chambers, intended, as in the Great Pyramid, to keep the superincumbent weight of the pyramid from crushing the burial chamber. The lower one had a flat roof (3) and the upper a pointed, "penthouse" roof of limestone blocks, each weighing nearly fifty tons. Above that, an enormous arch of brick, three feet thick, was built over the pointed roof to support the pyramid core (5).

All these precautions were in vain. As always, the tomb-robbers got through and rifled the chamber; and one does not know what most to admire, the skill of the architect who planned the last resting place of Amenemhat III, or the determined courage of the robbers who defeated him. Always the story is the same. As Cyril Connolly has written in the 'Sunday Times'.

". . . every Necropolis is the scene of an insect-like conflict between the Pharaoh—who begins his tomb on the day of his accession and is compelled to take his treasure with him that his jaws may function in a future life, and the tomb-robbers, full of cunning and unbelief. The God-king mines and counter-mines, constructs false doors, blind shafts, labyrinths of dummy passages, retires deeper and deeper into his pyramid as into an oak-gall. The probing antennæ pursue him; however many builders he immolates, his own priests are not always to be trusted. . . ."

Sir Thomas Browne had the answer three hundred years ago.

"To be pyramidally extant," he wrote, "is but a fallacy in duration."

CHAPTER FOURTEEN

THE TREASURE OF THE PRINCESSES

TRUE archæology is not treasure-hunting. The archæologist judges his work, and that of his fellow-excavators, not by the intrinsic, or even artistic, value of the objects found, but by the light which such objects throw on the historical period which he is investigating. "The science of observation, of registration, of recording," wrote Petrie, "was as yet unthought of; nothing had a meaning unless it was an inscription or a sculpture." He, and others like him, were not unduly disappointed when they found that the burial chambers beneath the pyramids which they were investigating had been entered and robbed a thousand or more years before their time. They had their triumphs if a piece of pottery—valueless to the dealer or the casual observer—gave them a clue to the dating of an epoch, filled a gap in knowledge, or even posed a problem which, generations hence, other archæologists would take up and solve.

For example, the story of Petrie's heroic attack on the pyramid of Amenemhat III, though it makes a dramatic story, is of far less importance, archæologically, than his detective work on the First Dynasty tombs at Abydos, where he had nothing to work on but a mass of ransacked ruin left by plunderers and speculators. And yet from this archæological junk-heap Petrie was able to trace the development of these proto-dynastic tombs from the simple brick-lined pit-graves of the dynasty before Menes (3200 B.C.) to the large elaborate tombs of the Second Dynasty kings with their surrounding chambers and galleries.

Yet only an archæological snob (and they exist) would attempt to belittle the wonder and excitement of those occasions when the excavator finds rare and beautiful objects—jewellery, ornaments, furniture which have been hidden from men's eyes for perhaps three thousand or more years. And the wonder is greatest of all when such things are found, not in forgotten tombs buried under deep layers of earth, but in pyramids which for four thousand years were known to be tombs, were known to have once contained treasure, and had been entered again and again in search of plunder. Yet even in the last seventy years such discoveries have been made.

One was made on March 7th, 1894, by Jacques de Morgan who, in 1891, had replaced Grébaut, the previous Director of the Service des Antiquités, in one of the periodical shake-ups which convulsed it. Petrie writes in his autobiography that "he was the son of Jack Morgan, a Welsh mining engineer, and brother of a Parisian dealer in antiquities. He knew nothing whatever about Egypt but, as a capable business man, made the most reputable head the French could find."

Petrie, who disliked Grébaut and tended to be prejudiced against the French, was probably a little unfair. De Morgan was a French civil engineer, probably of Welsh descent, who had previously explored the Caucasus, Persia and other sites in the Near East. He was a little younger than Petrie, whom he always treated fairly, as the latter admitted, and later he made some useful investigations into the predynastic antiquities of Egypt, which were also Petrie's particular field.[1] He was thirty-seven when he made his great discovery at Dashur.

The pyramid-field at Dashur lies some miles to the south of Saqqara, but north of the Fayum. It is most famous for its two great stone pyramids of the Third Dynasty, one of which—the northern pyramid—is almost as large as the Great Pyramid of Cheops, though far less well-known, while the other, called the "Blunted" Pyramid, changes its angle about half-way up its sides, the upper slope being less steep than the lower. It was probably built by Snofru, as his Horus-name *Neb-maat* was found by the late Abdessalam on a foundation stone on the north-east corner. But the

---

[1] The egotism of great archæologists is astounding. In his autobiography *Seventy Years in Archæology* covering the period 1880–1930 there is hardly a mention of the discoveries made by other archæologists during this period—not even the tomb of Tutankhamun.

builder of the larger, northern pyramid is still unknown.

Beside these stone monsters crouch the humbler, much ruined mud-brick pyramids of some of the Twelfth Dynasty kings, most of them mere heaps of rubble hardly distinguishable as pyramids. Here stand the pyramids of Senusret III—"Senusret is at peace", Amenemhat III—who, as we have seen, also had one at Hawara—and of Amenemhat II, known as "Sceptre of Amenemhat". All these were built between about 2000 and 1790 B.C.

In the early days of March 1894 de Morgan was excavating in the enclosure of the northern brick pyramid, in which he found fragments of sculptured blocks bearing the name of Senusret III (Sesostris), the great warrior king of the Twelfth Dynasty. After a great deal of labour he found the entrance in a court on the west side of the building, and eventually penetrated to the burial chamber, which was constructed of enormous blocks of Assuan granite and contained a fine sarcophagus—robbed, of course.

He then began to excavate the tombs of the royal family which had stood on the northern side of the pyramid. Their superstructures had practically disappeared, but he found a rock-cut gallery, entered from a pit at the north-east corner of the main pyramid.

In his *Fouilles à Dachour*, 1894–95, de Morgan wrote:

"The meticulous examination of the ground of these galleries disclosed, on the sixth of March, a rectangular cavity excavated in the rock at the foot of the sarcophagus. The terrain was loose, and the foot of one of the workmen sank into the middle of the debris. After a few blows with a pickaxe the hiding-place—for such it was—revealed its treasures; jewellery of gold and of silver, gems and precious stones were there, mingled with the fragments of a casket in which they had been enclosed. This square box, of about 30 centimetres along the side, existed only in a state of dust, but we found the gold leaf with which it had been encrusted, and the hieroglyphs of silver which had composed the name of the owner of the treasure."

Her name was the Princess Hathor-Sat, one of the daughters of Senusret III. De Morgan continues:

"The ancient people, at the time of the burial, knowing full well that the riches accumulated in the sarcophagus, in the offering chambers and on the mummies themselves, would one day fall a prey to robbers, had carefully hidden the *bijoux* of Princess Hathor-Sat in a place where no one would suspect their existence. It was thus that they escaped the ancient robbers, and that, thanks to the meticulous care with which the least dust was raised from the galleries, that they were discovered by the Department of Antiquities."

On the following day de Morgan discovered another, equally important *cache* in the tomb of Princess Merit, whose name was only known through being inscribed on her jewellery. It had been enclosed in a gold-encased casket as in the case of the other princess's jewellery, but the objects were more numerous. Then, on April 19th, near the pyramid of Amenemhat II, the delighted excavator discovered yet more royal treasures; this time they found the mummy of a royal princess—Nub-hotep; and jewels were found on her body and "in her winding sheet".

No royal jewellery of this remote period of Egyptian history had been found in modern times; the discovery was unique, and the objects of such beauty and splendour as to impress all who saw them with the high level of artistic achievement which the craftsmen of the Middle Kingdom had attained.

But de Morgan's triumphs were not yet over. In the latter part of the same year he led another expedition to Dashur, and this time concentrated on the pyramid enclosure of Amenemhat II, near which he had found the jewellery of the Princess Nub-hotep.

"On the 10th December," he wrote, "we made extensive soundings in the centre of the principal mound, instructing the workmen to dig down to the bedrock. After a few days the men raised a considerable cube of debris, and came upon the roof of a chamber, perfectly constructed. The so-called 'white *mastaba*' was in fact a pyramid, as Lepsius had thought."

But the pyramid had been thoroughly robbed by the ancients, who had, says de Morgan, opened the sarcophagus and broken the partitions which had once closed the offering chambers. Nothing had escaped them. Or had it ?

After establishing, from fragments of inscribed stelæ, that the pyramid was that of Amenemhat II, de Morgan commenced to make *sondages* (trial pits) close together in the pile of debris situated on the east of the pyramid. "On the 12th February, these soundings led to the discovery of an enormous rectangular cavity." Near this, one of the pits sunk by the ancient robbers had come within only six feet of the door of the chamber. But they had not gone down to a sufficient depth to find the monument, which was yet another tomb of a royal princess. In fact, two royal tombs were found, those of the Princesses Ita and Khnoumit, each containing splendid jewellery.

"The plunderers," wrote de Morgan, "were satisfied with their booty (obtained from the adjoining tombs) and thought they had discovered all the principal tombs adjacent to that of Amenemhat II. . . . It is this error of the ancient tomb-robbers to which we owe our possession of the splendid jewellery exhibited in the Museum at Giza." (Now in the Cairo Museum.)

Among these treasures, worn by royal ladies of Egypt nearly four thousand years ago, are the two lovely golden diadems of Princess Khnoumit, one a naturalistic design of tendrils, held together with florets of gold with hearts of carnelian, petals of lapis lazuli, and berries of the same stone—"the most charming and graceful head-dress ever seen," wrote Petrie.

The other diadem is as formal as the other is natural. "It consists," writes Baikie, "of double lyre motives, separated by rosettes, which uphold erect lyre motives. The whole is of gold, inlaid with lapis, carnelian, red jasper, and green felspar. In the case of the floral design it is almost miraculously fine. The florets are not stamped, but each gold socket is made by hand for the inserted stones. In no case, however small, was the polishing of the stone done in its *cloison*; it was always finished before setting."

There were also pectorals or breast ornaments of gold, one with the cartouche of Senusret II between two hawks, who wear the Double Crown, and another in which a vulture with outstretched wings overshadows the cartouche of Senusret III; again the materials are gold, lapis, carnelian and green felspar. All these lovely things are now in the Egyptian Museum at Cairo.

Nineteen years were to pass before a comparable discovery was made in an Egyptian pyramid, and although I have to break my chronological sequence I propose to deal with it here, because it, too, consisted of jewellery belonging to a Twelfth Dynasty princess. The discovery was made in one of the small pyramids adjoining that of Senusret II, the successor to Amenemhat II.

Senusret II built his pyramid at Illahun (sometimes called Lahun) on the edge of the Fayum. Petrie began excavating it in 1887–88, and spent many months of labour before he found his way inside. It was enclosed by two walls, one of stone and the other of mud-brick, and between these, on the south side, were four shaft-tombs made for members of the royal family. It was not until 1913 that Petrie again excavated in this pyramid enclosure, with the assistance of Mrs. (now Lady) Petrie, C. T. Campion, Rex Engelbach, Mr. F. Frost, Mr. Battiscombe Gunn, Mr. D. Willey, and Mr. and Mrs. Guy Brunton.

Brunton was thirty-five at this time. His interest in Egyptology had begun when he was a boy, and when he was eighteen he began to frequent the Edwards Library at University College, London—where Petrie was then Professor of Egyptology—and began to study the subject seriously.

Then he went to South Africa where he worked as a bank

clerk for several years. He had, Lady Petrie once told me, "long, delicate bank clerk's fingers." In South Africa he met and married a Miss Winifred Newberry, a gay, buoyant South African girl, who was also a skilful artist, best known, perhaps, for her magnificent portraits of the Pharaohs in her book *Great Ones of Ancient Egypt*.

Petrie had an extraordinary power of personality, and a gift for drawing disciples to him; young men would hear him give a lecture, in London or Manchester or some other provincial town, and come up to him afterwards and offer their services. Each year he would take out to Egypt one or two of these proselytes and train them. Some of them fell by the wayside, but many achieved high distinction as archæologists, and it is no exaggeration to say that the majority of British Egyptologists who have gained fame and honour during the past fifty years owed their early training to Sir Flinders Petrie. Brunton was one of them.

He gave up his job in South Africa and returned to Egypt to work for Petrie. In 1913 he was so skilful and experienced that Petrie allowed him to work practically without supervision. While Petrie was working in the large pyramid, Brunton was supervising the excavation of the tomb shafts in the outer enclosure. He had with him a handful of highly-trained workmen known as the "Qufti" because they came from Quft in Upper Egypt. One of them, a youth, was working in the sarcophagus chamber of the easternmost shaft-tomb under Brunton's direction. In his fascinating account, *The Lahun Treasure*,[1] Brunton wrote:

"At about 4.30 p.m., when I was some distance away north of the pyramid, I received a message from the Qufti in charge that some gold beads were discovered in the mud, and I hurried to the spot. Mr. Frost had already taken charge of the site, and Professor Petrie had removed all the local workers clear of the tomb, and the earth from it where they had been hunting for any gold beads which had been overlooked, and from which they

[1] *Lahun* I, *the Treasure*, by Guy Brunton. London School of Archæology in Egypt, London, 1920.

handed up a few. The remainder of the work was done entirely by myself, during the ensuing eight days."

What had happened was this. The sarcophagus chamber had, as usual, been robbed, but on one side of the small chamber was a narrow recess. Like the pyramid of Amenemhat, that of Senusret II had suffered from flooding, and the recess was choked with dried mud left by flood-water in very ancient times.[1] In this deposit of mud the Qufti lad had come across some tiny gold beads, and, thanks to his native honesty, and the training he had received from Petrie, had immediately reported the discovery. The Qufti, trained by Petrie, were completely reliable. The local workmen were less so, and were accordingly banned from this part of the workings. Brunton then examined the recess, and delicately probing in the mud, found that there were many other rich treasures waiting to be removed. Petrie, although in charge of the excavations, had sufficient faith in his gifted assistant to leave him to finish the job himself. Brunton continues:

"The work was carried out mainly from the front; it would have been better possibly to have done it from above, but the distance of the surface of the mud from the roof of the recess, only ten inches, made this out of the question. . . . I found the recess so low (only forty inches to the roof) that I could not even kneel in it but had as a rule to work lying flat—resting on my elbows. Of course, the continued succession of finds, day after day, was amazing and utterly unequalled. The whole of the clearing was done with a small penknife, or with a pin when there was a chance of finding small beads. The work of pricking out the small beads (there were over nine thousand five hundred of them) was so laborious that eventually any detached scraps of mud were examined in the camp. . . ."

Guy Brunton died in 1948, and the full account of his

[1] The Ancient Egyptians had anticipated this danger, and had dug a trench around the large pyramid to collect the flood-water pouring down its sides.

great discovery can be read in his own scholarly work, *Lahun I: the Treasure*, published in London in 1920. But I would like to supplement it by the personal memories of Lady Petrie herself—now eighty-seven—as she told them to me a few days before I began this chapter.

"For eight days and nights," she said, "Brunton hardly ever left that chamber. At night he slept near the recess, and whenever he was awake he kept probing away in the dried mud with his long, delicate fingers, removing object after object; golden crowns, with feathers and streamers of gold, eight hundred and ten gold rings, a pectoral, or chest-ornament with the name of King Senusret II; another with the name of Amenemhat III; golden lions' heads, golden *couchant* lions, amethyst ball-beads, gold and turquoise ball-beads, bracelets and anklets of gold, a silver mirror, toilet vases containing perfumed ointment, and even copper toilet razors, all belonging apparently to the Princess Sat-Hathor-Unet. In spite of their fragile condition, not a single object was damaged or even scratched during their removal." (See illustrations 18–21.)

Day after day, night after night, the precious objects were brought out of the tomb and taken to the mud-hut in which the Petries lived.

"They were laid out on my bed," Lady Petrie told me, "and they covered it completely. I shall never forget the sight—all the jewellery, the crowns, the pectorals, the bracelet, anklet and necklace beads, all glowing in the beauty of their brilliant colours; gold, the pale blue of lapis-lazuli, the red of carnelian, the amethyst of the necklace-beads."

The discovery had to be kept a close secret from the workmen, for if the news had reached the surrounding villages, there might have been an armed raid on the camp. Eventually, when the last bead had been removed and the treasure-cache was empty, the objects were sealed in a box and taken to Cairo by one of Petrie's staff. He handed over the box to Maspero, who had been reappointed Director of the Department of Antiquities, and who placed it, unopened, in his safe.

"Then," said Lady Petrie, "when the season was over, my husband and I went to Cairo and saw Maspero. He handed us the box, and we asked him to retire from his office for a while. Carefully we laid out the jewellery on his big desks and tables until they were covered; then we asked Maspero to come in. He took one look at the blaze of colour before him and exclaimed:

"Mais, c'est encore Dachour!"

*   *   *

When one looks at the beautifully reconstructed jewellery, now in the possession of the New York Metropolitan Museum of Art, it is difficult to realize the utter confusion in which they were found by Brunton. The plan diagram opposite this page shows the positions in which they were found. At first, because there was a good layer of mud *under* the jewellery, it was thought that it may have been placed there temporarily by the robbers when they plundered the sarcophagus, and that they intended to remove it later. But, as Brunton says, "mud was found *under* the Canopic Jars[1] (in which the viscera were placed) and, as these jars were undisturbed, we are forced to the conclusion that the mud was deposited *before* the burial."

Apparently, after the tomb was made but before the body and its furniture were deposited, storm water poured down the mouth of the tomb shaft from time to time, leaving a deposit of mud in the recess. The jewellery of the princess, some of which was originally enclosed in caskets, was placed on top of the mud, in the positions shown on Brunton's plan 8. In the top right-hand corner, furthest from the entrance, were the marks left by a plain wooden box (the wood had decayed) which may at one time have contained linen, or perhaps the princess's wig. But no remains were found in the space which the box had occupied. In the top left-hand corner, mixed up with the bulk of the jewellery, were the many fragments of ivory inlay which had once formed part of

[1] When they embalmed a body, the Ancient Egyptians removed the vital organs and buried them separately beside the sarcophagus in four jars, known as Canopic Jars.

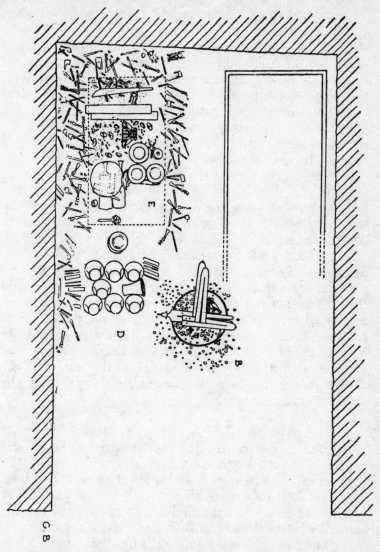

8. Brunton's diagram showing position in which the jewellery of
Princess Sat-Hathor-Unet was found

an ivory and ebony casket, ornamented with red carnelian and blue glaze.

It was in this area (E on the plan) that Brunton found nearly all the beads, the cowries (golden ornaments in the form of cowrie shells which were threaded on to a necklace) the bracelets and anklets, the toilet objects, the silver mirror and the magnificent pectoral of Senusret II.

In the area marked B on the plan, near the centre of the recess, was found the golden crown, lying on a bed of gold rings. "In only one case," writes Brunton, "could I discover any order. One of the lions was fixed in the ground with its head downwards. From its rump two lines of tiny beads extended, one from each threading-hole; and by moving the earth away, grain by grain, it was possible to get the arrangement, which was, counting from the lion, 7 turquoise, 3 gold, 5 carnelian, 3 gold, with the remainder disturbed. The other string was in the same order."

It was little clues like this which later enabled experts to thread together the necklaces and reveal them as they appeared when they adorned the neck of the princess Sat-Hathor-Unet. All the threads, had, of course, perished. As an example of the infinite care which Petrie and Brunton and the other archæologists lavished on the search for the tiniest fragments, here is Brunton's description of the crown (found in area B).

". . . it had been laid horizontally, sloping somewhat down to the North-west; the uræus ('sacred snake and emblem of royalty') pointed N.E. as shown in the plan. Of the rosettes, two were found after the crown had been taken out. One was sticking in the ground slightly away from the position of the circlet, and at the back . . . the other was standing on edge inside the circle.

"The piece of lazuli forming the head of the uræus was not in position, but was found later in washing the mud. One garnet eye was then still missing; this also turned up in the washing, but without its tiny gold setting. This again was found by Professor Petrie in his examination of the material above ground."

These passages from Brunton's straightforward technical description of the dig show the difference between scientific archæology and indiscriminate plunder. How many more treasures might have been preserved for us to-day if all Egyptian monuments had been excavated with such loving care!

Brunton was also able to make some interesting deductions after comparing the jewellery of Sat-Hathor-Unet with that of the princesses found by de Morgan at Dashur.

"The fact that the pectorals are of the same design is interesting. Princess Merit had two pectorals of Senusret III and Amenemhat III, but different in pattern. It looks as if a princess would choose her own design; Sat-Hathor-Unet, probably an elderly lady at the time, found the newer flamboyant designs were not to her taste, and so repeated her old favourite."

Sat-Hathor-Unet was the wife of Amenemhat III, who built the pyramid at Hawara described in the previous chapter.

". . . We may suppose that while Senusret III was the eldest son of Senusret II, Sat-Hathor-Unet was the daughter of his old age; she arrived at maturity shortly before his death, and so received jewellery from him. Amenemhat III, probably her nephew, and more or less of her own age, may have married her, long before his succession, and only given her the jewellery bearing his name when he had come to the throne, thirty-eight years after the death of Senusret II. When Sat-Hathor-Unet died, she chose to be buried close to her father at Lahun, rather than with her husband at Hawara, where his pyramid may not have been completed."

There remains the question "When was the tomb robbed, and how did the jewellery come to be overlooked?" Brunton's view was that after the burial there was a process of slow disintegration over a number of years, during which time no water entered the tomb.

"The wood gradually decayed; the threads stringing the beads rotted; the ivory inlay fell out and leant against the walls; the floor of the jewel-box dropped down between the legs, and the razors and the mirror lying flat on the bottom fell down with it."

Then came a year of exceptional rainfall, and the tomb was flooded. The roof of the shaft collapsed, and a flood of water and mud entered the tomb, washing the lighter objects about in the recess, and further breaking up the wooden sides of the casket.

"The legs of the casket, of stouter wood, floated up, and hence the golden feet are found at a high level. Probably many storm floods filled the chambers with water and each left its deposit of mud."

When, eventually, the robbers entered the tomb they opened the sarcophagus and cleared it out, leaving only a few planks from the coffins. But they did not touch the canopic jars, which were found intact, nor did they bother to explore the mud-filled recess "to the lasting joy of present and future generations".

It was on these alabaster jars, still standing untouched in their stone chest, that the explorers found the hieroglyphic inscriptions which gave the name of the royal owner of this rifled sepulchre. It read:

"*O Neit, spread thy protection over Duatmutef, who is in thee. She who has the honour with Duatmutef, the King's daughter, Sat-Hathor-Unet, true of voice.*"

CHAPTER FIFTEEN

FROM MENES TO MYCERINUS

I n Chapter Five I posed one or two problems connected
with the Giza pyramids which might interest the tech-
nically-minded reader. For instance, why are there three
chambers in the Great Pyramid, why had it an Ascending
as well as a Descending Gallery, and how was the former
closed? Again, why does the Second Pyramid of Chephren
have two entrances, one in the body of the pyramid, the
other some distance to the north in the rock, yet uniting
under the pyramid? Then there is the question of the two
sloping galleries leading to the large chamber in the Third
Pyramid, one of which communicates with the surface,
while the other, running above and parallel with the first,
merely loses itself in the masonry and has no outlet. There
is also the problem of the strange "Step Pyramid" at
Saqqara, so unlike the rest. When and by whom was it
built? Why was it built in tiers, instead of straight sides,
like most of the others?

These questions could only be answered satisfactorily
when scholars had discovered how the Pyramids had originated and how they were built; when they had surveyed
all, or nearly all, these monuments; when something was
known of the period which preceded that of the pyramid
builders; and, above all, when the builder of each pyramid
could be identified and the monuments arranged in their
correct chronological sequence.

The fact that most of these questions can now be
answered is not due to any one man, but to the combined
researches of scholars and excavators of several nations;
French, German, British, Italian, Swiss, American, and
Egyptian. For if there is any branch of science to which
the old truism could be applied, that "science is international", it is Egyptology.

To find the answers we have to go back to a period long

before the first pyramid was built in Egypt. In 1894 Petrie, with his assistant Quibell, was excavating on the west bank of the Nile opposite Koptos, between Nagadeh and Ballas, in Upper Egypt. There they found over three thousand shallow graves in the sand. In each lay a skeleton on its side, arms and legs drawn up to the body in an embryonic position, the head to the south, the face to the west. (See Illustration 22.) In these little graves were found small objects, ivory combs and bracelets, small statuettes of painted clay, and slate palettes carved to represent fish, antelopes, tortoises and birds' heads, some of which were like those represented in the later hieroglyphic inscriptions. At first Petrie thought that these people were later intruders who entered Egypt at about the time of the Sixth Dynasty (*circa* 2400 B.C.).

But not long afterwards Jacques de Morgan, then Director of the Service des Antiquités, excavated near Nagadeh a royal tomb containing objects bearing the name of Narmer or Menes, the founder of the First Dynasty (*circa* 3200 B.C.). Inside it were found objects of a style similar to those found in the later examples of the "pit-graves" discovered by Petrie; it then seemed pretty certain that these mysterious people were not later intruders, but the ancestors of the so-called "Ancient Egyptians" of the Dynastic periods, the men who built the Pyramids. Later, Petrie found other cemeteries of pre-dynastic date which he called "Amratean" and "Baderian", after the names of the places in which they were found. Among these peoples were some who, aided by superior weapons, had subdued their predecessors, and around 3200 B.C. there seems to have arisen a conquering people, whose leader, Narmer or Menes, founded the First Dynasty, as stated by Manetho. At this period the hieroglyphic writing was already in existence.

"When, thirty centuries before Christ, Menes founded the First Dynasty, most of the characteristic features of Egyptian civilization were already present. It is believed that hieroglyphic writing arose very rapidly just before the First Dynasty, and during the time of Menes we can almost see it developing before our eyes. . . . Although Menes chose to be buried near his native This, in Upper Egypt, he established his capital at Memphis, near what is now Cairo."[1]

Before the time of Menes, Egypt seems to have been divided into two territories, Upper and Lower Egypt, and Menes was the first king to unify by conquest the two kingdoms. Yet, more than two thousand years afterwards, the memory of the ancient division was retained in the title of the Pharaoh "King of Upper and Lower Egypt". The royal insignia which he wore on his crown, the hawk of Upper Egypt, and the snake (uræus) of Lower Egypt, commemorated the time when Egypt was divided into two Kingdoms.

One fact is clear from the presence, in the pre-dynastic pit-graves, of ornaments, arms, food-offerings, etc., that these people believed that they would enjoy an after-life in which they would need the same objects of daily use which they had needed on earth. Perhaps, also, because of the dryness of the soil, which preserved even un-embalmed bodies for centuries, there grew up a belief that the preservation of the body was essential if the soul was to survive.

Following de Morgan, Petrie also excavated at Abydos in the tombs of the First and Second Dynasty kings. He found that the oldest was a simple rectangular grave dug in the sand, 23 feet long, 16 feet wide and 10 feet deep. The walls were of brick and there was a wooden ceiling supported by props, with a mound of sand on the top. The tomb of King Djer, the largest of the royal sepulchres, was surrounded by offering chambers covering an area of about 48 by 38 feet. Densemti, the fifth king of the First Dynasty, had a larger tomb paved with granite, but the main body of the structure was still of mud-brick. But by the time of Khasekhemui, the ninth king of the Second Dynasty, the tomb had developed into a huge structure, 223 feet long and 54 feet wide, with 58 separate rooms built

[1] Cottrell, "The Lost Pharaohs".

around a central chamber *of stone*—the oldest stone structure known in the world.

"Only a belief in the survival of the body," wrote Budge, "can explain the presence of furniture and provisions. The King, being the successor of Horus and Osiris[1] and their living image on earth, had to be treated after death like those gods themselves."

Since Petrie's time, Professor Walter Emery, his successor as Professor of Egyptology at University College, London, has made some important excavations in tombs of the First and Second Dynasties. He has found, in the northern part of Saqqara, a number of large mud-brick tombs, similar to those found at Abydos. It will be remembered that after Menes unified Egypt, the kings used as their base the town of Memphis, which stood roughly on the borders of the two kingdoms. Saqqara was the cemetery of Memphis but it is not yet clear whether these Saqqara tombs were the actual sepulchres of the kings, or of high court officials. It is possible that each king had two tombs, one at Abydos, near the old capital of This in Upper Egypt, and another near the new capital of Memphis in Lower Egypt. Although Menes may have conquered Lower Egypt, it is doubtful if the unification of the Two Kingdoms was complete in his time; in fact the general belief to-day is that this did not occur until the beginning of the Third Dynasty.

However, these early tombs of the First and Second Dynasty kings have certain clearly recognizable features. Above ground there is a large oblong structure of mud-bricks, very solidly built, and with sloping sides and a flat top. Underneath this superstructure was a central burial chamber, sometimes lined with stone, surrounded by smaller magazines or store chambers which were intended to contain the food-offerings (contained in hundreds of stone jars) and the funerary furniture and equipment needed by the dead king in the after-life. The Arabs call

[1] For details of these gods, see "Egyptian Religion" in the Appendix.

these tombs *mastabas*—the Arabic word for "bench"—because they resemble in shape, though not of course in size, the mud-brick benches one finds outside the homes of the *fellahin*.

But Dr. George Reisner, one of the greatest of American archæologists, in his *magnum opus*, *The Development of the Egyptian Tomb*, notes:

> "In Upper Egypt up to this time (i.e. to the end of Dyn. II) the superstructure of the royal tombs and the private tombs were brick structures" (i.e. *mastabas*) "or built in open pits in the gravel and roofed with wood or brick corbel vaults. *At Memphis, in Dyn. II, the type developed was the deep stairway type with rock-cut underground chambers, on a complex plan in the larger tombs and with one chamber in the smaller.*" (Our italics.)

What was the reason for this change? Reisner says:

> "The Egyptian craftsmen had mastered the cutting of blocks of limestone to such an extent that they were able to quarry limestone blocks of almost any size and on royal demand excavate large pits and trenches (or stairways) in the rock."

The reason for this may have been that at Memphis, the new capital, there was an abundance of easily-worked limestone and workmen who were skilled in the art of cutting and shaping it. On both sides of the river there are limestone cliffs which have been systematically quarried for more than four thousand years.

Now we must return to the mysterious "Step Pyramid" at Saqqara, which had puzzled generations of explorers, which had been superficially surveyed by Pococke, measured by Perring, explored by Baron von Minutoli and Lepsius. The name of the unknown king whose name appeared in some of the galleries had been identified as *Neterkhet*; but this name does not appear in Manetho's list of kings.

However, as knowledge of Ancient Egyptian customs increased, it became known that the Pharaohs bore more than one title; in fact the royal titulary usually included several. There was the "Horus-name", the "Nebti-name" and others. Then, in 1890, Emile Brugsch, the German scholar who was one of Maspero's assistants, was doing a piece of routine translation of quite a late inscription on what is known as the Famine Stela of Sehel—so-called because it was found on the island of Sehel. Brugsch, and another German philologist, Steindorff, published their findings in a German journal. The inscription referred to a seven-year period of famine during the reign of Neter-khet, the king whose name appeared in the Step Pyramid. But beside it was another name—*Djoser*.

It was then known that the Pharaohs bore more than one name, and therefore this Djoser was another of Neter-khet's names. But the Greek form of the name Djoser was *Tosorthros*, and when they consulted Manetho's list the investigators found that he was mentioned as the first king of the Third Dynasty. Moreover, Manetho had stated that:

"Tosorthros reigned for 29 years. In his reign lived Imouthes (Imhotep) who because of his medical skill had the reputation of Aesculapius, *and was the inventor of the art of building in hewn stone*.[1] He also paid attention to writing."

At last the mystery was solved. The strange Step Pyramid at Saqqara, so unlike all the others, was probably the first pyramid;[2] in fact, as was subsequently established, it was the first large stone monument to be built in the world, in about 2,750 years before Christ. All the later pyramids, including that of Cheops, developed from it.

Since 1890 three distinguished archæologists have excavated and studied the Step Pyramid. The first two were J. Mallaby Firth and Quibell (the latter a pupil of Petrie) who worked on it for a great number of years. They explored the galleries, found thousands of beautifully made alabaster jars, and alabaster sarcophagi belonging to the

---

[1] Our italics.
[2] It is possible, though so far unproved, that the small "Layer Pyramid" and "Unfinished Pyramid" at Zawiyet-el-Eryan may have preceded it.

royal family. The third archæologist was Monsieur Jean
Philippe Lauer, who has devoted the last twenty-five years
of his life to its study and still lives in its shadow.

Those who wish to make a close study of this fascinating
monument should read Firth and Quibell's *The Step Pyramid* and Lauer's *Les Problèmes des Pyramides* besides his
most readable little monograph on the Step Pyramid itself
—*La Pyramide à Degrés.* Here I have only space to give a
bare outline of their discoveries.

The first fact to remember is that the Step Pyramid
began life, not as a pyramid, but as a stone-built *mastaba.*
But before this was built the architect planned the burial
chamber, which lay at the bottom of a seventy-foot pit
hewn out of the rock. At the base of this pit the builders
constructed a chamber of granite, not large enough to
enclose a sarcophagus, but just big enough to receive the
embalmed body of the king. The granite chamber was
sealed by a granite plug-block, shaped like the stopper of a
bottle, and weighing 3 tons. (See Perring's illustration 16
opposite page 129 and the plan opposite page 223.) The
pit was approached by a sloping cutting on the north side.

During the king's reign the structure was extended on
all four sides, but as the extension was on a lower level
than the original a step was formed. Again the architect
altered his plan, making the building oblong, but still
apparently he or the king was not satisfied. For a fourth
time he enlarged the building, and then did something
which no Egyptian tomb-builder had done before. On the
top of the original large, flat *mastaba* he built a series of
three others, each smaller than the one below it. Thus he
created the first known Step Pyramid, the father of all the
pyramids of Egypt.

Evidently Djoser was delighted with this novelty, for he
decided to make it even bigger. He extended the base still
more until it measured 385 feet. And on top of this he built
his final monument, six superimposed terraces, encased
with the fine limestone quarried from the Tura and Masura
hills on the opposite bank of the Nile.

Nor was this all. Djoser surrounded his pyramid with

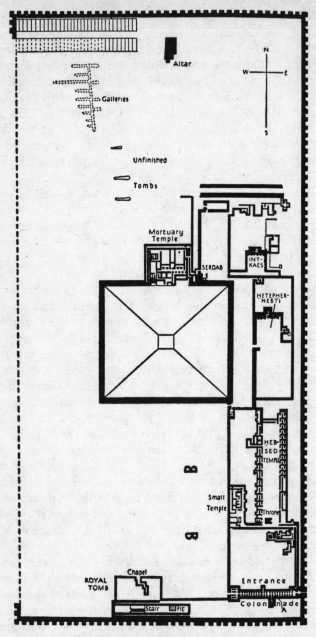

ŞAQQÂRA. STEP PYRAMID ENCLOSURE.
From FIRTH in *Ann. Serv.* xxviii, pl. iii.

9. Plan of Djoser's Step Pyramid

an enormous enclosure wall enclosing an area of 544 metres by 277 metres, a hundred times bigger than the area of the brick tomb at Nagadeh attributed to Menes. Within this courtyard the architect, Imhotep, erected the complex of dummy buildings described in Chapter One, and which seem to have been associated with the welfare of the king's spirit in the life after death.

Under the southern section of the great enclosing wall the architect built another tomb, also at the foot of an eighty-foot pit at the base of which was a sepulchral chamber of granite blocks. But this was so small that it could not have contained a body, although it had a stopper-like granite plug like that in the main burial chamber under the pyramid itself. The purpose of this Southern Tomb of Djoser has puzzled archæologists for years. We shall discuss its possible purpose in a later chapter.

Because the Step Pyramid is in a sadly ruined condition —the outer facing-stones of fine limestone having been removed by later quarriers—it was possible for archæologists to study closely its inner structure. They found that it was built of independent "skins" of masonry, inclining inwards at an angle of 75 degrees and resting on a central core of rubble (see sectioned view of pyramid diagram 15, opposite page 128). Moreover *the stone courses were laid at right-angles to the facing lines—i.e. the angle of the inclination at which the layers leaned on the central core.*

But perhaps the most interesting feature of the Step Pyramid, as shown by Firth and Quibell, Lauer and other scholars, was that the builders had not yet learned fully the technique of building in stone. In fact they were imitating, with stone blocks, the type of construction which their ancestors had used with mud-bricks.

If, after reading this chapter, readers will refer again to Chapter One, they will find examples of this in the dummy doors, the columns of stone which imitated bundles of reeds, and so on. Here is proof, if proof were not already available, that this is Man's first attempt to build monumentally in stone, at a time when the laws of stone construction had not yet imposed themselves, and earlier forms were therefore slavishly copied.

The more they studied the monument, the more certain the archæologists became that the tradition transmitted by Manetho was a true one; that Imhotep, the architect of Djoser, was *"the inventor of the art of building in hewn stone"*. The American archæologist Reisner, who made a close study of the building, wrote:

> "Whatever the architectural forms developed in the earlier stone buildings which I have inferred, the buildings of Djoser present a wonderful transition translation of the older brick architecture with wooden accessories into dressed limestone. This work is associated with the name of Imhotep, famous as a scribe, wise man, physician, and prime minister, but now revealed as a great creative architect. . . . This wonderful tomb and its overwhelmingly abundant funerary equipment reveals an astonishing mastery over the hard materials of the earth and an opulence in power without precedent in Egypt before this time. It shows the civilization of Egypt approaching its climax."[1]

*   *   *

Why was Djoser, or Neter-khet, able to erect this stupendous monument when his immediate predecessors, as far as can be ascertained, had to content themselves with structures of mud-brick? The answer seems to be that under Djoser, the first king of the Third Dynasty, Egypt was truly unified for the first time. The long struggle between the North and the South was over, and the Pharaoh had control over the entire land, over its materials and its manpower. From his time onwards for another five hundred years, the Pharaohs ruled securely from Memphis.

Once the early date of Djoser's pyramid had been established and its peculiar structure studied, other archæologists began to concentrate on this remote period. For example, in 1901, an Italian, Alessandro Barsanti, exca-

[1] *The Development of the Egyptian Tomb Down to the Accession of Cheops*, by G. A. Reisner, Cambridge Harvard University Press, 1936.

vated a small and inconspicuous structure at Zawiyet-el-
Eryan, about mid-way between Giza and Saqqara. Here
there were the remains of a small, ruined pyramid, called
the Layer Pyramid because, like Djoser's much greater
building, it was constructed with inclined layers of masonry,
and again, as in Djoser's monument, the courses of masonry
were at right angles to the angle of inclination of the layers.
It may have been built by Kha-ba, a little-known king of
the Third Dynasty, one of Djoser's successors. Later Professor Reisner excavated it more thoroughly than Barsanti.

He found that Kha-ba's "Layer" Pyramid has a core of
limestone against which lean fourteen skins of masonry of
the same material. It is about three hundred feet square.
The sarcophagus chamber is not at the bottom of a pit, as
in Djoser's pyramid, but cut out of the rock beneath the
structure, and approached by a stairway and passage from
an entrance on the north-east side.

Then Petrie excavated the great pyramid at Meidum,
attributed to Snofru, the last king of the Third Dynasty and
the father of Cheops. Few monuments in the whole of
Egypt are more dramatic than this steep-sided, tower-like
structure, with sides only a few degrees off the vertical, like
a medieval keep on a hill-top (see Illustration 32 opposite
page 177). But Petrie, and later Borchardt, were able to
show that originally this too had been planned as a step
pyramid, and that it was built of "accretion layers" leaning inwards at an angle of 73–75 degrees, the innermost
layer being the highest, the next lower, the next lower still,
and so on. But later the king or his architect seems to have
been dissatisfied, so the spaces between the steps were filled
in and cased with fine limestone. Thus the Meidum pyramid
presents two stages in the development of the pyramid,
viz.: (1) a step pyramid and (2) a true pyramid. Only the
fact that later generations had stripped the outer layers for
building material enabled its inner construction to be seen.

It was at the Meidum pyramid that the great German
archæologist, Ludwig Borchardt, found the remains of what
he believed to be a construction ramp, and thus helped to
solve the problem which had intrigued travellers from the

time of Herodotus; how did the Ancient Egyptians erect
these huge structures?

The Greek historian, who had the opportunity of talking
to the Egyptian priests, said that the pyramids were built
"in steps, battlement-wise, or, as some say, altar-wise".
But he also spoke of "machines" used for raising the stones,
and no machines are shown in any of the many ancient
pictures and reliefs showing buildings under construction.
Nor have any machines been found. But Diodorus got
nearer to the truth when he said that "the stone is said to
have been brought from a great distance in Arabia, *and
raised on mounds*" (our italics). Borchardt, and Petrie before
him, believed that the stone blocks were dragged up ramps
of sand and rubble built against the sides of the pyramid,
and extended as the building grew higher in order to main-
tain the same angle of inclination. It would only be necessary to have such a ramp on one side of the building. On
the other sides all that would be needed would be comparatively steep "foothold embankments" to enable the
labourers to climb up to their work. At Meidum, Borchardt
believed he could detect the remains of such a ramp, which
had not been dismantled, but not all archæologists supported him in this belief.

Ludwig Borchardt (1863–1938) was to Germany what
Petrie was to Great Britain. He studied Egyptology under
Erman, and visited Egypt first in 1895. His greatest
achievements were his excavations of the pyramids and
sun-temples at Abusir, where he proved that not only had
the Fifth Dynasty kings, Sahure, Nieuserre, Neferikare and
Nefer-efra built pyramids, but also temples to the sun-god,
in which the central feature was a "pyramidon"—an
emblem of Re standing in a great courtyard in which were
altars and offering tables. But he also did valuable work
at Giza, where he was able to find a solution to problems
which Petrie had left unsolved.

The chronological links between the Meidum pyramid and
the Great Pyramid of Cheops were the two great stone
pyramids at Dashur mentioned in Chapter Fourteen. One
of these, the so-called "Blunted Pyramid", has definitely

been attributed to Snofru, and either it or its northern neighbour may be the immediate predecessor of Cheops' monument. The "Blunted Pyramid" bears some points of resemblance to the Great Pyramid, especially in its internal arrangements. There is an entrance gallery on the north side (and another on the west), the first leading to a tall chamber with a corbelled roof very like that of the Grand Gallery in the Great Pyramid. I remember being struck by the resemblance when I visited this pyramid in 1947, when it had been opened by the late Abdessalam after being closed for many years. Another point of resemblance to the Great Pyramid is that it has two chambers, one in the rock beneath the pyramid, and the other within the masonry (see Illustration 24 opposite page 192).

Snofru's son, Cheops (Khufu), the first king of the Fourth Dynasty, decided to build his pyramid, not at Dashur or Saqqara, but further north, at Giza, where a high rocky knoll provided an ideal site. The reader will be by now so familiar with the monument as to need no description; but what is interesting is the manner in which Borchardt, after prolonged study, succeeded in solving some of the mysteries of its construction.

We have noticed that, in the case of Djoser's Step Pyramid, there were several changes of plan while the building was under construction. This, as we know from the study of many Egyptian monuments, was a habit of the Ancient Egyptians; nor is it surprising when one considers the time taken to erect a pyramid, and the changes which might occur during such a long period.

Borchardt was able to show that there were several distinct stages in the construction of the Great Pyramid. At first the architect seems to have planned a burial-chamber hewn out of the rock beneath the monument. He drove a corridor down through the rock, and commenced to hew out a chamber at a point beneath the spot at which the peak of the pyramid would be when it was completed. (See plan 2 opposite page 74.) Meanwhile, the lower stages of the pyramid were being built. It seems pretty certain that the Great Pyramid was built in the same manner as that of Snofru at Meidum, and Djoser at Saqqara, with inclined courses of masonry leaning on a central core, except that whereas the latter had courses at right angles to the angle of slope, the "accretion walls" of Cheops' pyramid were built with horizontal courses.

Then there was a change of plan. When the lower part of the building was already built, it was decided to construct the burial chamber *inside* the pyramid. So work on the rock-cut chamber was stopped, and the workmen began to drive a corridor upwards *through the already existing masonry*.

The proof of this, as Borchardt pointed out, is that the masonry in the lower part of the Ascending Gallery is laid horizontally, and the corridor is driven through it, whereas higher up the masonry is laid at the same angle as that of the corridor. Borchardt suggested that the point at which the change occurred marked the level which the pyramid had reached when it was decided to construct the tomb-chamber inside the pyramid instead of under it.

After ascending for a certain distance, the builders levelled off the corridor, and constructed the so-called "Queen's Chamber" exactly beneath the intended peak of the pyramid (see Plan 2). They also began to make "air channels" leading from this central chamber, but after a comparatively short distance they stopped. Once again there was a change of plan.

This time the architect extended the Ascending Gallery but also heightened it and gave it a magnificent corbelled roof; this was the Grand Gallery with its ramp down the centre and its "benches" on each side. At the top of this they built the Ante-Chamber with its portcullis blocks, and the mighty King's Chamber of granite, with the five "relieving chambers" above. Before the roof was put on they introduced the sarcophagus into the burial chamber (it was too large to be taken up the Ascending Gallery) and, at the same time, before the Grand Gallery was roofed, they stored within it the granite plug-blocks with which they intended to seal the Ascending Corridor after the mummy of the king had been placed within its sarcophagus.

Petrie, as we have seen, proved that these granite blocks could not have been stored anywhere in the pyramid except in the Grand Gallery, but this left him with the unlikely supposition that the funeral procession, when it climbed up to the King's Chamber, must have made its way over the top of these blocks.

It was Borchardt who finally solved this mystery. If readers will refer back to Chapter Three, page 89, they will find that the seventeenth-century English explorer, Greaves, had remarked of the Grand Gallery:

"Upon the top of these benches near the angle, where they close, and join the wall, are little spaces cut in right-angled parallel figures, set on each side opposite to one another; *intended, no question, for some other end than ornament.*" (Our italics.)

Greaves was correct in his supposition, and it is strange that no other archæologist up to the time of Borchardt guessed the purpose of these "little spaces". There are twenty-eight of these holes cut at regular intervals in the upper surface of each side-ramp of the Grand Gallery. There were also other peculiar features un-noted by Petrie. Small blocks of stone had been inserted in the side-walls opposite the holes, each with a slot in its surface. There is also a long continuous groove nearly an inch deep extending along the entire length of both sides of the Grand Gallery. Borchardt decided that these holes and slots were made to hold wooden uprights supporting a wooden platform, the sides of which fitted into the long grooves. In fact, he even made a theoretical reconstruction of this timber structure, and found that it would have sufficed to support the granite plugs, so that the funeral procession could pass up the gallery without hindrance.

When the king had been buried, the plug-blocks were slid down the Ascending Gallery from the top, and the extraordinary fact is that, although they fitted the space to within one quarter of an inch, they did not jam on the way down. Probably some kind of lubricant was used. The lower part of the Ascending Gallery was made very slightly smaller than the upper part so that the plugs were wedged firmly into position and could slide no further. Then, as we have seen, the workmen made their escape down the vertical shaft or "well" and so out of the pyramid via the Descending Gallery, which they afterwards closed with rubble. A glance at Plan 2 opposite page 74 will make this procedure clear.

The purpose of the "air-channels" has never been satisfactorily explained. They may have been simply ventilation shafts to keep air flowing through the pyramid while it was open, or they may have been for some ritual purpose. Nobody knows.

There remained the problem of the so-called "girdle-stones". In the upper part of the Ascending Gallery, where the masonry is laid at the same angle as that of the corridor, there are, at regular intervals of 17 feet 2 inches, large stones *through which the corridor has been hewn*. We have seen that the Step Pyramid of Djoser at Saqqara, the "Layer" Pyramid at Zawiyet-el-Eryan, and the Meidum Pyramid, were all built of layers of masonry diminishing in height from the centre outwards and leaning on a central core. Each layer was cased with fine limestone. Borchardt was able to prove that this method was still used by builders of the Sixth Dynasty—the pyramid of Sahura at Abusir is built in this fashion—and he suggested that the same method of internal construction was used in the Great Pyramid. If so, the so-called "girdle-stones" observed in the Ascending Gallery each formed part of one of these internal casings. It must be stated, however, that some authorities, e.g., Somers Clarke and Rex Engelbach, do not accept Borchardt's view. Even so, as I. E. S. Edwards remarks in his *Pyramids of Egypt*, it does not follow that such casings do not exist elsewhere in the Great Pyramid.

Once it was realized that the builders of the Pyramids sometimes changed their plans while the buildings were under construction, it was possible to understand the apparent anomalies in the substructures of the Second and Third Pyramids. Take first the Second Pyramid (Plan 10,

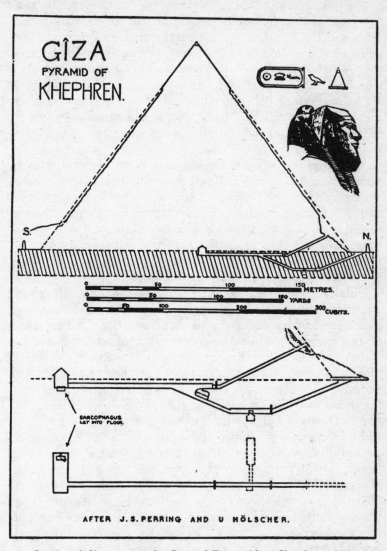

GÎZA
PYRAMID OF
KHEPHREN.

S.

N.

METRES.
YARDS
CUBITS.

SARCOPHAGUS
LET INTO FLOOR.

AFTER J.S. PERRING AND U HÖLSCHER.

10. Sectional diagram of the Second Pyramid of Chephren (Khafre)
showing the layout of the subterranean galleries

opposite page 230). It has two entrances, one beginning in the masonry of the northern face, the other cut out of the rock a little distance to the north, both galleries joining beneath the pyramid. The lower gallery, after descending through the rock, levels out and leads to a recess opposite which is a sloping passage leading to an unfinished chamber. But the corridor continues beyond this and rises again to join the upper gallery which proceeds horizontally until it reaches the real burial chamber lying under the apex of the pyramid.

Why was this? Edwards suggests that "it is to be supposed that, when the (lower) chamber and corridor were constructed, it was planned to build the Pyramid some 200 feet further north, both the chamber and the entrance would have occupied their customary position. A possible reason for the change of plan was the discovery of a suitable rock foundation for the causeway concealed beneath the sand on a line south of the one chosen."

Finally let us look again at Plan 5 of the Third Pyramid opposite page 136. Here again there are two descending galleries of which the lower one starts in the northern face of the pyramid, while the second is a blind alley which, leaving the central chamber at a point above the first, planes upwards through the rock and then is blocked by the masonry of the pyramid. To understand the reasons for this it must be remembered that these galleries were cut before the pyramid was built above them. The first gallery to be made was the upper one. Probably at first a smaller pyramid was envisaged, the entrance to which would have been near the point where the upper gallery ends. But then Mycerinus decided to build a larger pyramid, and in order that the entrance should be in the usual place, low down on the northern face, they deepened the central chamber and cut a second sloping corridor below the first. The third and last alteration in the design was the addition of two chambers, one for storing objects such as furniture, etc., and the other a new burial chamber; the one in which Vyse and Perring found the basalt sarcophagus of Mycerinus and, nearby, the bones which may be those of the king.

CHAPTER SIXTEEN

GREATNESS AND DECLINE

T H E greatest period of pyramid-building was undoubtedly that of the Fourth Dynasty (2720–2560 B.C.), and it reached its peak in the reign of Cheops. The Great Pyramid remains the greatest pyramid, and except for the Second Pyramid of Chephren, nothing remotely comparable to it was built afterwards.

After the turn of the twentieth century it was the turn of the distinguished American archæologist Reisner to study the Giza group, and he did outstanding work, particularly in the pyramid of Mycerinus and among the *mastabas*. George Andrew Reisner was born in Indianapolis in 1867. Educated at Harvard, he became Hearst Lecturer and Director of the Hearst Expedition to Egypt in 1906–7, and Director of the Archæological Survey of Nubia in 1907–9. But he will probably be best remembered for his work at Giza, where he led the Harvard-Boston expedition, which for twenty-three years excavated two-thirds of the cemetery west of Cheops' pyramid, the area of the smaller pyramids and east of the Great Pyramid as far as the Sphinx. Street after street of tombs, the sepulchres of the nobles, high court officials and members of the royal families were carefully cleared, excavated, photographed, drawn and planned. It was a monumental work.

It is important to remember that the Pyramids did not stand in isolation. Each had its causeway leading up from the river, and its two temples, the Valley Temple near the river and the Mortuary Temple adjoining the pyramid itself. And nearby, arranged in orderly rows, were street after street of *mastabas*, the tombs of the nobles, Viziers, Chiefs of the Treasury, officers of the royal household, attending the kings in death as they had in life. In the First, Second and Third Dynasties, the kings themselves built *mastabas*, but after Djoser the kings were almost invariably buried in pyramids, the earlier form of tomb being used by the nobles. Some were built of mud-bricks, but during the Fourth Dynasty they were usually of stone (see Illustration 4 opposite page 48).

It fell to the Harvard-Boston expedition to discover the only unplundered tomb of a royal personage of the Old Kingdom ever found, that of Queen Hetepheres, the wife of Snofru and the mother of Cheops himself. During Reisner's absence in America, one of his staff, a photographer, was trying to stand his tripod on what appeared to be rock when, to his surprise, he noticed that the spiked legs of the tripod were sinking into the "rock". On examination this was found to be a plaster covering, made to look like rock, but concealing a shaft filled with masonry. It took thirteen days to clear the shaft, which was eighty-five feet deep, and at the bottom the excavators found, on the south side, a wall of masonry. Alan Rowe, one of Reisner's staff, removed one of the topmost blocks and thrust a candle through the hole, and looked into a chamber which had not been seen by human eyes for five thousand years.

Inside was a sealed alabaster sarcophagus and a confused mass of objects which required months of patient effort to sort out. There were thousands of tiny fragments of gold inlays—some no bigger than a postage stamp—which had once covered the surface of wooden furniture, the wood having decayed. There were sheets of gold inlaid with faience, lion-legs which had supported a throne, the remains of a gold-encased canopy, a set of silver anklets inlaid with a butterfly pattern in lapis-lazuli, and toilet jars inscribed with the names of the queen's cosmetics, such as *sti-hab* (festival perfume), *wadj* (green eye-paint) and *hatet-tjenu* (prime Libyan oil). There were also depilatory razors, gold dishes and a manicure instrument pointed at one end for cleaning the nails and rounded at the other for pushing back the cuticle.

"On 28th February an area was reached covered with fragmented gold inlays. Altogether there were eight layers and their recording and removal took four months.

One of the Expedition staff, Dunham, lay on a mattress supported by a beam and carefully picked up the tiny fragments with pincers and placed them on a tray without disturbing the rest of the deposit. One day in February he came upon a row of hieroglyphs on a bar of decayed wood. In March they were carefully removed on a tray and eagerly examined by the Expedition. They read:

"*Mother of the King of Upper and Lower Egypt, follower of Horus, Guide to the ruler, favourite lady whose every word is done for her, daughter of the god of his body, Hetepheres.*"

In spite of the fact that the shaft was filled from top to bottom with rubble which had never been disturbed, the sarcophagus proved to be empty, and must therefore have been empty when it was placed in the chamber. Although the lid had been replaced it showed signs of having been forced. Reisner, by a process of brilliant deduction from the condition and placing of the objects, concluded that this was a re-burial. Originally, the queen may have been buried near her husband's pyramid at Dashur; then the tomb was robbed, but incompletely. The body was stolen but the rest of the furniture was left—perhaps because the thieves were interrupted. Reisner suggested that Cheops, hearing of the robbery, but being kept in ignorance of the fact that his mother's body had disappeared, gave orders for Hetepheres and her funerary furniture to be reburied in a secret *cache* near his own new pyramid, which was then under construction. The evidence of haste in the construction of the shaft, and the fact that the workmen left their copper tools behind, mixed up with the queen's furniture, suggests that the officials were in a desperate hurry to re-bury the sarcophagus before the king found out that it was empty.

This, the only royal funerary furniture of the Fourth Dynasty ever found, has been painstakingly reconstructed on new wooden foundations, and now forms one of the finest exhibits on view in the Cairo Museum. If the *ka* of Queen Hetepheres ever visits that Museum, she can see her jewellery and furniture exactly as she knew them in life; the gold-encased bed given her by her husband, Snofru, and bearing his name in gold hieroglyphs; her carrying-chair, her throne, her silver anklets, and her make-up box with the alabaster toilet jars still in position. Above them stands the great collapsible canopy once hung with curtains, which the queen took with her on her journeys. (See Illustration 25 opposite page 192.) The beauty, strength and simplicity of these objects is in keeping with the dignity of the kings and queens of the pyramid age, the founders of Egypt's greatness. Beside them, the art of the Eighteenth Dynasty, as represented by the over-ornamented tomb-furniture of Tutankhamun, seems by comparison lush and decadent.

Before we move on to the later dynasties, I would like to summarize, very briefly and incompletely, some of the conclusions of such archæologists as Petrie, Borchardt, Junker, Reisner and others regarding the methods by which the pyramids were built in the Fourth Dynasty. There is, for example, their incredibly accurate orientation—in the case of the Great Pyramid so precise that compass errors can be checked against it. The methods used are not fully known, but the Ancient Egyptians were skilled astronomers, and one method would have been to sight on a star in the northern heavens and bisect the angle formed by its rising position, the position from which the observation was made, and the setting. This would give true north, after which the other cardinal points could be easily established.

How did they establish a level base-line for the foundations? Mr. Rex Engelbach, a pupil of Petrie and for many years Keeper of the Cairo Museum, made a close study of Ancient Egyptian technical methods and his book *Ancient Egyptian Masonry* is probably the best introduction to the absorbing subject of pyramid construction. Engelbach believed that the builders "ran a watercourse along and about the surface to be levelled, then measured down from the surface at many points simultaneously, thus establishing datum points to which the complete surface would eventually be reduced." And he pointed out that if this method was used it would explain the slight error which exists in the level of the platform which runs partly under the Great Pyramid. Although it is on a perfect plane, the whole surface slopes up about six inches from the north-east to the south-west corner. If a north-east wind had been blowing when the points were checked, this would have produced the error.

We have seen that the builders of Djoser's pyramid used relatively small stones in imitation of the mud-bricks with which earlier tombs were constructed. But the Ancient Egyptians soon learned that this method was uneconomic, and before long they were using blocks of limestone weighing sixteen tons and more. Moreover, they were able to cut and face them with such precision that—as Petrie pointed out when he surveyed the Great Pyramid—the joints between the limestone casing-stones were accurate to within one five-hundredth of an inch, not only at the surface, but over an area of thirty-five square feet. And although these great megaliths were brought almost into contact, ("the mean opening of the joint was one fiftieth of an inch") the joints were cemented throughout.

How were the stones quarried in the days when blasting powder was unknown, and when there were no iron or even bronze tools? The limestone blocks were cut out of the virgin rock with copper chisels, and at many places in Egypt one can see the ancient quarries and study the methods of the Ancient Egyptian workmen. For instance, in the rocky hills which border the eastern bank of the Nile opposite Memphis are the quarries of Tura and Masura, from which the pyramid-builders quarried the fine limestone for the casing-blocks of the Pyramids. These quarries are wide, horizontal galleries cut out of the rock, some of them hundreds of feet in depth. The roofs are supported by columns of natural rock left purposely by the quarriers (see Illustration 26 opposite page 193). The rock was cut in such a way that the blocks left the quarry roughly in the shape required, the final cutting and polishing being done by skilled masons, probably near the pyramid itself. The illustration opposite page 193 will show how the quarrying was done. The workmen started at the top of the rock wall, first cutting out a ledge deep enough for a man to work in, and then worked downwards, cutting slots at the back and sides until eventually the block was detached on all sides except the base. Then a few sharp blows of a chisel applied to the base and the block split off. Having cleared one horizontal row of blocks, the quarrymen then started to remove a row below, and so on down the wall until they reached the floor. The marks left by the copper chisels can be clearly seen in these ancient quarries.

Even hard rock like granite was quarried in this way, except that in order to split off the blocks, the workmen made slots at the base into which they drove wedges. In some cases these wedges were of wood which they soaked with water. The expansion of the wood split the rock. Engelbach tried this method at Assuan and found that it worked. Much of the hard granite used in the Pyramids came from Assuan, in Upper Egypt, from whence it was brought six hundred miles down the river.

The accurate shaping and polishing of the stones was probably done on the site of the pyramid by masons who were permanently employed throughout the year (Petrie found the remains of their barracks near the Second Pyramid) but unskilled labour would have sufficed to drag the stones from the east bank, bring them across the Nile in barges, and then haul them up to the pyramid plateau. Herodotus stated that one hundred thousand men laboured twenty years to build the Great Pyramid, and implies that Cheops oppressed the people, forcing all to labour for the achievement of his megalomaniac ambition. But Petrie pointed out that for three months of each year the flooding of the Nile compelled the field-labourers to be temporarily idle, and that if they were used during this period to transport the stone for the pyramid, Cheops was only making use of this idle labour without detriment to the country's economy. Petrie also calculated from the number and weight of the blocks and the number of men required to move each, that one hundred thousand men could have built the pyramid in twenty years, as Herodotus said.

The next question is how were these huge blocks

manœuvred into position and laid with such accuracy? Did the Egyptians possess machines, as Herodotus suggests? The answer seems to be no. In none of the tomb-paintings and sculptured reliefs depicting the process of building is any mechanical device shown. Nor, as Engelbach has pointed out, is there any evidence that the Ancient Egyptians possessed lifting tackle, such as the pulley-block which the medieval masons used for raising stone blocks. If they had used such devices some of the stones would have shown the marks of the tongs or "lewises". There are no such marks. An interesting fact which he also demonstrated was that in the structures of Ancient Egyptian ships, the yards are *pushed up from below*, and not hauled up over a pulley. On the other hand, it seems fairly certain that, in the interior of the Pyramids, lifting tackle was sometimes used; for example, for lowering the granite plug-block into its hole in the top of Djoser's burial chamber, and perhaps for lowering the lids of sarcophagi. But as regards the building of the Pyramids, there is no evidence that the Egyptians used any mechanical devices more elaborate than the lever, the roller and the inclined plane. Incredible as it may seem to modern minds, accustomed to every kind of labour-saving machinery, it now seems certain that these colossal monuments were raised by nothing more than muscle-power, assisted by a few simple mechanical contrivances. Even the granite beams—each weighing nearly fifty tons—which roof the King's Chamber, could have been raised by a squad of men levering alternate ends of each beam and placing packing blocks beneath them until they had attained the required height.

But the organization of man-power must have been superb. No mere disorderly mob could have raised such monuments in a hundred years, let alone twenty. There is evidence of this organization in the marks painted on some of the blocks before they left the quarries. From these it seems that the men were organized in gangs or crews of between eight hundred and a thousand men. For instance, here are the names of some of the crews who quarried the stones for the pyramids of Cheops and Mycerinus:

"The crew, Cheops excites love"
"The crew, the White Crown of Knmw-Khui (Cheops) is powerful"

—and most curious of all—

"The crew, Mycerinus is drunk."

Other marks have been translated as follows:

"This side up"
"To be taken away"
"For the royal tomb (per nwb)".

Having hauled the blocks from the quarries, floated them across the Nile (probably during the inundation period when the river was widest), dragged them up to the pyramid plateau, where they were shaped by the masons, how did the builders get them into position on the monument? The general belief among archæologists to-day is that the process was as follows:

First the foundation platform would be made, and then the builders would lay the first courses of masonry. Then they would build, against one side of the pyramid, a supply ramp up which the stones were hauled on wooden sledges.

"As the Pyramid rose in height, so the ramp was increased both in height and length; simultaneously the top surface would become progressively narrower to correspond with the constantly diminishing breadth of the Pyramid face. If the angle of incline of the Pyramid were 52 degrees, the two side faces of the ramp would also slope at the same angle of 52 degrees, so that any risk of 'land-slides' would be eliminated. The three sides of the pyramid not covered by the supply ramp would have foot-hold embankments of sufficient width at the top to allow for the passage of men and materials, but, since they were not required for raising the stones from the ground, their gradient in the exposed outer surface could be as steep as would be compatible with firmness. Wooden baulks, some of which have been found *in situ* by the American excavators at Lisht, would be placed on the top surface both of the supply ramp and the foot-hold embankments in order to provide a firm roadway for the passage of sledges bearing the stone blocks."[1]

Petrie has noted that the blocks, in spite of their great size, were cemented throughout, although their weight alone would have been sufficient to keep them in position. Engelbach has suggested that as the blocks were not lowered from above, but pushed into position *from the front*, the purpose of this cement or mortar was to act as a lubricant, making it easier to slide the rocks into position.

Herodotus also states that "the upper portion of the pyramid was finished first, then the middle, and then the part which was nearest the ground", and this statement has puzzled many people. But it is perfectly explicable if we assume that when the builders had finished laying the inner blocks of the pyramid, and the construction ramp reached to the top of the monument, they then started laying the outer casing-stones of polished limestone at the top, removing the ramp as they worked their way downwards, until the pyramid stood alone and unencumbered. For, as Diodorus had truly said (see Chapter Two, page 56):

"The same number of hands which raised the mounds, restored the work to its original state."

* * *

The German contribution to pyramid study did not end with Borchardt. At Giza, Junker worked over the *mastabas*, and Uvo Hölscher, with George Steindorff, dug the pyramid complex of Chephren, builder of the Second Pyramid, between 1909 and 1910. Their work on this pyramid and its temples was equal to that of Borchardt at Abusir.

Not all the Fourth Dynasty kings built their tombs at Giza. One of them, Dedefre, built his pyramid at Abu Roash, to the north. Another, Shepseskaf, erected a peculiar monument near Saqqara known as the Mastabat Faraun. This was excavated by Mariette, who wrongly

[1] *The Pyramids of Egypt*, by I. E. S. Edwards, London, 1947.

attributed it to Unas, a Fifth Dynasty king. The man who first correctly identified it was the Swiss archæologist, Gustave Jequier, whose work deserves the highest praise. The Mastabat Faraun is built in the form of a huge sarcophagus, but its corridors and chambers are so like those under the Third Pyramid of Mycerinus as to leave no doubt that they were made shortly afterwards. In fact, it is known from an inscription that Shepseskaf contributed to the completion of the pyramid complex of his father, Mycerinus.

The fact that Shepseskaf built his tomb so far from Giza, and that it was not a pyramid, has led to the suggestion that he may have quarrelled with the priesthood of Re at Heliopolis. It may be significant that, unlike his predecessors, Dedef*re*, Khaf*re* (Chephren) and Menkau*re* (Mycerinus), he did not incorporate the name of the god in his own name. Such struggles between royal and priestly power occurred throughout Egyptian history; another example is Amenophis IV, who rebelled against the priesthood of Amun and changed his name to Akhnaten.

If such a rebellion did take place it was not lasting, for the kings of the following dynasty, the Fifth, were closely identified with the worship of the sun-god, and the names of some of them—Sahure, Nieuserre, Neferikare—suggest this. It was these three kings who built the sun-temples at Abusir excavated by Ludwig Borchardt. A legend preserved in an ancient papyrus—the Papyrus Wetcar, now in the Berlin Museum—states that the first three kings of this dynasty were triplets begotten of Re by the wife of a priest of Re. There may be a germ of truth in this; perhaps the first king, Userkhaf, came from a priestly family.

Once again the kings built pyramids, though far inferior in size to those of the preceding dynasty. In construction, too, they are of poor quality, being made of small stones covered with a coating of fine limestone. The same is true of the pyramids of the Sixth Dynasty, built by such kings as Teti, Pepi I and II, and Merenre I and II. They are important, however, as links in the chain of development, and in particular because some of them contained the famous Pyramid Texts. The Swiss archæologist, Jequier, who excavated the Mastabat Faraun, found another set of texts in the Pyramid of Pepi II, which he published. Jequier, though less well known than such men as Petrie, Borchardt and Reisner, deserves special credit for his pains-taking work in reconstructing, often from quite small frag-ments, whole scenes on temple walls. He also excavated the Pyramid of Aba and two very interesting Middle King-dom pyramids, one built by Kenjer, of the Thirteenth Dynasty, and the other by an unknown king.

Since Maspero's day, two other scholars have increased our understanding of the Pyramid Texts. One is Professor Lacau, who is still living. Lacau first pointed to a pecu-liarity of the texts which throws a very interesting light on the mentality of the Ancient Egyptians. As the texts were in hieroglyphs, they had sometimes to include representa-tions of human beings, animals, birds and reptiles. These, besides being parts of words, could become, through the power of magic, actual embodiments of the creatures them-selves. This introduced a serious difficulty, because it would not do for the dead king to be surrounded by destructive creatures such as scorpions, etc. Even fish were dangerous because they fed on dead bodies.

The priestly scribes overcame this difficulty in various ingenious ways. The scorpion was represented without its dangerous tail. The bodies of animals were cut in half. Human beings were deprived of all except heads and arms. In other cases the dangerous signs, e.g., for fish, were omitted altogether or replaced by other, harmless signs having the same phonetic value.

The period of the Seventh to the Tenth Dynasties (2270–2100 B.C.) was one of anarchy and confusion. Historians call it the First Intermediate Period. The unity which had been achieved by the Kings of the Fourth Dynasty was lost, and Egypt, as on other occasions during her long history, became the prey of warring nobles—the *nomarchs* of the various provinces. It was not until 2100 B.C. that power passed to a family of provincial nobles whose seat was at Hermonthis, in Upper Egypt. Nearby was a small pro-vincial town called No by the Egyptians and Thebes by the

Greeks, which became the leading city of the south under
its monarch, Intef. His son, of the same name, assumed
royal honours and founded the Eleventh Dynasty with
which begins the period which Egyptologists call the Middle
Kingdom. But the transfer of power to the south did not
take place immediately. Amenemhat I, the first king of the
Twelfth Dynasty, founded its capital at Ijtowe, which
means "She who has captured the Two Lands". From this
city near modern Lisht, he was able to secure a more effec-
tive control of the northern nomarchs. With Amenemhat I,
a new period of prosperity and power began, during which
the kings could once again build pyramids, though far inferior to those built by the Memphite kings.

These were the pyramids at Dashur, Hawara, Illahun,
Lisht and other places excavated by Petrie, de Morgan and
others, as described in Chapters Thirteen and Fourteen.
Of Amenemhat I an inscription states:

"... he restored that which he found ruined; that which
a city had taken from its neighbour; while he caused city
to know its boundary with city, establishing their land-
marks like the heavens, distinguishing their waters according to that which was of old, because he so greatly
loved justice." (Breasted's translation.)

The pyramids built by these kings—the Amenemhats and
the Senusrets—were those with the cunningly concealed
entrances and complicated galleries which gave so much
trouble to Petrie and his fellow-archæologists. It was near
them that de Morgan and Brunton found the glorious royal
jewellery at Dashur and Illahun.

One of the most remarkable of the Twelfth Dynasty
pyramids was that of Senusret I at Lisht, near which the
ancient capital of Ijtowe probably stood. Though excavated
superficially by Maspero in 1882, and more thoroughly by
Gustave Jequier and J. E. Gautier in 1894, the most complete excavation was carried out for the Metropolitan
Museum of New York by the distinguished American
archæologists Ambrose Lansing and Albert Lythgoe, and
the British scholar Arthur Mace who was closely associated

with them. The Metropolitan Museum expedition worked there intermittently from 1906 to 1934, clearing not only the pyramid, its enclosure and temple, but much of the adjoining cemetery. In the Mortuary Temple some magnificent statues were found, each standing in a recess and representing the king as the god Osiris. Around the pyramid itself, which was approximately 350 feet square, were two enclosure walls, between which were nine smaller pyramids for the royal family, each with its own enclosure wall and miniature mortuary temple. All the tombs had been robbed in antiquity, but the whole pyramid complex, like that of Amenemhat I, the predecessor of Senusret, provided impressive evidence of the power and wealth of these Twelfth Dynasty kings, though they were far inferior to those of the Fourth Dynasty.

After this brief period of prosperity, Egypt again fell into anarchy, and for two hundred years was ruled by Asiatic invaders, the so-called Hyksos ("Shepherd") Kings. When, with the rise of the Seventeenth Dynasty, the country entered on its imperial age—the period of the Eighteenth and Nineteenth Dynasties—the days of pyramid-building in Egypt were over. A few small pyramids were built in the necropolis of Thebes, the capital, but these soon gave way to rock-cut tombs hollowed out of the Theban hills; their temples, instead of adjoining the tombs, were built some distance away on the western side of the hills, facing the valley. Conservative though they were, even the Ancient Egyptians had become convinced at last that the pyramid, boldly proclaiming itself as a royal tomb, stood no chance of defeating the hereditary skill of the tomb-robber; weight of masonry, granite portcullises and blocking-stones, "puzzle-passages", secret entrances, blind alleys, all failed in their turn.

So the kings of the Eighteenth Dynasty tried a new method of protecting their royal dead, by rock-cut tombs burrowed out of the mountainside behind Thebes. The location was carefully guarded; the workmen few compared with those needed to build a pyramid; the architect-designer was a close confidant of the Pharaoh.

"I attended to the excavation of the cliff-tomb of His Majesty alone," boasted the architect of Tuthmosis I in his own tomb-inscription, *"no one seeing, no one hearing. . . . I shall be praised for my wisdom in after years."*

Over sixty such "secret" tombs were made in or near the Royal Valley. All were cunningly made; some had concealed entrances, others had false passages leading nowhere, while the entrance to the real burial chamber was concealed behind an apparently solid wall, or beneath the pavement. All were crammed with a wealth of gold and jewels; golden coffins, golden ornaments, gold-encased furniture, treasures of a richness and splendour which even the pyramid-builders would have envied. And all—except one—were robbed, and even that escaped by an accident. The "probing antennae" of the tomb-robber reached the Pharaoh in the end.

     *   *   *

After the Seventeenth Dynasty (1600–1555 B.C.) no more royal pyramids were built in Egypt, although the pyramidal form was occasionally employed in small private tombs. Then, eight centuries after the last pyramid had been built in Egypt, the form suddenly appeared again—this time in the Sudan.

The Sudan—anciently called Ethiopia—was conquered, and several times lost and reconquered by the Ancient Egyptians. It was a great source of wealth, especially in slaves, ivory and precious metals; and Egyptian temple reliefs often show ranks of Negro slaves in the train of a Pharaoh returning in triumph after victories in the south. But in the eighth century B.C. the tables were turned, and an Ethiopian leader, Piankhi, led his armies into Egypt, and subsequently three Ethiopian kings occupied the throne of Pharaoh; Shabaka, Shabtaka and Taharka. This, however, can hardly be accounted a foreign conquest, for the Ethiopians had been Egyptianized for centuries and worshipped the same gods as the Egyptians. These Ethiopian kings had their capital at Napata, between the Third and Fourth Cataracts, and up to the time of Piankhi were buried in *mastaba*-type tombs.

After their conquest of Egypt, and probably as a result of seeing the Giza pyramids, they adopted the pyramid form for their royal tombs, and continued to do so for nearly one thousand years. The honour of excavating these monuments belongs to the nation which came latest into the field of Egyptology—America. Professor George Reisner, the discoverer of the tomb of Hetepheres, spent many seasons between 1900 and the outbreak of the First World War excavating, not only at Napata, but at Nuri and Meroe, later capitals of the Ethiopian kings. His three great books, *Excavations at Napata*, *Known and Unknown Kings of Ethiopia* and *The Royal Family of Ethiopia* added a new chapter to the long history of pyramid building. Though the Ethiopian pyramids were far smaller than most of those built in Egypt, there are many points of similarity. They were built of stone, and show various stages of development. That of Piankhi was built over a pit, at the foot of which lay a corbelled burial-chamber approached by a stairway, which was closed with rubble after the funeral. Taharka, the last king of the Twenty-fifth Egyptian Dynasty (712–663 B.C.) built a more elaborate pyramid with a burial chamber divided by pillars into three aisles. The pyramids of his successors were even more complex; one had religious texts inscribed on the walls of its chambers.

An innovation was the burial of horses, which Reisner discovered in the cemetery at Kuru; twenty-four horses were found, adorned with silver trappings and beads. These, no doubt, were killed at the time of the funeral. With one exception no horse-burials have been found in Egypt.

Although they were defeated first by the Assyrians under Asshubanipal, and later by the Abyssinians, the Ethiopian kings, driven first to Napata and then to Meroe, continued down to A.D. 350 to build pyramids. It was not until after the time of the Emperor Constantine, when the Ancient religion had given way to Christianity, and the ancient language had been forgotten, that the last pyramid was built in Africa—3,000 years after the first.

CHAPTER SEVENTEEN

SUNRISE

I HAVE tried to tell the story of pyramid exploration through twenty-six centuries, from the Saites of the seventh century B.C. to Goneim in the twentieth century A.D. One can liken it to a journey begun at sunset and ending at sunrise. At first the traveller still has the help of the fading light of past knowledge. The Saitic kings, though living more than two thousand years after the first pyramid was built, could read the inscriptions, knew the names of the builders, whom they revered as gods, and understood the purpose of the monuments.

Then came Herodotus and the Greek travellers, who knew Egypt in twilight, when the ancient culture was dying. When the Romans came the sun had almost set, and the darkness of ignorance had begun to enshroud the Pyramids. By the time of the Arab invasion all was lost; the language, the religion, the history of the Ancient Egyptians were incomprehensible to the invaders, and even among the indigenous population survived only in folk memories and traditions.

The seventeenth and eighteenth centuries were like the hour before the dawn; it was not yet light, but there was a hint of the coming glory. Then, at the beginning of the nineteenth century, with the decipherment of the hiero-glyphs, the sun appears again above the horizon, and with each discovery made by the great explorers—Vyse and Perring, Mariette, Maspero, Borchardt, Petrie, and the philologists, Champollion, Birch, Erman, and the rest—the light broadens, the shadows shrink and almost disappear, until, by the middle of the twentieth century, we probably know more about the Pyramids and their builders than even the Saites knew.

Is it full daylight now? Is there anything more to be learned? There is.

From time to time, new discoveries are made, sometimes
by design—as in the case of the "new" pyramid and the
great *mastaba* tombs excavated by Professor Emery at
Saqqara—at other times by accident. A recent example of
the latter kind was the finding by Kemal el Malakh, at
Giza, of what appear to be the remains of a funerary boat
buried in a great pit on the southern side of the Great
Pyramid. In 1954 Malakh, an architect employed by the
Department of Antiquities, was clearing the sand and
debris from the pyramid in order to make a road for
tourists. He came upon an ancient wall running parallel
with the side of the monument, and just in front of it,
between the wall and the pyramid, two rows of large limestone blocks let into the rock, and evidently concealing pits.
Such pits are known by other examples near the Great
Pyramid—there is an illustration of one opposite page 273
—and Borchardt shows several in his map of the Giza
pyramids. But the others were empty when found.

On removing some of the limestone roofing blocks the
Department of Antiquities revealed a mass of timber filling
the pit and roughly in the shape of a boat (see Illustration
38, opposite page 273.) The first reports of the discovery
suggested that this was indeed a boat, decked, with a prow
and stern-post, and a large steering oar placed at one end.
There were also signs of coils of rope such as are still used
for hauling along the Nile. At one end was what had clearly
been the prow shaped from wood to form a stylistic flower,
but this had been detached and lay on the deck along with
a perfectly preserved three-hundred-foot rope, planks and
pieces of rotting linen. When the second lot of blocking
stones were removed in November 1954, some of the spec-
tators stated that they could scent a faint aroma arising
from the well-preserved woodwork of cedar originally
brought from Mount Lebanon more than five thousand
years ago. Hieroglyphic inscriptions found on the roofing
blocks bore the name of Dedefre, the successor to Cheops,
who presumably finished the work after his predecessor's
death.

When I saw the woodwork through a peephole in one of

the blocks, in June 1954, it certainly had the appearance of a complete boat, but since other blocks have been removed, and archæologists have had an opportunity of making a closer examination, some have expressed the opinion that this is not a finished vessel, but a mass of timbers which may have formed part of a boat. The prow or bowsprit was standing in a perpendicular position as if possibly the boat had been made too long for the pit, and that the prow—if it is a prow—had been jammed in.

What earlier observers thought to be decks were actually panels formed of several boards with cross-bracing. These were piled up one above the other, forming several layers and covering almost the entire length of the structure, but from the western end it is possible to see—say these ob- servers—that they rest on loose woodwork of all kinds, and no hull is visible. The whole leaves the impression of a mass of lumber laid out to give the general appearance of a boat.

Where the mass of piled-up woodwork begins there are several poles, each about five feet long and ending in a bulb or bud. These seem to be tent or canopy poles, known from the furniture of Queen Hetepheres and from boat models dating from the Middle Kingdom. They were intended to support the roof of the deck cabin.

But if it eventually established that the Giza pits contain not boats but the fragments of what were once boats, this need cause no surprise. In the earlier tombs, and in the galleries beneath the Step Pyramid, excavators have some- times found fragmented jars and other food-vessels which, from their context, must have been deliberately smashed at the time of burial. It has been suggested that this was done to prevent the jars ever being used by living persons. The vessels were in fact "killed" and buried beside the dead person for the use of his *ka*, to which their broken condition was apparently no handicap. I suggest, as a theory only, that the boats may have been broken up or left unassembled for the same reason.

Only closer examination can provide the answers to the problems which have been raised by this discovery, one of the most remarkable made in Egypt for many years. There is also the second row of roofing-blocks to the west of the first. These probably conceal a second "boat". But the task of raising these ponderous blocks, each of which weighs about nineteen tons, is prodigious. A structure will have to be built over the pits to protect their contents, and then there is the problem of preserving the wood, which has been sealed from the air for more than fifty centuries.

Although this accidental discovery has received widespread and deserved publicity, it should be remembered that the existence of such boat-pits has been known for many years, and at Dashur, de Morgan found two complete boats, with oars, buried in the sand near the pyramid of Senusret II; they have been on view in the Cairo Museum for many years. But these were of the Twelfth Dynasty, whereas the newly-opened pit at Giza definitely belongs to the Fourth Dynasty.

There have also been attempts to connect the Giza "boat" with the cult of the sun-god, Re. They have been described as "Solar Boats", intended to transport the king on his daily journey across the heavens by day and through the underworld by night. Romantic though this theory is, there is at present no archæological evidence to support it.

We know, of course, that the kings who were followers of the Re cult, believed that in the after-life they would accompany the sun-god on his heavenly journeys. There is evidence of this in the Pyramid Texts:

"*King Pepi takes to himself an oar; he rows Re to the West.*"

And in the much later tombs of the Eighteenth and Nineteenth Dynasties at Thebes there are representations of this heavenly barque being dragged through the caverns of the underworld. But the king also needed a boat to take him to Abydos, the sacred shrine of Osiris, and some have suggested that boats, or model boats, found in or near tombs, may have been intended for this purpose. There are so many doubtful points, that it is prudent to suspect anyone who tries to give you a too facile explanation of the Ancient

Egyptian religion. It is still imperfectly understood, which is why the works of serious students of Egyptology abound in such phrases as "it may be that" and "it is possible that".

The second type of discovery is that made by archæologists who deliberately set out to throw light on the little-known periods of Egyptian history. There are serious gaps in our knowledge, especially with regard to the very early Dynasties, from the First to the Third. Before and since the Second World War, Professor Walter Emery, of University College, London, has concentrated on the First and Second Dynasty cemeteries of northern Saqqara, working on behalf of the Egypt Exploration Society for the Government of Egypt. Two large mud-brick *mastabas* have been unearthed, one bearing the name of King Aha, who may be Narmer (or Menes), the other that of Djet. Petrie also discovered tombs at Abydos bearing the names of these kings, but it is not yet certain whether the kings were actually buried at Saqqara or Abydos. It may be that these Saqqara tombs are those of high officials whose names also appear in association with those of the kings.[1] Both sepulchres had been plundered in antiquity, but stone jars and other funerary remains were found, with fragments of gold leaf which may once have adorned the central chamber. Emery has also shown that the mud-brick walls show signs of intense heat, which suggests that at some time the contents had been burned, either by enemies of the dead kings, or by later intruders who wished to drive away their spirits in order to make room for their own dead.

When I saw the tomb of Djer (if it is his tomb) in 1954, Emery had opened the whole of the structure, and it was possible to see that in many small cells, each a few feet square, built in the outer walls of the *mastaba*, there were small pathetic piles of human bones, no doubt the slaves of the royal household who were slain at the time of their master's burial. This barbarous practice was abandoned shortly afterwards, and there is no evidence of it having been practised by the pyramid-building kings.

[1] Professor Emery is of the opinion that the Saqqara *mastabas* were the actual tombs of the Kings.

What lies in the future? As I did not feel competent to answer fully this question, I decided to put it to Mr. I. E. S. Edwards of the Egyptian Department of the British Museum. Mr. Edwards is the author of *The Pyramids of Egypt*, one of the most authoritative and readable accounts of pyramid study published in English in recent years.[1] I am deeply indebted to him for the generous help and advice he has given me during the writing of this book.

"In spite of all that has been achieved during the past century, a great deal of work still remains to be done before we can trace the complete architectural history of the Pyramids and the temples belonging to them. Thanks to the efforts of the archæologists whose work Mr. Cottrell has described, we are fairly well-informed about the chief architectural features from the Great Pyramid onwards until the end of the Old Kingdom (say from 2500 to 2250 B.C.).

"Unfortunately, a very different state of affairs prevails when we come to consider the period before the Great Pyramid. Only odd links in the chain of monumental evidence have been found and the gaps are often too wide to be bridged by conjecture. The difficulties begin with the pyramids of Snofru, Cheops's father and predecessor on the throne. Contemporary evidence shows that he possessed two Pyramids, one of which is described as his 'Southern Pyramid'.

"Recent excavation by the Antiquities Service has proved that the so-called Bent or 'Blunted' Pyramid at Dashur was one of his 'Two Pyramids', but we do not know whether it was the 'Southern Pyramid' or its northern companion. Two other Pyramids—one lying to the south of the Bent Pyramid at Meidum and one to the north at Dashur—possess about equal claims, on the evidence at present available, to be considered each as the second Pyramid of Snofru. The task which confronts us therefore is to discover from new evidence which of these two Pyramids in reality belonged to Snofru and, secondly, to find the name of the owner of the remaining Pyramid.

"In all probability a partial—and perhaps complete—

[1] I quote his reply in full.

solution to this problem will be forthcoming when the temples of the northern Pyramid at Dashur are excavated. At present, the remains of the Mortuary Temple on the east side of this pyramid lie deep beneath not only sand but also heavy blocks which successive despoilers have pushed down the face of the monument. Only by mechanical means not hitherto available can the superincumbent masonry be lifted and the walls of the temple uncovered. When this is done there is every hope that the name of the owner will be revealed. If it should prove to be some other king than Snofru there will be no need to re-examine the Meidum Pyramid and it will be safe to regard the latter as Snofru's 'Southern Pyramid'.

"But supposing the northern Pyramid at Dashur proves to be Snofru's, what more can be done at Meidum, the temples of which have already been excavated without yielding contemporary evidence that it belonged to Snofru, although its walls bear inscriptions by visitors who lived only 250 years after that king's death, which show that they regarded it as the pyramid of Snofru? The only visible hope in this case lies in uncovering the surviving blocks of the outer casing which are now buried beneath vast accumulations of sand at the base of the Pyramid. Such blocks sometimes bear the name of the king, for whom the monument was built, scribbled on them in red ink. It would not be a very difficult task and the chance thus provided of settling the problem of ownership would certainly seem to justify the expense of the operation.

"Even without the precise knowledge which we should like to possess regarding the Pyramids of Dashur and Meidum, it is clear that they are all closely related chronologically. The known Pyramids of the preceding period, including the famous Step Pyramid of Djoser, are far more difficult to place in their proper sequence. The recently discovered incomplete pyramid at Saqqara seems to be later than Djoser's, and may have followed it directly, as its discoverer believes. There are, however, three other pyramids which, on the basis of our present knowledge, seem to belong to pre-Snofru times. Two of these are situated at Zawiyet-el-Eryan, between Saqqara and Giza, and one at El Kuleh about 45 miles south of Luxor.

"The pyramids at Zawiyet-el-Eryan, which have been tentatively ascribed to two obscure kings, have already been excavated first by Barsanti and later by Reisner, but neither has yielded conclusive evidence of its owner's identity. This is particularly regrettable in the case of the so-called Layer Pyramid because its design suggests that it may ante-date Djoser's Pyramid. Fortunately, however, there is still hope that the problem will be solved when a group of brick tombs in the vicinity of the two Pyramids have been thoroughly excavated. They have hardly been touched yet by archæologists, but there they lie, under the sand, waiting, perhaps, to answer our problems. Experience has shown that tombs so placed were generally occupied either by relatives of the dead king or by priests whose lives were devoted to the duties of performing the funerary cult, and among the objects which were normally buried with them were some inscribed with the king's name.

"If these tombs were systematically cleared they should enable us to identify the owners of the nearby pyramids, and if the relative positions of these kings are known from the king-lists, then the Pyramids themselves can be placed in their correct sequence.

"But the most puzzling monument of all is the Pyramid of El Kuleh, which lies, not at Giza, Saqqara, or Dashur, but more than five hundred miles to the south, near Luxor. Nothing is at present known about it, except its dimensions —it covers nearly 350 square yards—and the fact that a few small objects found near it have been dated to the Third Dynasty or perhaps somewhat earlier. Up to now it has defied such efforts as have been made to find its entrance, and a very considerable amount of excavation may be necessary before it gives up its secret. Apart from the question of its owner, why, we ask, was this solitary pyramid, alone among those attributed to the Old Kingdom, built in Upper Egypt and not near Memphis, like all the others?

"These examples do not represent by any means all the work which must be done before we can feel that our information is as complete as surviving records will allow. When all these excavations have been carried out there will probably still be missing links in the chain of evidence and antecedents will still be required before we can trace the whole process of Pyramid evolution. At present it is hard to pinpoint the places where this information will be found, but I believe that it lies somewhere beneath the sand at Saqqara and perhaps in the early-Dynastic cemetery which Professor Emery is now excavating for the Egyptian Government on behalf of the Egypt Exploration Society."

There we must end our story, with the hope that our troubled world may eventually be allowed a sufficient period of tranquillity to permit the Masperos, Petries and Borchardts of the future to carry out their peaceful attack on the remaining mysteries of the Egyptian Pyramids. To achieve this requires time, the co-operation of the best archæological brains of several nations and the funds—private or public, national or international—to enable the work to be properly carried out.

Of one thing we may be certain. If and when the last veil is withdrawn, and the Pyramids have no more to tell us, that will not be the end of their attraction. Their great bulks, serene against the Egyptian sky, will continue to stir the hearts of future generations by their bold defiance of time, and their affirmation of Man's longing for immortality.

THE END

March 24th, 1955

AN OUTLINE OF EGYPTIAN RELIGION

THROUGHOUT this book there are occasional references to Egyptian deities such as Re, Osiris, etc. Since the Pyramids were not only sepulchral but also, in a sense, religious buildings, some knowledge of the main elements of Egyptian religion can help us to understand them. At the same time, it should be understood that the religious beliefs of the Ancient Egyptians are so bewilderingly complex that it is impossible in a brief chapter to describe them in detail. Readers who wish for fuller information should read Erman's *Egyptian Religion* or one of the more recent works on the subject such as those by Professor Czerny and Professor Mercer.

I am indebted to Messrs. Evans Brothers for permission to publish part of my summary of Egyptian religion from my book *The Lost Pharaohs*.

Before Egypt became unified, each of its many local tribes had their local gods, of which some were deified chieftains, the "great father" of the tribe or community. Others were birds, animals or reptiles. Some were totems, such as trees, rocks or pillars. For instance, there was Sobk, the crocodile-god, Ape(t), the hippopotamus-goddess, Bes, the god of music, singing and dancing, Ubaste, the cat-goddess of Bubastis, and Sakme(t), the lioness-goddess of Memphis. Over two thousand of these primitive gods have been recorded.

By the time of the pyramid-builders the chief deity was the sun-god, Re, who was served by a powerful priesthood at On (later called Heliopolis). Gradually this priesthood assumed greater influence over the court, until in the Fifth Dynasty (2560–2420 B.C.) the name of the reigning king always included the name of the god—e.g., Sahure, Neferirkere, Nieuserre. These were the kings who built, near modern Abusir, elaborate sun-temples to the god which were excavated by Borchardt, as described in Chapter Fifteen.

As the cult of Re became predominant, other priesthoods began to identify their local gods with him. For instance, Amun, the ram-headed god of Thebes, was pronounced to be a manifestation of Re and his name was changed to Amun-Re. He became the chief god of

Egypt after the capital was transferred to Thebes. But the most interesting development of the Middle Kingdom (when the Twelfth Dynasty pyramids were built) was the rise of the Osiris-cult.

To understand this we must take a brief backward glance at Egypt's pre-history. Like most primitive peoples the Egyptians had their folk-myths which explained the origin of the world. They believed that in the beginning only the ocean existed, and on this ocean appeared an egg (in some versions a flower) from which was born the sun-god. He had four children, Geb and Shu, Tefnut and Nut. Planting their feet on Geb, Shu and Tefnut raised their sister Nut to the heavens. Thus Geb became the earth, Shu and Tefnut the atmosphere, and Nut the sky.

For example, the inscription on the coffin of King Menkaure (Mycerinus), mentioned in Chapter Eight, also contains the words:

> "*Thy mother Nut spreads herself over thee in her name of 'Secret of the Sky'. She has caused thee to be as a God in thy name of God, O king of Upper and Lower Egypt, Menkaure, living for ever . . .*"

and the king is also described as being:

> "*Born of the sky, conceived of Nut, heir of Geb of whom he is beloved.*"

Geb and Nut had four children, Osiris and Isis, Nepthys and Seth. Osiris succeeded to the throne of his father and governed the world wisely and justly, aided by his sister Isis, whom he married. Seth, jealous of his brother's power, plotted to destroy him and eventually succeeded, afterwards cutting the body of Osiris into pieces which he buried in several parts of Egypt. The head he buried at Abydos (the burial place of the First and Second Dynasty kings). The faithful Isis recovered the scattered fragments of her husband's corpse, and with the aid of the jackal-headed god Anubis, who subsequently became the god of embalmment, re-animated it. Though unable to return to his life on earth, Osiris passed to the Underworld, where he became the god of the dead and later judge of souls. Isis bore a son, Horus, who took revenge on his uncle, Seth, defeating the usurper in battle and winning back his father's throne.

This legend became the most popular of all Egyptian folk-myths. It never lost its hold on the people, because of its human appeal, Isis becoming the type of loyal wife and mother, Horus the ideal son. In the Middle Kingdom it developed into the leading cult, and

Abydos, the supposed burial place of the head of Osiris, became a place of pilgrimage. Every year thousands flocked to Abydos to watch a dramatic re-enactment of scenes in the life of Osiris, and to follow the procession of the god's body to his supposed tomb.

The two boats found near the pyramid of Senusret II at Dashur may have been intended for the king's use in the after-life when he made his annual pilgrimage to Abydos.

These two main elements in Egyptian religion, the Re-cult and the Osiris-cult, continued side by side. The King was identified with Osiris, becoming himself "and Osiris"; e.g., Menkaure is referred to on the same coffin inscription as "Osiris, King of Upper and Lower Egypt, Menkaure", and in time, with the gradual democratization of Egyptian religion, every dead Egyptian, not only the king, identified himself with Osiris.

To make matters more confusing, the kings also identified themselves with Horus, the son of Osiris, and the "hawk of Horus" became a kingly emblem.

Among the other deities mentioned from time to time is the goddess Hat-hor, sometimes represented in the form of a cow. In one of her aspects she was the goddess of love and beauty, so it is not surprising to find her name incorporated in that of the Princess Sat-Hathor-Unet, whose jewellery was found by Brunton in her pyramid adjoining that of her father at Illahun. The face of the goddess is incorporated in the handle of her mirror and in other objects. As H. E. Winlock remarks in his book, *The Treasure of El Lahun*, referring to the gold plumes on the princess's crown:

"The high plumes were an attribute of the goddess Hat-hor, who was in some of her manifestations a patroness of love and of beauty, and the attributes of that goddess would naturally be thought appropriate to the ladies of the king's harim."

But the presiding deity during the greatest period of pyramid building—the Old Kingdom—was undoubtedly the sun-god Re, and it is not difficult to see why he assumed such predominance. Perhaps nowhere in the world does the sun's daily journey across the heavens have such dramatic importance as in Egypt. The sky is clear and usually cloudless, and the sight of the bright orb rising above the eastern hills at daybreak, and sinking at sunset behind the hills of the west—the home of the dead—so impressed the Egyptians that they came to believe that "all might, majesty and power" were embodied in the solar disc. More than a thousand years after the first pyramid was built, the Pharaoh Amnophis IV (Akhenaten) expressed this in a poem which is inscribed in the tombs of some of his nobles:

"When thou risest in the eastern horizon
Thou fillest the land with thy beauty
Thou art beautiful, great, gleaming and high over every land.
Thy rays, they embrace the lands to the limits of all thou hast made.
Thou art Re and bringest them all,
Thou blindest them (for) thy beloved son
Thou art afar off, yet thy rays are on the earth;
Thou art in the faces (of men) yet thy ways are not known. . . ."

Some Egyptologists, for example, Mr. I. E. S. Edwards, have suggested that the shape of the pyramid itself may have been a representation of the downward-thrusting rays of the sun, in stone. In his book, *The Pyramids of Egypt*, Edwards writes:

"When standing on the road to Saqqara and gazing westwards . . . it is possible to see the sun's rays striking downwards . . . at about the same angle as the slope of the Great Pyramid."

He then quotes Pyramid Text No. 523:

"Heaven has strengthened for thee the rays of the sun in order that thou mayest lift thyself to heaven as the eye of Re."

Was the pyramid a representation of the sun's rays? In support of this theory, Edwards mentions that the Egyptian name for a pyramid was $M(e)r$. If it could be proved that this word was a compound word consisting of the prefix M which conveys the meaning of "place" and a known root composed of the two consonants r which means to "ascend" $m/e/r$ would then mean "place of ascending". But there is no positive proof of this derivation.

In this book I have tried to explain the conventional theory of the origin and development of the pyramid, from the *mastaba*, through the Step Pyramid to the "true pyramid". But let us suppose that, as Edwards suggests as a *tentative* theory, there were *two* rival religious cults, that of the Step Pyramid and the True Pyramid. This would explain why Snofru built one of each. Then when the latter cult triumphed he changed his Meidum building from a Step Pyramid to a straight-sided building—after which all his successors seem to have built true pyramids, with the possible exception of Dedefre, successor to Cheops. Instead of building at Giza where there was plenty of room, Dedefre constructed at Abu Roash a now-ruined building which *may* have been a Step Pyramid. Was he, perhaps, the last die-hard adherent of the old faith?

THE DYNASTIES OF ANCIENT EGYPT

1st and 2nd Dynasties . . . . . *c.* 3200–2780 B.C.

In 3200 B.C. Menes combined in unity for the first time the Kingdoms of Upper and Lower Egypt.

OLD KINGDOM—2780–2100 B.C.

3rd Dynasty	2780–2720 B.C.
4th Dynasty	2720–2560 B.C.
5th Dynasty	2560–2420 B.C.
6th Dynasty	2420–2270 B.C.
7th to 10th Dynasty (The First Intermediate Period)	2270–2100 B.C.

THE MIDDLE EMPIRE—2100–1700 B.C.

11th Dynasty	2100–2000 B.C.
12th Dynasty	2000–1790 B.C.
13th Dynasty	1790–1700 B.C.

HYKSOS PERIOD—*c.* 1700–1555 B.C.

14th to 16th Dynasties	*c.* 1700–1600 B.C.
17th Dynasty	1600–1555 B.C.

NEW EMPIRE—1555–712 B.C.

18th Dynasty	1555–1350 B.C.
19th Dynasty	1350–1200 B.C.
20th Dynasty	1200–1090 B.C.
21st Dynasty (Tanites)	1090–945 B.C.
22nd Dynasty	945–745 B.C.
23rd Dynasty	745–718 B.C.
24th Dynasty	718–712 B.C.

LATE EGYPTIAN PERIOD—712–525 B.C.

25th Dynasty . . . . . .   712–663 B.C.
26th Dynasty . . . . . .   663–525 B.C.

PERSIAN DOMINATION—525–332 B.C.

27th Dynasty . . . . . .   525–438 B.C.
28th Dynasty . . . . . .   438–399 B.C.
29th Dynasty . . . . . .   398–379 B.C.
30th Dynasty . . . . . .   378–332 B.C.

GRÆCO-ROMAN PERIOD—332 B.C.–A.D. 638

 (i) Alexander the Great and Ptolemies . .   332–30 B.C.
 (ii) Roman Period . . . . .   30 B.C.–A.D. 395
 (iii) Byzantine Period . . . . .   A.D. 395–638

BIBLIOGRAPHY

All the following books are of value to the study of the Pyramids, but those marked * are probably more assimilable by the non-specialist reader.

Baikie, James, *Egyptian Antiquities in the Nile Valley.*

*Belzoni, G., *Narrative of the Operations and recent discoveries within the Pyramids, Temples, Tombs and Excavations in Egypt and Nubia.*

Borchardt, L., *Die Entstehung der Pyramide an Baugeschichte der Pyramide bei Meidum nachgeweisen.* Berlin, 1928.

Borchardt, L., *Die Pyramiden, ihre Enstehung und Entwicklung.* Berlin, 1911.

Borchardt, L., *Eineges zur dritten Bauperiode der grossen Pyramide bei Gise.* Berlin, 1932.

Borchardt, L., *Gegen die Zahlenmystik an der grossen Pyramide de Gise.* Berlin, 1922.

*Breasted, J. H., *History of Egypt.* London, 1924.

*Browne, *Travels in Africa, Egypt and Syria.* London, 1746.

*Brunton, Guy, *Lahun I: The Treasure.* London, 1920.

*Carter, H., *Report on the Tomb of Menthuhotep I. Annales du Service des Antiquités,* Vol. II. Cairo, 1901.

*Cottrell, L., *Life Under the Pharaohs.* London, 1955.

*Cottrell, L., *The Lost Pharaohs.* London, 1950.

*de Morgan, J., *Fouilles à Dachour.* Vienna, 1895–1903.

*de Morgan, J., *Recherche sur les Origines de l'Egypte.* 1896.

*Diodorus Siculus.

*Drioton, E. (and J. P. Lauer), *Sakkara, the Monuments of Zoser, Institut Français de l'Archœologie Orientale,* 1939.

*Edwards, I. E. S., *The Pyramids of Egypt.* London, 1947.

*Emery, W. B., *The Tomb of Hemaka.* Cairo, 1938.

*Emery, W. B., *The Tomb of Hor-Aha.* Cairo, 1939.

*Engelbach, R., *Ancient Egyptian Masonry.*

*Erman, A., *The Religion of the Egyptians* (translated by A. M. Blackman). London, 1927.

*Erman, A., *Die Religion der Agypter.*

Firth, C. M., Quibell, J. E. and Lauer, J. P., *The Step Pyramid.* Cairo, 1935.

Firth, C. M. and Gunn, B., *The Teti Pyramid Cemeteries*, Cairo, 1926.

*Greaves, J., *Pyramidographia*. London, 1646.

*Grinsell, L., *Egyptian Pyramids*.

*Halls, J. J., *Life of Henry Salt*. London, 1834.

*Herodótus, *History* (translated by Rawlinson). London, 1858.

Holscher, U., *Das Grabdenkmal des Konigs Chephren*. Leipzig, 1219.

Howard-Vyse, R. and Perring, J. S., *Operations Carried on at the Pyramids of Gizeh*. London, 1840–42.

Jequier, G., *Douze ans de fouilles dans la Necropole Memphite*. Neuchatel, 1940.

Jequier, G., *Le Mastabat Faraoun*. Cairo, 1928.

Jequier, G., *Le Monument funéraire de Pepi II*. Cairo, 1936–41.

Junker, H., *Grabungen auf dem Friedhof des Alten Reiches bei den Pyramidem von Giza* (Vols. 1–4). Vienna, 1929–41.

Lacau, P., *Suppressions des noms divins dans les textes de la chambre funéraire*. *Annales du Service des Antiquités*, Vol. 26. Cairo, 1926.

*Lauer, J. P., *Les problèmes des pyramides*.

*Lauer, J. P., *The Step Pyramid*. Service des Antiquités, Cairo.

*Lucas, A., *Ancient Egyptian materials and industries*. London, 1934.

*Lythgoe, A. M., "The Treasure of Lahun", *Bulletin of the Metropolitan Museum of Art*. New York, December 1919.

*Mace, A. C., "Excavations on the north pyramid at Lisht", *Bulletin of the Metropolitan Museum of Art*, Vol. 9. New York, 1914.

*Petrie, W. M. F., *The Pyramids and Temples of Gizeh*. London, 1883.

*Petrie, W. M. F., *Illahun, Kahun and Gurob*. London, 1890.

*Petrie, W. M. F., *Kahun, Gurob and Hawara*. London, 1890.

*Petrie, W. M. F., *Naqada and Ballas*. London, 1896.

*Petrie, W. M. F., *Royal Tombs of the 1st and 2nd Dynasties*. London, 1901–2.

*Petrie, W. M. F., *Seventy Years in Archæology*. London, 1932.

Petrie, W. M. F., Mackay, E. and Wainwright, G., *Meydum and Memphis III*. London, 1910.

*Pliny, *Natural History*.

*Pococke, R., *Travels in Egypt*. London, 1755.

*Reisner, G., "Excavations at Napata, the capital of Ethiopia", *Bulletin of the Museum of Fine Arts*, Vol. 15, No. 89. Boston, 1917.

*Reisner, G., "Known and unknown kings of Ethiopia", *Bulletin of the Museum of Fine Arts*, Vol. 16, No. 97.

*Reisner, G., "Hetepheres, mother of Cheops", *Bulletin of the Museum of Fine Arts*, Vols. 25, 26 and 30. Boston, 1927–32.

Reisner, G., *The development of the Egyptian tomb down to the accession of Cheops*. Harvard University, 1936.

*Sandys, *Travells*. London, 1610.

Selim Bey Hassan, *Excavations at Sakkara* (1937–38). Cairo, 1938.

Sethe, K., *Die altagyptischen Pyramiden texte*. Leipzig, 1908–22.

*Shaw, *Travels in Barbary*.

*Strabo, *Geographia*.

*Winlock, H. E., *The Treasure of El Lahun*. New York, 1934.

INDEX